THE NEW
PEOPLEMAKING

THE NEW PEOPLEMAKING

BY

VIRGINIA SATIR

Science and Behavior Books, Inc.
Mountain View, California

Library of Congress Card Number: 88-061241

ISBN: 0-8314-0070-6

Cover design by Sharon Smith
Illustrations by Barry Ives
Editing by June Schwartz and Rain Blockley
Interior design by Gary Head
Typesetting by Miller Freeman Composition Services
Printed in the United States of America by Haddon Craftsmen

To my daughters, Mary and Ruth, and their
children—Tina, Barry, Angela, Scott, Julie, John and
Michael—who helped to texture me,
and
to the members of the Avanta Network who came on board
to create new possibilities in the world.

Contents

Preface

When *Peoplemaking* was first published in 1972, I invited readers to share their responses to the book and their experiences with it. As a result, I have received hundreds of letters, each containing something useful: thoughtful reflections, impressions, questions, suggestions, and constructive criticisms. People requested new topics as well as an expansion and clarification of old ones.

This revision is my response to you, the readers. You asked me to discuss:

> Adolescence
> Life in the older years: retirement and transitions
> Peace in the world
> Spirituality

I have added these as new chapters.

You also asked for a deepening of understanding of one-parent, blended, and gay-parent families; healthy pairing; sexuality; and the family of the future. I am adding what I have learned in these past fifteen years, weaving it into the fabric of existing chapters. This book cannot do justice to the full range of concerns in these families, however, and I refer you to the bibliography for further information.

I am immensely gratified that you responded so generously. That means lots of people out there care about families. You may also be pleased to know that *Peoplemaking* has now been translated into many languages, including Japanese, Hebrew, Chinese, and Braille. It is obviously widely read, and I hope you keep writing to me with your reactions.

My basic message has been and is that a strong link exists between life in the family and the kind of adults that that family's children become. Since individuals make up society, it seems very important that we develop the strongest and most congruent people possible. It all starts in the family. In time, having congruent people at the helm will change the character of our society.

The New Peoplemaking is one of my efforts to make a positive difference toward enabling congruent adults. Using many experiences with families all over the world, I have written this book to support, emphasize, educate, and empower the family. We know there are better ways to deal with ourselves and each other. We have only to put them into practice. Each of us who does contributes toward a stronger, more positive world for all of us.

Each of us can make a difference; each of us is needed. The difference we can make begins when we develop high self-esteem as individuals. A big hope I have for this book is that it will help each of us empower and commit ourselves to congruence. Our congruent experiences and modeling will lead to creative ways to understand each other, care for ourselves and each other, and give our children a sturdy foundation from which they can develop strength and wholeness.

It is important to remember that every bit of energy we use to fight with ourselves and each other divides and diffuses the energy we could use for discovery and creativity. After all, when the fight is over, we still have to go back to the bargaining table. We can find easier and more effective ways to handle conflict; we can benefit from it rather than destroying ourselves.

I believe we are living in a most historic time. Most of you who are reading this book will live to see the year 2000.

A new evolution in humankind is afoot. All people who are working toward becoming more fully human will be bridges to that new time. We are the transition people.

I see small signs of this everywhere. For the planet and its inhabitants to survive, we must develop our ability to live together in harmony. For me, this means learning how to be congruent, and that leads to becoming more fully human.

Oftentimes, it has to get very dark before the light comes. We are in pretty dark places right now. Our destructive past and the shadow of extinction by nuclear weapons, together with the pain of the present, remind us of our ability to be lethal. We also need to remember that we have the resources to be nurturing. The hope lies in our choices.

It is urgent that we nourish and develop the buds of sanity and humanness that are emerging. What we have going for us is a fantastic know-how of technical development and proven intellectual ability. We know how to probe and investigate practically everything. Our challenge now is to develop human beings with values—moral, ethical, and humanistic—that can effectively utilize this development. When we achieve that, we will be able to enjoy this most wonderful planet and the life that inhabits it.

WE ARE ON THE WAY.

Editor's Note

To me, Virginia Satir's writings are like homemade bread. They are yeasty, hearty, and nourishing. They promise much, taste wonderful, digest well, and thoroughly satisfy.

So why revise this book? Virginia describes the new material in her preface. I want to emphasize her devotion to peace in the world. By dipping into her own spiritual life, Virginia courageously tackles the difficult task of writing about peace and spirituality.

Working with Virginia is a blessing for which I am deeply grateful. I also wish to thank Ann Austin Thompson, who carefully reviewed the manuscript; Betsy and Ellen Stevens, who brought a daughter's and mother's point of view to the new chapter on adolescence; and M. Ruth Whitcomb, who particularly attended to the chapter "The Later Years."

June Y. Schwartz

I

Introduction

When I was five, I decided that when I grew up I'd be a "children's detective on parents." I didn't quite know what I would look for, but I realized a lot went on in families that didn't meet the eye. There were a lot of puzzles I did not know how to understand.

Now, many years later, after working with some thousands of families, I find there are still a lot of puzzles. I have learned from my work, and learning opens up new possibilities and new directions for discovery. It is now clear to me that the family is a microcosm of the world. To understand the world, we can study the family: issues such as power, intimacy, autonomy, trust, and communication skills are vital parts underlying how we live in the world. To change the world is to change the family.

Family life is something like an iceberg: most people are aware of only about one-tenth of what is going on—the tenth that they can see and hear. Some suspect there may be more, but they don't know what and have no idea how to find out. Not knowing can set the family on a dangerous course. Just as a sailor's fate depends on knowing that the bulk of the iceberg is under the water, so a family's fate depends on understanding the feelings and needs that lie beneath everyday family events. (What goes on *under* the table?)

Through the years I have also found ways to approach solutions to many puzzles. I would like to share them with you in this book. In the chapters that follow we will be looking at the underside of the iceberg.

In this age of expanding knowledge about this very small world of elementary particles and this very large world of extragalactic astronomy, we are also learning new things about people's relationships with people. I believe that historians a thousand years from now will point to our time as the beginning of a new era in the development of humankind, the time when people began to live more comfortably with their humanity.

Over the years I have developed a picture of what human beings living humanly are like. They are people who understand, value, and develop their bodies, finding them beautiful and useful. They are real and honest to and about themselves and others; they are loving and kind to themselves and others. People living humanly are willing to take risks, to be creative, to manifest competence, and to change when the situation calls for it. They find ways to accommodate what is new and different, keeping that part of the old that is still useful and discarding what is not.

When you add all this up, you have physically healthy, mentally alert, feeling, loving, playful, authentic, creative, productive, responsible human beings. These are people who can stand on their own two feet, love deeply, and fight fairly and effectively. They can be on equally good terms with both their tenderness and their toughness, and can know the difference between them.

The family is the context in which a person with such dimensions develops. And the adults in charge are the *peoplemakers.*

In my years as a family therapist, I have found that four aspects of family life keep popping up:

The feelings and ideas one has about oneself, which I call *self-worth*

The ways people use to work out meaning with one another, which I call *communication*

The *rules* people use for how they should feel and act, which eventually develop into what I call the *family system*

The way people relate to other people and institutions outside the family, which I call the *link to society.*

No matter what kind of problem first led a family into my office—whether an unfaithful wife or depressed husband, a delinquent daughter or a schizophrenic son—I soon found that the prescription was the same. To relieve their family pain, some way had to be found to change these four key factors. In all of the troubled families I noticed that:

Self-worth was low.

Communication was indirect, vague, and not really honest.

Rules were rigid, inhuman, nonnegotiable, and everlasting.

The family's link to society was fearful, placating, and blaming.

I have had the joy of knowing relatively untroubled families, especially in my workshops where families develop their nurturing potential. In these vital and nurturing families, I consistently see a different pattern:

Self-worth is high.

Communication is direct, clear, specific, and honest.

Rules are flexible, human, appropriate, and subject to change.

The link to society is open and hopeful, and is based on choice.

The changes all rest on new learnings, new awareness, and a new consciousness. Everyone can achieve these.

No matter where a surgeon studies medicine, he can operate on any human being anywhere in the world, because the internal organs and the limbs will be in relatively the same place. Through my work with families, troubled and nurturing, in most of the continents of the world, I have learned that families everywhere deal with the same issues. In all families,

Every person has a feeling of worth, positive or negative; the question is,

Which is it?

Every person communicates; the question is,

How, and what happens as a result?

Every person follows rules; the question is,

What kind, and how well do they work for her, or him?

Every person is linked to society; the question is,

In what way, and what are the results?

These things are true whether the family is a *natural* one, in which the man and woman who sired and conceived the child continue to care for that child until the child is grown; a *one-parent* family, in which one parent leaves the family by death, divorce, or desertion, and all of the parenting is done by the remaining parent; a *blended* family, whose children are parented by step-, adoptive, foster, or gay parents; or an *institutional* family, in which groups of adults rear groups of children, as in institutions, communes, or extended families. Today, children are being brought up in many configurations.

Each of these family forms has its own special problems and possibilities, and we will return to them later. Basically, the same forces will be at work in all of them: *self-worth, communication, rules, and links to society.*

This book will help you discover how these elements operate in your own family and point to some new directions you can take to change. Think of my words as the voice of someone who has accumulated experience from sharing the happiness and sorrow, the hurt and anger, and the love, of many families, including my own.

This book is not about blaming parents. People are always doing the best they can. Developing a family is the hardest, most complicated job in the world. The very fact that you are reading this tells me that you care about yourself and the well-being of your family. I hope we can discover a better life together as a family—that we can really experience seeing the lights come on in each other's eyes when we meet.

Relationships are the living links that join family members. Through exploring the many parts of these relationships, you can come to an understanding of the system in which you now live and can create new vitality and joy of teamwork with one another.

From time to time, as you read, you will come upon suggested experiments or exercises designed to give you new experiences and new ways to understand what may be happening to you. I hope you will do each one as you come

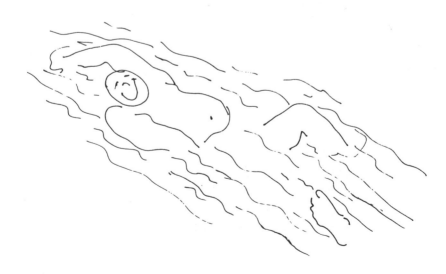

to it, even if at first it seems simple or foolish. Knowing something begins a change; experiencing makes it happen. These experiments are positive, concrete steps your family can take to become less troubled and more nurturing. The more members of your family who take part, the more effective the results will be. Remember, you learn to swim better when you get into the water.

If you feel shy or doubtful about inviting family members to participate in these exercises with you, become thoroughly familiar with what you are asking, feel it from your heart, and present your wish simply and directly. If you feel enthusiastic and hopeful about what you are asking, you will probably communicate a sense of excitement, which will make the invitation attractive and encourage your family to go along with you. By setting your request in a simple, straightforward question—"Will you participate with me in an experiment that I think might be useful to us?"—you maximize the opportunity for a positive response.

Badgering, demanding, or nagging people to go along turns the transaction into a power struggle, which usually works in the opposite direction from what one is trying to accomplish. Things may be so ruptured at this point that nothing can be done. However, chances are good that if your family members still live under the same roof, they will be willing to at least try if they are approached properly. Have patience and faith.

I have seen much pain in families. Each family has moved me deeply. Through this book I hope to ease that pain in families whom I may never have a chance to meet personally. In doing so, I also hope to prevent the pain from continuing into the families their children will form. Some human pain is unavoidable, of course. I see two kinds of pain: one is the pain of recognition of problems, and the other is the pain of blame. The first we can't avoid; the second we can. We can direct our efforts to change what we can and to work out creative ways to live with what we can't change.

THE SERENITY PRAYER

God grant me the serenity to accept
the things I cannot change,
Courage to change the things I can,
And wisdom to know the difference.
—*Reinhold Niebuhr*

Just reading this book may evoke some or both kinds of pain for you because it can bring back memories. After all, facing ourselves and learning how to take some responsibility for ourselves have their painful moments. If you think there may be a better way of living together as a family than the way you are living now, though, you'll also find this book rewarding.

2

What's *Your* Family Like?

Does it feel good to you to live in your family right now? This question seemed not to have occurred to most of the families I have worked with until I posed it. Living together was something they took for granted. If no family crisis was apparent, everyone assumed everyone else was satisfied. Perhaps many family members didn't dare face such a question. They felt stuck in the family, for better or for worse, and knew no ways to change things.

Do you feel you are living with friends, people you like and trust, and who like and trust you?

This question usually brought the same puzzled replies. "Gee, I've never thought about that; they're just my family"—as though family members were somehow different from people!

Is it fun and exciting to be a member of your family?

Yes, there really are families whose members find home one of the most interesting and rewarding places they can be. But many people live year after year in families that are a threat, a burden, or a bore.

If you can answer "yes" to these three questions, I am certain you live in what I call *a nurturing* family. If you answer "no" or "not often," you probably live in a family that is more or less troubled. This does not mean that you have a bad family. It only means that people aren't very happy and have not learned ways to love and value one another openly.

After knowing hundreds of families, I find that each one can be placed somewhere along a scale from *very nurturing* to *very troubled*. I see many similarities in the way nurturing families operate. Troubled families, too, no matter what their problems, seem to have much in common. I would thus like to draw for you a word picture of these two types of families, as I have observed them. Of course, neither picture will fit any specific family exactly, but in one or the other you may recognize some part of your own family in action.

The atmosphere in a troubled family is easy to feel. Whenever I am with such a family, I quickly sense discomfort. Sometimes it feels cold, as if everyone were frozen; the atmosphere is extremely polite, and everyone is obviously bored. Sometimes it feels as if everything were constantly spinning, like a top; I get dizzy and can't find my balance. Or it may be an atmosphere of foreboding, like the lull before a storm, when thunder may crash and lightning strike at any moment. Sometimes the air is full of secrecy. Sometimes I feel very sad and cannot find an obvious reason. I realize that's because the sources are covered up.

When I am in any of these troubled atmospheres, my body reacts violently. My stomach feels queasy; my back and shoulders soon ache, as does my head. I used to wonder if the bodies of these family members responded as mine did. Later, when I knew them better and they became free enough to tell me what life was like in their family, I learned that they did indeed have the same sensations. After having this kind of experience over and over again, I began to understand why so many members of troubled families were beset with physical ills. Their bodies were simply reacting humanly to a very inhuman atmosphere.

Perhaps you will find the reactions I describe here surprising. Everybody—every body—has physical reactions to individuals around him or her. Many people are not aware of it: we were taught as we grew up to turn off these feelings. With years of practice we may turn them off so successfully that we are totally unaware of reacting until, hours later, we have a headache, an aching shoulder, or an upset stomach. Even then we may not understand why. As a therapist I have learned to be tuned in to these feelings in myself and to recognize signs of them in other people. They tell me a good deal about what is actually going on. I hope this book will help you learn to recognize these useful clues in yourself. The first step of change is to recognize what is happening.

In troubled families, people's bodies and faces tell of their plight. Bodies are either stiff and tight, or slouchy. Faces look sullen, or sad, or blank like masks. Eyes look down and past people. Ears obviously don't hear. Voices are either harsh and strident, or barely audible.

There is little evidence of friendship among individual family members, little joy in one another. The family seems to stay together through duty, with people just trying to tolerate one another. Now and then I see someone in a trou-

bled family make an effort at lightness, but the words fall with a thud. More often humor is caustic, sarcastic, even cruel. The adults are so busy telling the child and each other what to do and what not to do that they never get to enjoy themselves as persons. It often comes as a great surprise to members of troubled families that they actually *can* enjoy one another.

Seeing whole families who were trying to live together in such an atmosphere, I used to wonder how they managed to survive. I discovered that in some families, people simply avoided one another; they became so involved in work and other outside activities that they rarely had much real contact with other family members. It is very easy to live with others in a house and not see them for days.

It is a sad experience for me to be with these families. I see the hopelessness, the helplessness, the loneliness. I see the bravery of people trying to cover up—a bravery that can prematurely kill. Some still cling to a little hope, some still bellow or nag or whine at each other. Others no longer care. These people go on year after year, enduring misery themselves or, in their desperation, inflicting it on others. I could never go on seeing these families unless I had hope that they could change, and most of them have. The family can be the place where one finds love and understanding and support, even when all else fails; where we can be refreshed and recharged to cope more effectively with the world outside. But for millions of troubled families, this is merely a dream.

In our urban, industrial society, the institutions we live with have been designed to be practical, efficient, economical, profitable—but rarely to protect and serve the human part of human beings. Nearly everyone experiences either poverty, discrimination, pressure, or other negative consequences of our inhuman social institutions. For people from troubled families, who find inhuman conditions at home, too, these difficulties are even harder to bear.

No one would intentionally pick this troubled way of living. Families accept it only because they know of no other way.

Stop reading for a few minutes and think about some families you know that would fit the description "troubled." Did the family you grew up in have some of these characteristics: Was your family at times cold, deadening, superpolite, secretive, confusing? What are the characteristics of the family you are living in now? Can you discover any signs of trouble that you haven't been aware of before?

How different it is to be in a nurturing family! Immediately, I can sense the aliveness, the genuineness, honesty, and love. I feel the heart and soul present as well as the head. People demonstrate their loving, their intellect, and their respect for life.

I feel that if I lived in such a family, I would be listened to and would be interested in listening to others; I would be considered and would wish to consider others. I could openly show my affection as well as my pain and disapproval. I wouldn't be afraid to take risks because everyone in my family would realize that some mistakes are bound to come with my risk-taking—that my mistakes are a sign that I am growing. I would feel like a person in my own right—noticed, valued, loved, and clearly asked to notice, value, and love others. I would feel free to respond with humor and laughter when it fits.

One can actually see and hear the vitality in such a family. The bodies are graceful, the facial expressions relaxed. People look *at* one another, not *through* one another or at the floor; and they speak in rich, clear voices. A flow and harmony permeate their relations with one another. The children, even as infants, seem open and friendly, and the rest of the family treats them very much as persons.

The houses in which these people live tend to have a lot of light and color. Clearly a place where people *live,* these homes are planned for their comfort and enjoyment, not as showplaces for the neighbors.

When there is quiet, it is a peaceful quiet, not the stillness of fear and caution. When there is noise, it is the sound of meaningful activity, not the thunder of trying to drown out everyone else. Each person seems to know that he or she will have the chance to be heard. If one's turn doesn't come now, it is only because there isn't time—not because one isn't loved.

People seem comfortable about touching one another and showing their affection, regardless of age. Loving and caring aren't demonstrated by carrying out the garbage, cooking the meals, or bringing home the paycheck. Instead, people show their loving and caring by talking openly and listening with concern, being straight and real with one another, and simply being together.

Members of a nurturing family feel free to tell each other how they feel. Anything can be talked about—the disappointments, fears, hurts, angers, criticisms, as well as the joys and achievements. If Father happens to be bad-humored for some reason, his child can say frankly, "Gee, Dad, you're grouchy tonight." The child isn't afraid that Father will bark back, "How dare you talk to your father that way!" Instead, Father can be frank, too: "I sure am grouchy. I had a terrible day today!"

Nurturing families can make plans. If something interferes with the plan, they can readily make adjustments, often with a sense of humor. This way they are able to handle more of life's problems without panicking. Suppose, for example, that a child drops and breaks a glass. In a troubled family, this accident could lead to a half-hour lecture, a spanking, and perhaps sending the child away in tears. In a

nurturing family, more likely someone would remark, "Well, Johnny, you broke your glass. Did you cut yourself? I'll get you a Band-Aid, and then you can get a broom and sweep up the pieces. I'll get you another glass." If the parent had noticed that Johnny had been holding the glass precariously, he might add, "I think the glass dropped because you didn't have both hands around it." Thus the incident would be used as a learning opportunity (which raises the child's self-worth) rather than as a cause for punishment, which puts that self-worth in question. In the nurturing family it is easy to pick up the message that human life and human feelings are more important than anything else.

These parents see themselves as empowering leaders, not as authoritative bosses. They see their job primarily as one of teaching their children how to be truly human in all situations. They readily acknowledge to the child their poor judgment as well as their good judgment; their hurt, anger, or disappointment as well as their joy. The behavior of these parents matches what they say. How different from the troubled parent who tells the children not to hurt each other, but slaps them whenever displeased.

Parents are people; they are not automatically leaders the day their first child is born. They learn that good leaders are careful of their timing: they watch for an opportunity to talk to their children when they can really be heard. When a child has misbehaved, the father or mother moves physically close to offer support. This helps the offending child overcome fear and guilt feelings and make the best of the teaching the parent is about to offer.

Recently, I saw a mother in a nurturing family handle a troublesome situation very skillfully and humanly. When she noticed that her two sons, ages five and six, were fighting, she calmly separated the boys, took each by the hand, and sat down with one son on either side of her. Still holding their hands, she asked each of them to tell her what was going on; she listened to one and then the other intently. By asking questions she slowly pieced together what had happened: the five-year-old had taken a dime from the six-year-old's dresser. As the two boys talked about their hurts and feelings of injustice, she helped them make new contact with one another, return the dime to its rightful owner, and pave the way for better ways of dealing with each other. Furthermore, the boys had a good lesson in constructive problem-solving.

Parents in nurturing families know that their children are not intentionally bad. If someone behaves destructively, parents realize some misunderstanding has arisen or someone's self-esteem is dangerously low. They know people learn only when valuing themselves and feeling valued, so they don't respond to behavior in a way that will make people feel devalued. Even when it is possible to change behavior by shaming or punishing, the resulting scar is not easily or quickly healed.

When a child must be corrected, as all children must at one time or another, nurturing parents rely on being clear: asking for information, listening, touching, understanding, using careful timing, and being aware of the child's feelings and natural wishes to learn and to please. These things all help us to be effective teachers. Children learn from the modeling of direct behavior.

Rearing a family is probably the most difficult job in the world. It resembles two business firms merging their respective resources to make a single product. All the potential headaches of that operation are present when an adult male and an adult female join to steer a child from infancy to adulthood. Parents in a nurturing family realize problems come along, simply because life offers them, and they will be alert to creative solutions as each new problem appears. Troubled families, on the other hand, put all their energies into the hopeless attempt to keep problems from happening; when they do happen—and, of course, they always do—these people have no resources left for solving the crisis.

Nurturing parents realize change is inevitable: children change quickly from one stage to another, nurturing adults never stop growing and changing, and the world around us never stands still. They accept change as part of being alive and try to use it creatively to make their families still more nurturing.

Can you think of a family that you would call nurturing at least part of the time? Can you remember a time recently when your family could be described as nurturing? Try to remember how it felt to be in your family then. Do these times happen often?

Some people may scoff at my picture of the nurturing family and say it isn't possible for any family to live that way. Unfulfilling family living is so habitual that it's easy to think there's no other way. To these people I would say, I have had the good fortune to know many nurturing families intimately, and *it is possible.* The human heart is always seeking love.

Some may protest that there just isn't time to overhaul their family lives. To them I would say, their survival may depend on it. Troubled families make troubled people and thus contribute to the devaluing of self, which is linked to crime, mental illness, alcoholism, drug abuse, poverty, alienated youth, terrorism, and many other social problems. Giving ourselves full permission to make the family a place to develop people who are more truly human will reflect itself in a safer and more humanly responsive world. We can make the family a real place for developing real people. Each of us is a discovery, and each of us makes a difference.

Everyone who holds a position of power or influence in the world was once an infant. How he or she uses power of influence depends largely on what that person learned in the family while growing up. When we help troubled families become nurturing—and nurturing ones become even more nurturing—each person's increased humanity will filter out into government, schools, businesses, religions, and all the other institutions that contribute to the quality of our lives.

I am convinced that any troubled family can become a nurturing one. Most of the things that cause families to be troubled are learned after birth. Since they are learned, they can be unlearned, and new things can be learned in their place. The question is, how?

First, you need to recognize that your family sometimes *is* a troubled family.

Second, you need to forgive yourself for past mistakes and give yourself permission to change, knowing that things can be different.

Third, make a decision to change things.

Fourth, take some action to start the process of change.

As you begin to see the troubles in your family more clearly, it will help you to realize that whatever may have happened in the past represented the best you knew how to do at the time. There is no reason for anyone to go on feeling guilty or blaming others in the family. Chances are that the causes of your family pain have been invisible to all of you—not because you don't want to see them but because either you don't know where to look or you have

been taught to view life through mental glasses that keep
you from seeing.

In this book you will begin to take off those glasses and
look directly at the things that cause joy or pain in family
life. The first is self-worth.

3
Self-Worth: The Pot Nobody Watches

Self-esteem is a concept, an attitude, a feeling, an image; and it is represented by behavior.

When I was a little girl, I lived on a farm in Wisconsin. On our back porch was a huge black iron pot, which had lovely rounded sides and stood on three legs. My mother made her own soap, so for part of the year the pot was filled with soap. When threshing crews came through in the summer, we filled the pot with stew. At other times, my father used it to store manure for my mother's flower beds. We came to call it the "3-S pot." Anyone who wanted to use the pot faced two questions: What is the pot now full of, and how full is it?

Long afterward, when people told me about themselves—whether they felt full, empty, dirty, or even "cracked"—I thought of that old pot. One day many years ago, a family was sitting in my office struggling to find words to tell each other how they felt about themselves. I remembered the black pot and told them the story. Soon the members of the family were talking about their individual "pots," whether they contained feelings of worth or of guilt, shame, or uselessness. They told me later how useful this metaphor was to them.

Before long this simple shorthand word was helping many families express feelings that had been difficult to talk about before. A father might say, "My pot is high today," and the rest of the family would know that he felt on top of things, full of energy and good spirits, secure in the knowledge that he really mattered. Or a son might say, "I feel low-pot." This told everyone that he felt he did not matter, he felt tired or bored or bruised, not particularly lovable. It might even mean he had always felt he was not good; that he had to take what was handed to him and could not complain.

Pot is a plain word in this use, almost a nonsense word. Many of the words professional people use to talk about self-worth sound sterile and lack life-and-breath images. Families often find it easier to express themselves in pot terms and to understand when other people express themselves this way. They seem suddenly more comfortable, released from our culture's taboo against talking about one's feelings. A wife who might hesitate to tell her husband that she feels inadequate, depressed, or worthless can say frankly, "Don't bother me now—my pot is dragging!"

In this book when I say "pot," I mean *self-worth* or *self-esteem;* I use these words interchangeably. (If you prefer another playful word that suits you better, use it.) As I said earlier, every person has a feeling of worth, positive or negative. As with my old family pot, the questions are: is my self-worth negative or positive at this point, and how much of it is there?

Self-esteem is the ability to value one's self and to treat oneself with dignity, love, and reality. Anyone who is loved is open to change. Our bodies are no different. In my many years of teaching young children, treating families of all economic and social levels, meeting people from all walks of life—from all the day-to-day experiences of my profession and personal living, I am convinced that the crucial factor in what happens both *inside* people and *between* people is one's self-worth, one's pot.

Integrity, honesty, responsibility, compassion, love, and competence—all flow easily from people whose self-esteem is high. We feel that we matter, that the world is a better place because we are here. We have faith in our own competence. We are able to ask others for help, yet we believe we can make our own decisions and are, in the end, our own best resources. Appreciating our own worth, we are ready to see and respect the worth of others. We radiate trust and hope. We don't have rules against anything we feel. We also know that we don't have to act on everything we feel. We can choose. Our intelligence directs our actions. We accept all of ourselves as human.

Vital people feel high-pot most of the time. True, all of us experience times when we would just as soon chuck it all, when fatigue overwhelms us and the world has dealt out too many disappointments too quickly, when the problems of life suddenly seem more than we can manage. But vital people treat these temporary low-pot feelings as just what they are: a crisis of the moment. This crisis might well be the birth pains of some new possibility for us. We may feel uncomfortable at the time but do not have to hide. We know we can emerge from this crisis whole.

When people feel they have little worth, they expect to be cheated, stepped on, and depreciated by others. This opens the way to becoming a victim. Expecting the worst, these people invite it and usually get it. To defend themselves, they hide behind a wall of distrust and sink into the terrible feeling of loneliness and isolation. Thus separated

from other people, they become apathetic, indifferent toward themselves and those around them. It is hard for them to see, hear, or think clearly, and therefore they tend to step on and depreciate others. People who feel this way build huge psychological walls behind which they hide, and then defend themselves by denying they are doing this.

Fear is a natural consequence of this distrust and isolation. Fear constricts and blinds us; it keeps us from risking new ways of solving our problems. Instead, we turn to still more self-defeating behavior. (Fear, incidentally, is always fear of some *future* thing. I have observed that as soon as a person confronts or challenges whatever she or he is afraid of in the present, the fear vanishes.)

When persons with constant low-pot feelings experience defeat, they often label themselves as failures. "I must be worthless or all these terrible things would not be happening to me" is often the inside response. After enough of these reactions, the self is vulnerable to drugs, alcohol, or other flights from coping.

Feeling low is not the same as low pot. Low pot essentially means that when you experience undesirable feelings, you try to behave as though those feelings did not exist. It takes a lot of high self-worth to acknowledge your low feelings.

It is also important to remember that persons of high self-esteem can feel low. The difference is that people who are feeling low don't label themselves as worthless or pretend that their low feelings do not exist. Nor do they project their feeling on someone else. Feeling low is quite natural from time to time. It makes a big difference whether one condemns one's self or sees this low time as a human condition with which one needs to cope. I shall be frequently calling your attention to this process of coping.

Feeling low and not admitting it is a form of lying to yourself and others. Devaluing your feelings this way is a direct link to devaluing yourself, thus deepening the conditions of low pot. Much of what happens to us is the outcome of our attitude. Since it is attitude, we can change it.

Relax for a moment now. Close your eyes and feel your condition now. How are you feeling about yourself? What has happened or is happening at the moment? How are you responding to what is happening? How are you feeling about how you are responding? If you are feeling tight, give yourself a message of love, physically relax yourself, and consciously be in touch with your breathing. Now open your eyes. You will feel stronger as a result.

This simple remedy will help build your sense of worth: in moments you can change your state of feeling. You then meet any event with a clearer mind and a firmer personal foundation.

Invite your family members to try the following experiment with you. Take a partner, then tell one another your feelings ("Right now, I feel scared/tight/embarrassed/happy/etc."). Each partner simply thanks the other without judging or commenting. You thus hear one another's feelings so you can know each other better. We need a lot of practice to break the taboo against sharing our feelings. *Practice as much as you can with people you trust.*

Now, tell each other what makes you each feel low, or high. You may find new dimensions to the people you have been living with all these years and feel closer or more real to them as a result. When you have finished the exercise, give yourself permission to share what happened for you.

An infant coming into the world has no past, no experience in handling itself, no scale on which to judge his or her own worth. The baby must rely on experiences with people and their messages about his or her worth as a person. For the first five or six years, the child's self-esteem is formed almost exclusively by the family. After the child starts school, other influences come into play; the family remains important. Outside forces tend to reinforce the feelings of worth or worthlessness the child learned at home: the confident youngster can weather many failures, in school or among peers; the child of low self-regard can experience many successes yet feel a gnawing doubt about his or her own value. Even one negative experience can have effects out of all proportion to the event.

Every word, facial expression, gesture, or action on the part of a parent gives the child some message about self-worth. It is sad that so many parents don't realize what messages they are sending. A mother may accept the bouquet clutched in her three-year-old's hand and say, "Where did you pick these?"—with her voice and smile implying, "How sweet of you to bring me these! Where do such lovely flowers grow?" This message would strengthen the

child's feeling of worth. Or she might say, "How pretty!" but add in a judgmental voice, "Did you pick these in Mrs. Randall's garden?", implying that the child was bad to steal them. This message would make the three-year-old feel wicked and worthless.

What kind of self-worth is your family building in the children and reinforcing in the adults? You can begin to find out with this next experiment.

Tonight, when the family has settled around the table for dinner, notice what is happening to your feelings about yourself when other members speak to you. There will be some remarks to which you have no special response. However, you may be surprised to find that even "Pass the potatoes, please" can give you a feeling of value or depreciation, depending on the speaker's tone of voice, facial expression, timing (did the message interrupt you, or ignore something you said?), and how good you are feeling about yourself. If you are feeling good about yourself, you may find that you have a lot of options for how you respond. If you are feeling low, however, you might find that your options are limited (see chapter 6 on communication).

Halfway through dinner, change the perspective. Listen to what you are saying to others. Try to be in the other's shoes and imagine how you might feel if you were talked to as you are doing now. Would you, for instance, feel loved and valued?

Tomorrow night explain this little game to the other members of the family and invite them to join you. It will be helpful to read this chapter aloud before you do this as a family. After dinner, talk together about what you discovered and how you felt.

Feelings of worth can flourish only in an atmosphere in which individual differences are appreciated, love is shown openly, mistakes are used for learning, communication is open, rules are flexible, responsibility (matching promise with delivery) is modeled and honesty is practiced—the kind of atmosphere found in a nurturing family. It is no accident that the children of families who practice the above usually feel good about themselves and consequently are loving, physically healthy, and competent.

Conversely, children in troubled families often feel worthless, growing up as they must amid "crooked" communication, inflexible rules, criticism of their differentness, punishment for their mistakes, and no experience in learning responsibility. Such children are highly at risk of developing destructive behavior toward themselves and/or others. Much of an individual's potential is held in abeyance when this happens. If this has happened to you, I hope you are now taking steps to free that energy. The basic tools and directions for doing so are contained throughout this book, especially in the chapters on communication and self-esteem.

These same differences in self-worth can be seen in adult family members. It is not so much that the family affects the adult's sense of self (although that certainly happens) as that parents with high self-esteem are more likely to create nurturing families, and low-self-worth parents to produce troubled families. The system evolves out of the architects of the family: the parents.

After years of working with families, I find that I can no longer blame parents, no matter how foolish or destructive their actions may be. I do hold parents responsible for accepting the consequences of their acts and learning to do differently. This is a good first step to improving the whole family situation.

Happily, it is possible to raise anyone's self-esteem, no matter what one's age or condition. Since the feeling of low worth has been learned, it can be unlearned, and something new learned in its place. The possibility for this learning lasts from birth to death, so it is never too late. At any point in a person's life, she or he can begin to learn higher self-worth.

I mean this to be the most important message in this book: *there is always hope that your life can change, because you can always learn new things.* Human beings can grow and change all their lives. It is a little harder as we grow older, and sometimes takes a little longer. It all depends on how set we choose to be in our ways. Knowing that change is possible and committing oneself to changing are first big steps. Some of us may be slow learners, but we are all educable.

This bit of prose contains my feelings and ideas about self-worth.*

My Declaration of Self-Esteem

I am me.

In all the world, there is no one else exactly like me. There are persons who have some parts like me, but no one adds up exactly like me. Therefore, everything that comes out of me is authentically mine because I alone chose it.

I own everything about me: my body, including everything it does; my mind, including all its thoughts and ideas; my eyes, including the images of all they behold; my feelings, whatever they may be: anger, joy, frustration, love, disappointment, excitement; my mouth, and all the words that come out of it: polite, sweet or rough, correct or incorrect; my voice, loud or soft; and all my actions, whether they be to others or to myself.

I own my fantasies, my dreams, my hopes, my fears.

I own all my triumphs and successes, all my failures and mistakes.

Because I own all of me, I can become intimately acquainted with me. By so doing, I can love me and be friendly with me in all my parts. I can then make it possible for all of me to work in my best interests.

I know there are aspects about myself that puzzle me, and other aspects that I do not know. But as long as I am friendly and loving to myself, I can cou-

*Reprinted by permission of (and available in poster form from) Celestial Arts. The poster is called "I Am Me."

rageously and hopefully look for the solutions to the puzzles and for ways to find out more about me.

However I look and sound, whatever I say and do, and whatever I think and feel at a given moment in time is me. This is authentic and represents where I am at that moment in time.

When I review later how I looked and sounded, what I said and did, and how I thought and felt, some parts may turn out to be unfitting. I can discard that which is unfitting, and keep that which proved fitting, and invent something new for that which I discarded.

I can see, hear, feel, think, say, and do. I have the tools to survive, to be close to others, to be productive, and to make sense and order out of the world of people and things outside of me.

I own me, and therefore, I can engineer me.

I am me and I am okay.

4

Self-Worth: The Source of Personal Energy

Let us imagine that inside each one of us is a power center responsible for maintaining life and hooked up to a universal power source. Each center has a generator that produces energy to continue life. The center is fueled by our breath, which comes from a central energy source. Without breath, there is no life.

The generator has many valves that control the rate of each person's energy, its quantity, and the directions in which it is channeled. Let us further imagine that what controls the valves are the knowledge and feelings that we have about ourselves. Our body language and activities reflect our thoughts and emotions. When we appreciate and love ourselves, our energy builds. When we use this energy positively and harmoniously to make a smoothly running system within each self, it creates a strong foundation from which that self can cope creatively, realistically, and compassionately with what life presents.

Another way of expressing this is: "When I feel good about myself and like myself, the chances are excellent that I will be able to meet life from a position of dignity, honesty, strength, love, and reality." This is the state of high self-esteem.

On the other hand, if a person's feeling toward him- or herself is one of depreciation, limitation, disgust, or any other negative attitude, the energy becomes diffused and fragmented. The self weakens, becoming a victim defeated by life: "If I do not like myself, I devalue and punish myself. I meet life from a position of fear and impotence, creating a state in which I feel victimized and act accordingly. I punish myself and others blindly. I become interchangeably subservient and tyrannical. I hold others responsible for my actions." In the accompanying psychological state, a person feels he or she doesn't count, feels a constant threat of rejection, and lacks the ability to look at her- or himself, others, and events in perspective. This is a state of low self-esteem.

A person who does not value him- or herself will expect someone else—a wife, husband, son, or daughter—to be responsible for bestowing that value. This often leads to endless manipulations that usually backfire on both parties.

To many, it may seem radical or even destructive to hear that it is essential for human beings to love and value themselves. To many people, loving one's self is selfishness, and thus an act against another, a war between people.

To avoid being against others, people have been taught to love others *instead* of themselves. This results in self-depreciation. The question also arises, if one does not love self, how can one know how to love others? We have plenty of evidence that loving oneself makes it possible to love others; self-worth and selfishness are not the same.

Being selfish is a form of upsmanship in which the message is some variation of "I am better than you." Loving oneself is a statement of value. When I value myself, I can love others as equally valuable. When I don't like myself, my feelings for others may be envy or fear.

We may also fear being criticized for seeming self-centered. I have found that the first step toward diminishing fear is to acknowledge it openly. You might say, for example, "I am afraid you will reject me if I tell you I like myself." Then check on your perception: "Is that true?" Ninety-five percent of the time, the answer will be, "No, I don't reject you; I feel you are brave to say so." It is amazing what happens when we confront our own monster—Fear of Rejection—especially in this simple way.

Good human relations and appropriate and loving behavior stem from persons who have strong feelings of self-worth. Simply stated, persons who love and value themselves are able to love and value others and treat reality appropriately. Having a strong sense of self-worth is the way to become more fully human, to having health and happiness, gaining and maintaining satisfying relationships, and being appropriate, effective, and responsible.

When one cares for oneself, one will not do anything to injure, degrade, humiliate, or otherwise destroy oneself or another, and will not hold others responsible for one's actions. For example, people who care for themselves would not abuse themselves through the use of drugs, alcohol, or tobacco or allow themselves to be physically or emotionally abused by others. People who care for themselves would not violate their relationships to others through violence.

Those who do not love themselves can easily become instruments of hate and destruction by unscrupulous people. They essentially give away their power, which often leads to emotional slavery. Perpetual placating exemplifies this.

The stronger one's self-worth, the easier it is to have and maintain the courage to change one's behavior. The more one values oneself, the less one demands from others. The less one demands from others, the more one can feel trust. The more one trusts oneself and others, the more one can love. The more one loves others, the less one fears them. The more one builds with them, the more one can know them. The more one knows another, the greater is one's bond and bridge with them. Self-worth behavior will thus help end the isolation and alienation between persons, groups, and nations today.

I invite you to look at two human facts.

FACT 1. Everyone has fingerprints and each set of fingerprints is unique, belonging only to that person. I REALLY AM THE ONLY ONE EXACTLY LIKE ME IN THIS WHOLE WORLD. THEREFORE I AM GUARANTEED TO BE DIFFERENT FROM EVERYONE IN SOME WAYS.

FACT 2. All human beings have the same basic physical ingredients—feet, arms, heads, etc.—and they are the same relative to each other. Therefore, I AM LIKE EVERYONE ELSE IN SOME BASIC PHYSICAL WAYS.

However, since I am also unique, I am different from *and* the same as everyone else in many ways.

These perspectives are very important in the development of self-esteem. Every person is a discovery. There is no way we can morally fashion one person in another's image. This means not asking a child to live in a parent's image or vice versa.

When I can acknowledge that I am a unique being, with the sameness and differentness of every other human being, then I can stop comparing myself to anyone else, and thus stop judging and punishing myself.

I can then learn about me. Many people act as though they think sameness creates love, and differentness creates dissension and difficulties. If we hold that view, we have no way of feeling whole. We will always feel split. I contend that we meet on the basis of our sameness and grow on the basis of our differences.

It is in honoring all parts of ourselves and being free to accept those parts that we lay the groundwork for high self-esteem. To do otherwise is to thwart nature. Many of us have created serious problems for ourselves by failing to understand that we are unique beings. We have tried instead to stuff ourselves into a mold so we will be like everyone else.

Some styles of parenting are based on comparison and conformity. This almost always results in low self-esteem. Accepting our uniqueness is one important foundation of self-esteem. Parents need to join the child in discovering who she or he is.

Let us think of a child as the outcome of two seeds that have joined. These seeds carry the physical resources of individuals who have preceded the child. These include tendencies and talents as well as physical characteristics. Each sperm and egg are channels from the past to the present.

Each of us has a different reservoir from which we draw. Whatever our heritage, it is our response to and our use of that heritage that make us different. We come into the world with a specific set of attributes, a unique cluster of variables selected from myriad possibilities of people who have preceded us.

Maybe another way of looking at this is: the sperm from any man contains physical manifestations of all the people who came before him, that is, his mother, his father, his grandmother, his grandfather—all those people connected by blood to him. The egg of any woman likewise contains physical manifestations of all who came before her. These are the initial resources from which we all draw.

Each person thus becomes a study in uniqueness and needs to be discovered and responded to in terms of that human specialness. Each human being is like an unlabeled

plant seed. We sow it and then wait to see what the plant turns out to be. Once it arrives, we have to discover its needs, what it looks like, how it flowers, and so forth. If we as adults have not yet discovered this for ourselves, now is a good time to start.

Perhaps the greatest challenge to parents is to plant our seeds in good faith and then wait to see what kind of plants they will become. The goal is to have no preconceptions about how a child should be. Instead, parents need to accept the fact that the plant will be unique unto itself. The child will have sameness as well as differentness in relation to each parent and every other human being. This makes parents discoverers, explorers, and detectives, rather than judges and molders. Parents can use time, patience, and observation to learn about the new treasure that has come into the world.

All individuals constantly shift and change. One is physically different at sixteen from what one has been at five or will be at eighty. This also applies to experience: a woman yet to bear a child is different from one who has given birth. Given this continual process of change, I strongly suggest we consciously keep discovering who we are. *We might call this our Updating Program. Reacquaint yourself with yourself and other family members. Bring yourselves up to date with the changes and growths that have taken place.*

Families who know about updating having found it helpful to arrange such a time every few months or so. *Take a Saturday morning or a Sunday afternoon. The topic is "What new has been happening to me lately?" Everyone has a chance to share, not just the children. Leadership can rotate among the members.*

It is important to keep a context of unconditional love and an uncritical attitude. The growths can include new bodily growth ("I grew three inches"), new skills ("Look, Ma, no hands [as I ride a bicycle]"), new views, new questions, and new jokes.

Don't forget the celebration party afterward. You will probably find these times can be very enjoyable. You might try creating a funny or romantic theme, for instance.

This process gives everyone's self-esteem a boost. We can each be seen as we now are, not as we were five months or two years ago. This also helps us put the past in perspective.

I have heard teenagers say, "But I am not a child anymore." This time-honored assertion of change is a good reminder. Staying up-to-date with each other furthers understanding and develops new opportunities for connection and excitement. Sometimes what is discovered is painful. That, too, is part of life and also needs airing.

I have a metaphor that families have found helpful. Think of a circular fountain that has hundreds of jet holes. Imagine each of these little holes as a symbol of growth in ourselves. As we grow, more of these jets open. Others are finished and close down. The fountain design keeps changing. It can always be beautiful; we are dynamic beings in constant movement.

Each of our fountains is in play even in infancy. The psychological reservoir from which an infant draws self-esteem is the outcome of all the actions, reactions, and interactions between and among the persons who care for that infant.

Coming into the world with a clean slate, the infant's sense of value and worth is a by-product of adults' handling. Adults can be unaware that the way they touch a child can contribute to the child's self-esteem. Children learn self-esteem from the voices they hear, the expressions in the eyes of the adults who handle them, the muscle tones as they are held, the way adults respond to their cries.

If the infant could talk, the words might be, "I am loved," "I am unnoticed; I feel rejected; I feel lonely," "I am most important," "I don't count. I am a burden." These are all forerunners to later messages of self-worth.

For parents starting out with new babies, giving attention to the following will greatly enhance the opportunity to develop self-worth of the babies.

1. Teach yourself to be aware of how you touch. If you were on the other end of your touch, how would it feel? When you touch your child, imagine what the child is learning. Is your touch hard, soft, weak, wet, loving, fearful, anxious? Tell your child what you are feeling.

2. Teach yourself to be aware of the expressions in your eyes. Then acknowledge them: "I am angry," "I am scared," "I am happy," and so forth. The important thing is to give your child straight emotional information from you about you.

3. Very young children tend to think all events occurring around them are because of them. That includes both good and bad events. One significant part of teaching self-esteem is to differentiate accurately between those events that belong to the child and those that belong to someone else. When you talk to your child, be very specific about whom your pronouns represent.

   For example, a mother, upset with one child's behavior, may say, "You kids never listen to me!" This is heard and believed by all her children present, though she is intending the message for one in particular.

4. Support children's ability and freedom to comment or ask questions, so that each person can verify what's going on. In the example above, the child with freedom to inquire can ask, "Do you mean me?"

All events, actions, voices, and the like that occur around infants are registered within them and, at some level, have meaning. Regressing adults to childhood through hypnosis validates these conclusions. Infants often register these events without the context that could adequately explain them. Without understanding these circumstances, the events become foundations for later false conclusions and consequent behavior.

I recommend that parents tell their infants what is going on, clearly indicating the context and the persons involved. When you and your spouse have had a fight, for instance, both of you could go to your infant's bed or playpen and take turns telling the child what is happening. This is particularly important if your child's name has been used by either of you in the fight. For example,

MOTHER (*picking up child from crib, holding the child lovingly*): Your father and I just had a fight. I wanted to take you over to my mother's house tonight. Your father is objecting. I have a short fuse. I got very angry and called him names.

FATHER (*holding the child and looking directly at him or her*): Your mother and I just finished a big fight. We still get mad when we have opposing ideas. I want to be home tonight, and your mother wants to go out. It is important for you to know that you are not the cause of this fight. We do it all by ourselves.

Being angry is different from describing anger; the tone of voice changes. I have seen babies as young as four months crying as their parents fight. When the fight was over and the parents talked to the child in the manner I've described, the child started smiling and went off to sleep.

Events do not have to be negative to confuse a child. They can be positive: "Your grandmother is coming today," or "Your father won a million dollars in the lottery." Events trigger emotional responses. Events color the emotional context. Tell your infants about that, too.

Infants do not differentiate *context from event, and event from self,* unless they are given help. The goal is to verbalize and clarify so that the child can know what is going on.

Another way to help a young child gain self-worth is to speak directly at eye level, using the child's name, touching lovingly, and carefully enunciating "I" and "you." When you do this, take the time to center yourself and be fully present for the child. Do not be thinking about something else. These directions will enable you to make full contact with the child, to successfully convey your love.

Self-esteem is further taught by calling attention to your child's sameness and differentness. Introduce this in the spirit of discovery, not in the context of competition or comparison (see "My Declaration of Self-Esteem" at the end of the previous chapter).

Self-esteem also is taught when you offer a child many opportunities to stimulate his or her interest and then patiently guide the child to a sense of mastery.

You, the parent, also teach self-esteem by how you manage discipline. When you become aware of the need to strengthen your child's self-worth while at the same time being very realistic, your efforts will produce the courage and strength to reshape behavior. A child treated with high esteem responds well to guidance.

For example, you have asked your child of three to pick up his or her toys. Your child does not respond immediately, proceeding as if you had not spoken. With the goal of heightening self-esteem, you recognize the communication has not been completed and recall that if one is immersed in thought or activity, people's voices can be faint.

You may also realize that your child's reaction might be a response to the hard tone in your voice. Or perhaps you made your request in an incongruent or nagging way. In addition, you may recognize that your child is playing around with power.

You can handle all these possibilities effectively by contacting the child at eye level, touching her or him in a loving way, and then, in a light but firm voice, saying that it is time to put things away. Become the cheering section while this is going on, turning the whole episode into a happy learning event.

Supporting self-worth helps a child toward creative amends-making and accepting the consequences of his or her behavior. This is another way to approach discipline as a chance for learning. Perhaps the most erosive effect on self-esteem comes from adults who shame, humiliate, deprive, or punish children for unacceptable behavior.

A self that is clearly loved and valued will learn new ways more easily.

Adults are the initiators, teachers, and models for self-esteem. However, we can't teach what we don't know. When wise people learn that they don't know, they can set out to learn. When people arrive at parenthood without high self-esteem themselves, they have new opportunities to gain it as they guide their children.

Many of us parents still suffer from the low self-esteem we learned growing up. It can be a bit of a bind when we ask ourselves to teach what we were never taught. However, the fortunate part is that self-worth can be reshaped at any age. Once one discovers one has low self-worth, is willing to acknowledge that condition, *and* is willing to change, one can achieve high self-worth. Developing self-worth takes time, patience, and the courage to risk new things. Investing in these efforts means we can release vast, untapped resources through developing value feelings for ourselves.

I often fantasize what would happen if, after tonight's sleep, everyone woke up with high self-esteem. I think our world would be very different. People would be able to treat themselves and each other with love, with kindness, and with reality.

5
Your Self Mandala

This chapter is aimed at further exciting you about yourself and, through your example, at exciting those around you, especially your family members, about being a human being and being alive.

I want to interest you in learning more about how your various parts work, and what a treasure you really are. Humans are wonderfully made.

To start, imagine that you are looking through spectacles that have eight lenses. Each lens reflects an essential part of yourself:

Your body   — your physical part

Your thoughts   — your intellectual part

Your feelings   — your emotional part

Your senses   — your sensual parts: eyes, ears, skin, tongue, and nose

Your relationship — your interactional part

Your context   — your space, time, air, color, sound, and temperature

Your nutrition   — the liquids and solids that you ingest

Your soul   — your spiritual part

Through the first lens, you will see the physical body with all its parts and systems. If you have never seen the in

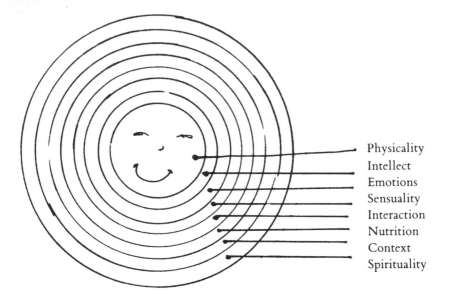

Physicality
Intellect
Emotions
Sensuality
Interaction
Nutrition
Context
Spirituality

side of a human body, and most of us have not, find a good anatomy book in which you can see pictures of your bones, muscles, internal organs, together with all the different systems (respiratory, circulatory, etc.). Let yourself be awed and amazed at how wonderfully your body is engineered and what a treasure house of resources it contains. If you can find a videotape of this in the library, so much the better.

Apply this information to your own body. Are you, its owner, meeting its needs? Are you listening to it? It will tell you when you are tired, hungry, or over-stressed, or alert you to any part of you that needs special care.

The second lens shows your intellect, the cognitive part of your brain. This lens tells you about the information you take in, the thoughts you have, and the meaning you give them. From this cognitive and rational part, you can get answers to such questions as, "What do I understand? How do I learn new things? How do I analyze situations and solve problems?"

We are just beginning to learn about the fantastic feats of learning that our brains and minds can accomplish. I have listed some interesting books on this subject and related subjects in the bibliography.

The third lens is that of your emotions, your feelings. How free are you to recognize and acknowledge them? What restrictions do you put on your feelings? How do you express them? Can you be friendly to all your feelings, knowing that how you deal with them makes the difference? All feelings are human. They bring texture, color, and sensitivity to life. Without feelings, we would be robots. Your feelings show you your current temperature. Your feelings *about* these feelings show you where your self-worth is in relation to your feelings.

The fourth lens lets you know how you sense yourself. What is the physical condition of your sense organs? What freedoms do you give yourself to look, hear, touch, taste, and smell? What restrictions do you place on these wonderful parts of yourself? Can you allow yourself to let the restrictions go? Many of us were taught as children that we could only look at, touch, or listen to certain things. That often resulted in limiting our use of our senses. To acknowledge, honor, and fully and freely use our senses is the main way we interact with the outside world and stimulate ourselves internally. We need a lot of sensual food to create interest for our senses. In turn, this bathes the inner psychological self.

The fifth lens shows how you interact with the people in *your* world. Your interaction shapes the nature of your relationships. How do you evaluate the quality of your various relationships? How do you use your power? Do you give it away and become a victim? Do you use it to become a dictator? Do you use it to develop harmony within yourself and with others, thus becoming an empowering leader? In other words, do you use your power to nurture yourself or others, or to threaten? Do you team up with family members or others to do things together? Do you have fun, make jokes, and generally use good humor to make your life and that of others lighter and happier? Remember that humor and love are two very powerful healing forces.

The sixth lens has to do with nutrition. What kind of food and drink do you put into your body? Do you understand that you need good nutrition to feed your body? Current research shows a relationship between what one eats and drinks and how one feels and acts.

The seventh lens has to do with your context. This refers to the sights and sounds, the feel of things, the temperature, the light, the color, the quality of air, and the space where you live and work. Each of these factors has an important effect on your life. For example, the kind of light and the amount of light have a great deal to do with your health. We are also beginning to see a relationship between color, sound, and music, and what happens in the human body.

The eighth lens has to do with your spiritual connection. This represents your relationship to your life force. How do you regard your life? Do you honor it? Do you use your spiritual connection in your daily life?

Each of these eight parts performs a different task and can be understood separately. However, within a person, no part can function by itself. All parts are interacting with all other parts all the time. This is another way of saying that whatever happens to one part affects all others.

The following figure shows the eight parts as though they were separate discs. All of them come together at the center which is represented by the Self, which is YOU.

Imagine each disc as a different color. You might even want to make one. Just cut out eight discs from colored paper, each one graduated in size.

Place your picture in the center, on a separate disc. You can call this your Self Mandala. Give yourself time to think about what you know and how you use your various parts. For example, you have very likely already experienced what happens to you when you eat something to which you are allergic, or when you are faced with criticism from someone, or are angry and cannot express it. These negative outcomes are manifestations of how our parts behave.

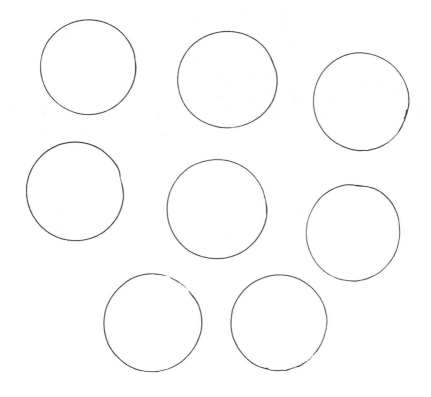

Considering our parts as interacting with one another was a foreign concept, especially to Western medicine, until forty years ago. Then physicians began to realize that inharmonious interaction among mind, emotion, and body was a large factor in the development of ulcers. This produced a new specialty, named psychosomatic medicine. Following the line of reasoning that led to this finding, it is equally possible that harmonious interaction among these three parts leads to health.

This was a wonderful start. We are now learning that all eight parts influence and are influenced by each other. We need to learn as much as we can about how this works, we are only beginning to have technology that helps us understand this process. For instance, we can now monitor the effect of negative thoughts on chemical responses in the body.

Learn all you can. Articles about some of our technology read like science fiction. Equally fantastic developments are under way in science, particularly physics.

A whole new world of information is opening up. Today we hear a lot about stress and its negative effects on the body, mind, and emotions. Now that you know these interrelationships exist, you can learn how to observe yourself and what happens to you. You will begin to see many things that you were unaware of before.

As we increase our knowledge of ourselves, developing and maintaining health becomes paramount. To create the best possible scenario for our total health and well-being we would:

1. Give our body good care, attention, exercise, and love.

2. Develop our intellect through learning how we learn and surrounding ourselves with stimulating ideas, books, activities, learning experiences, and opportunities to engage in dialogue with others.

3. Give ourselves permission to become so friendly with our feelings that they work for us instead of against us.

4. Develop our senses, learn about their care, and think of them and use them as vital avenues to bring things into ourselves.

5. Develop harmonious ways of problem-solving, nurturing, and conflict resolution; and develop congruent and healthy relationships.

6. Learn what our nutritional needs are and provide for them; remember that each person's body is unique. Eating strawberries gives one person hives; another will have a taste treat.

7. Provide the place where you live and work with the kinds of sights, sounds, temperature, light, color, quality of air, and space that more fully support life.

8. Engage yourself with what it means to be alive, to be a part of the universe, to fully manifest yourself and to know that there is a life force outside yourself.

As we pay more attention to our total health, we will certainly arrive at a more joyous, responsible, and effective life. Perhaps even a greater reward will be developing a closer connection between ourselves and our planet. We are at this time in the shadow of nuclear weapons which could herald the end of our existence on the planet as we know it today.

On a television program not so long ago, I saw a picture of a nuclear weapon and, within another few minutes, a

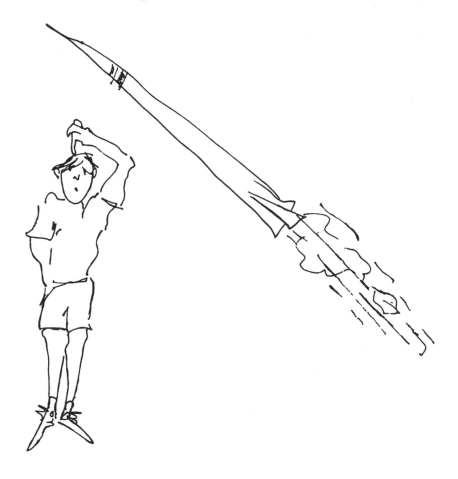

picture of a space ship launching. The two were remarkably similar in their forms but very different in their goals. One was to destroy, the other to discover.

We are blessed with fine endowments as human beings. It remains for us to choose how we will use these resources. I believe we have the energy, intelligence, information, will, love, and technology that can help us make the kinds of choices that will further our evolutionary process. Human beings do have a higher nature. By really knowing and appreciating ourselves in all our parts, we can reach that higher nature.

6

Communication: Talking and Listening

I see communication as a huge umbrella that covers and affects all that goes on between human beings. Once a human being has arrived on this earth, *communication is the largest single factor determining what kinds of relationships she or he makes with others and what happens to each in the world.* How we manage survival, how we develop intimacy, how productive we are, how we make sense, how we connect with our own divinity—all depend largely on our communication skills.

Communication has many facets. It is a gauge by which two people measure one another's self-worth. It is also the tool by which the "pot level" can be changed. Communication covers the whole range of ways people pass information back and forth: it includes the information they give and receive, the ways that information is used, and how people make meaning out of this information.

All communication is learned. Every baby who comes into this world comes only with raw materials—no self-concept, no experience of interacting with others, and no experience in dealing with the world. Babies learn all these things through communication with the people who are in charge of them from birth on.

By the time we reach the age of five, we probably have had a billion experiences in sharing communication. By that age we have developed ideas about how we see ourselves, what we can expect from others, and what seems to be possible or impossible for us in the world. Unless something powerful changes those conclusions, that early learning becomes the foundation for the rest of our lives.

Once we realize all communication is learned, we can set about changing it if we want to. First, I want to review the elements of communication. At any point in time everyone brings the same elements to the communication process.

We bring our *bodies*—which move and have form and shape.

We bring our *values*—those concepts that represent each person's way of trying to survive and live a "good" life (the *oughts* and *shoulds* for self and others).

We bring our *expectations* of the moment, gleaned from past experience.

We bring our *sense organs*—eyes, ears, nose, mouth, and skin, which enable us to see, hear, smell, taste, touch, and be touched.

We bring our *ability to talk*—words and voice.

We bring our *brains*—the storehouses of our knowledge, including what we have learned from past experience, what we have read and been taught, and what has been recorded in both hemispheres of our brains. We respond to communication like a film camera equipped with sound. The brain records pictures and sounds in the present, between you and me.

This is how it works. You are face to face with me. Your senses take in what I look like, how I sound, what I smell like, and, if you happen to touch me, how I feel to you. Your brain then reports what this means to you, calling on your past experience, particularly with your parents and other authority figures, your book learning, and your ability to use this information to explain the message from your senses. Depending on what your brain reports, you feel comfortable or uncomfortable; your body is loose or tight.

Meanwhile, I am going through something similar. I too see, hear, feel something, think something, have a past, and have values and expectations; and my body is doing something. You don't really know what I am sensing, what I am feeling, what my past is, what my values are, or exactly what my body is doing. You have only guesses and fantasies, and I have the same about you. Unless the guesses and fantasies are checked out, they become the "facts" and as such can often lead to miscommunications and traps.

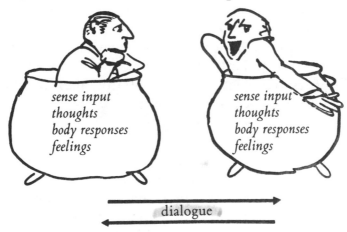

This is a picture of communication between two people.

To illustrate the sensory message, the brain's interpretation of it, and the consequent feelings and feelings *about* the feelings, let's consider the following. I am in your presence; you are a man. I think, "Your eyes are very wide apart, you must be a deep thinker"; or, "You have long hair, you must be a hippie." To make sense out of what I see, drawing on my experience and knowledge, what I tell myself influences me to have certain feelings both about myself and about you before a word is spoken.

For example, if I tell myself you're a hippie, and I'm afraid of hippies, then I might feel fear in myself and anger at you. I might get up and leave this frightening situation, or I might slug you. Then again, perhaps I would tell myself you look like a scholar. Since I admire smart people, and feel you are like me, I might want to start a conversation. On the other hand, if I felt myself to be stupid, your being a scholar might make me feel ashamed, so I would bend my head and feel humiliated. In other words, I make you up by how I interpret you. You can easily not know anything about how I am perceiving you. My responses to you might not make sense to you.

Meanwhile you are also taking me in and trying to make sense out of me. Perhaps you smell my perfume and decide I am a nightclub singer, which is offensive to you; so you turn your back. On the other hand, maybe my perfume would make you decide I am a neat gal, and you would search for ways to contact me. Again, all this takes place in a fraction of a second before anything is said.

With whom am I now having the pleasure, you or my picture of you?

I have developed a set of games or exercises that will help deepen your awareness and appreciation of communication. As with the rest of this chapter, these emphasize looking, listening, paying attention, getting understanding, and making meaning.

It is best to try these games with a partner. Choose any member of your family you wish. You will all learn and grow if you all take part. *If no one wishes to join you, then try it alone in your imagination.*

Sit directly in front of your partner, close enough to be able to touch easily. You may not be used to doing what I'm going to ask you to do; it may even seem silly or uncomfortable. If you feel that way, try to go along anyway and see what happens. No one, as far as I know, has ever been even slightly damaged.

Now imagine you are two people, each with a camera, photographing the other. This is how it is when two people are face to face. Other people may be present, but only two people can be eye to eye at any moment in time.

A picture must be processed to see what actually was photographed. Human beings process their pictures in the brain, which interprets them; then action follows from that.

Now, to start the exercise. *First, sit back comfortably in your chair and just look at the person in front of you. Forget what Mama and Papa said about its being impolite to stare. Give yourself the luxury of fully looking. Don't talk while you are doing*

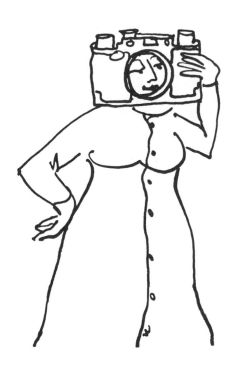

this. Notice each movable part of the face. See what the eyes, eyelids, eyebrows, nostrils, facial and neck muscles are doing, and how the skin is coloring. Is it turning pink, red, white, blue? You'll observe the body, its size and form, and the clothing on it. And you'll be able to see how the body is moving—what the legs and arms are doing, how the back is held.

Do this for about one minute and close your eyes. See how clearly you can bring this person's face and body to your mind's eye. If you've missed something, open your eyes and pick up on the details you may have overlooked.

This is the picture-taking process. Our brains could develop the picture as follows: "His hair is too long. He should sit up straight. He is just like his mother"; or, "I like her eyes. I like her hands. I don't like the color of her dress. I don't like her frown." Or you may ask yourself, "Does he frown all the time? Why doesn't he look at me more? Why is he wasting himself?" You may compare yourself to her. "I could never be as smart as she is." You may remember old injuries: "He had an affair once; how can I trust him?"

This is part of your internal dialogue. Are you aware that dialogue of some kind is going on in your head all the time? When your senses are focused on something, this inner dialogue is emphasized.

As you become aware of your thoughts, you may notice some of them make you feel bad. You may also notice that your body responds. Your body may stiffen, your stomach get butterflies, your hands become sweaty, your knees weak, and your heart beat faster. You may get dizzy or blush. If, on the other hand, you're having thoughts that make you feel good, your body may relax. Your thoughts and your body responses have strong influences on each other.

All right. We're ready to go on with the exercise. You have really looked at your partner. Now close your eyes. Does she or he remind you of anyone? Almost everyone reminds one of someone else. It could be a parent, a former boy- or girlfriend, a movie star, a character in a fairy tale or literature—anybody. If you find a resemblance, let yourself be aware of how you feel about that other person.

Chances are that if the reminders are strong, you'll sometimes get that person mixed up with the one in front of you. You could have been reacting to your partner or someone else. In this case, your partner will be in the dark and feel unreal about what is happening.

After about a minute, open your eyes and share what you've learned with your partner. If you found another person while your eyes were closed, tell your partner who it was, what part of him or her reminded you of your partner, and how you feel about this. Of course, your partner will do the same thing.

When this kind of thing happens outside this exercise context, communication is taking place with shadows from the past, not real people. I have actually found people who lived together for thirty years treating one another as someone else and constantly suffering disappointment as a result. "I am not your father!" finally cries the husband in a rage.

As mentioned, your responses to someone take place almost instantly. What words come out depend on how free you and your partner feel with one another, how sure you are about yourself, and how aware you are in expressing yourself. Let as much be said as is possible. Don't push either yourself or your partner.

So you have looked at your partner, and you have become aware of what is going on inside you. *Now, close your eyes for a minute. Let yourself become aware of what you were feeling and thinking as you looked: your body feelings and also how you felt about some of your thoughts and feelings. Imagine telling your partner all you can about your inner space activity. Does the very thought of it make you quake and feel scared? Are you excited? Do you dare? Put into words all you want to and/or can about your inner space activity, talking quietly and with a sharing attitude about what went on within you.*

How much of your inner space activity were you willing to share with your partner? The answer to this question can give you a pretty good idea of where you stand in terms of freedom with your partner. If you quaked at the thought of sharing, you probably didn't want to tell much. If you had negative feelings, you probably wanted to hide them. If there is very much of this negative kind of response, you've probably been troubled about your relationship. If you felt you had to be careful, could you let yourself know why? Could you be honest and direct?

Here is another important exercise related to the one you have just finished. I call it *bringing yourself up to date.*

All family members have a history with each other. Sometimes things have occurred in the past that never got talked about, leaving old hurts and fantasies still around. Something in us human beings seeks closure of unfinished business.

Give yourself permission to finish unfinished business. Having done that, you can bring yourself up to date with each family member and start out on a clean slate. Old unfinished business is often a barrier to full acceptance in relationships. Get in the habit of doing the following when the need arises.

Invite one family member to join you. Remember this is not a confrontation. It is more like closing the books on an old subject, with understanding. If your invitation is accepted, choose a comfortable place to sit, position yourself at eye level, calm yourself, and breathe consciously. Now, tell your family member that there are some things you would like to clear up, make straight, or close. Perhaps all you will have to do to finish is put words to what this is. In some cases more will be required: for example, if your unfinished business includes assumptions, you may want to ask some questions.

The dialogue might go something like this. "Two weeks ago Monday, I told you that I would go for a walk with you. I didn't do it. I forgot. I want you to know that I want to work on keeping my promises." Or, "Last night I felt angry when you chose someone else, rather than me. I don't feel angry anymore. Could you tell me why you did not choose me?" Or, "I feel so proud of your performance at the concert yesterday. I guess I was feeling a little jealous and I did not tell you."

Many families have told me this keeping-up-to-date exercise has prevented many possible rifts, healed rifts that exist, deepened bonds between family members, and has led to more understanding of each other.

When you have finished what you wanted to say, invite your family member to share his or her feelings and any further thoughts on the matter. Close the exercise with a thank-you and a sharing of your feelings now that things are resolved.

It is important to remember that any invitation is open to acceptance as well as rejection. If the family member you ask does not accept your invitation, thank that person for at least hearing you and wait for another time.

Having done exercises about the picture-taking process, now we are ready for the sound part of your camera to become active. When your partner starts breathing heavily, coughing, making sounds, or talking, your ears report it to you. Your hearing stimulates past inner space experience just as seeing does.

Listening to another person's voice usually puts other sounds in the background. The voice may be loud, soft,

high, low, clear, muffled, slow, or fast. Again, you have thoughts and feelings about what you hear. You notice and react to voice quality—sometimes to the extent that the words may escape you and you have to ask your partner to repeat them.

I'm convinced few people would talk as they do if they knew how they sounded. Voices are like musical instruments: they can be in or out of tune. Since the tunes of our voices are not born with us, we have hope. If people could really hear themselves, they might change their voices. I am convinced most people don't hear how they really sound but only how they *intend* to sound.

Once a woman and her son were in my office. She was saying in loud tones to him, "You are always yelling!" The son answered quietly, "You are yelling now." The woman denied it. I happened to have my tape recorder on, and I asked her to listen to herself. Afterwards she said rather soberly, "My goodness, that woman sounded loud!"

She was unaware of how her voice sounded while she was talking; she was aware only of her thoughts, which were not getting over because her voice drowned them out. You all probably have been around people whose voices were high-pitched and harsh, or low and barely audible, or who talked as if they had a mouthful of mush; and you have experienced the resultant injury to your ears. A person's voice can help you or hinder you in understanding the meaning of her or his words.

Share with your partner how her voice sounds to you, and ask her to do the same.

When more of us know how to hear our voices, I think they will change considerably. *Listen to yourself on a tape recorder; prepare yourself for a surprise. If you listen to it in the presence of others, you will probably be the only one who feels your recorded voice sounds different. Everyone else will say it's right on. Nothing is wrong with the tape recorder.*

Now let us go farther in exploring communication. This time it will have to do with touch. To help you find the next exercises more meaningful, consider what I am about to tell you about touch.

Just as breath is our link to life, touch is the most telling means of conveying emotional information between two people. Our most concrete introduction to this world was through the touch of human hands, and touch remains the most trusted connection between people. I will believe your touch before I believe your words. Intimate relationships are turned on or off by the way people experience touch.

Remind yourself of how many ways you use your hands: to lift, to caress, to hold, to slap, to balance. Every touch has a feeling connected with it, including love, trust, fear, weakness, excitement, and boredom.

I teach people to become aware of what their touch feels like to someone else. The way to do this is to ask, "How do you feel when I touch you as I do?" We have very little training in learning to feel our touch. For many people, the above question might seem awkward. After you try it for awhile, you can see its value.

Another part of touching consists of telling someone else how his or her touch feels to you. It is important to remember that until someone calls our attention to it, many of us are unaware of what our touch feels like. I am reminded of the many times loving, enthusiastic people have left blood in my hands: I was wearing rings when they were squeezing my fingers in a hearty handshake.

I believe also that most parents never intend to injure their children when they hit them. They are altogether unaware of the power of their slap. Many parents are horror-stricken when they see the results of what they have done. This applies particularly to individuals who are taught to be physically strong without being taught to be aware of their effect on other people, especially children.

I knew a police officer who broke three of his wife's ribs when he was hugging her after a period of absence. I know this man had no hostile feelings toward his wife. He just had no idea of his strength.

I want to emphasize that we need to learn to feel our touch as well as think it. This part of our education has been neglected for most of us. We can change this if we take our courage to ask, "How do you feel when I touch you as I do?" *The next time you greet someone by shaking hands, or caress someone, let yourself become aware of what is happening as you touch that person. Then check out your observations with him or her: "Just then, I felt . . .. How about you?"*

Now we're ready for another exercise. *Again sit within touching distance of your partner and look at each other for one minute. Then take each other's hands and close your eyes. Slowly explore the hands of your partner. Think about their form, their texture. Let yourself be aware of any attitudes you have about what you're discovering in these hands. Experience how it feels to touch these hands and be touched by them. See how it feels to feel the pulses in your respective fingertips.*

After about two minutes, open your eyes and continue touching at the same time you are looking. Let yourself experience what happens. Is there a change in your touching experience when you look?

After about thirty seconds, close your eyes, continue to touch, and experience any possible changes. After a minute, disengage your hands with a parting but not a rejection. Sit back and let yourself feel the impact of the whole experience. Open your eyes and share your inner space with your partner.

Try this variation: one person closes his or her eyes, and the second person uses hands to trace all the parts of the first one's face, keeping awareness on the touch. Reverse this and then share your experience.

At this point in the experiment, many people say they become uncomfortable. Some say their sexual responses get stirred up, and it is like having intercourse in public. My response is, "It was your hands and faces you were touching, nothing else!" Some say they feel nothing; the whole thing seems stupid and silly. This saddens me as it could mean these people have constructed walls around themselves so they get no joy from physical contact. Does anyone ever really outgrow the wish and need for physical comforting and contact?

In the past ten years, people have begun to be more receptive about their touching needs. Hug passes and hug coupons have begun to appear in many places. Hugging is a nonsexual, very human way to get and give nurture. It is gradually spreading to men as well. Their skins get just as hungry as women's skins. Maybe if people had more permission to gratify their needs for touching, they would not commit so much aggression.

I have noticed that when couples gradually begin to enjoy touching each other, their relationships improve in all areas. The taboo against touching and being touched goes a long way to explain the sterile, unsatisfying, monstrous experiences many people have in their sexual lives. This taboo also does much to explain to me why young people often get into premature sex. They feel the need for physical contact and think the only avenue open to them is intercourse.

As you went through these experiments, you probably realized that they are subject to individual interpretation. When our hands touch, you and I feel the touch differently. It is important for people to tell each other how the other's touch feels. If I intend a loving touch and you experience it as harsh, I want to know that. Not knowing how we look or sound, or how our touch feels to someone else is very common, and since we often intend that which does not come across, we encounter unnecessary disappointment and pain in our relationships.

Now try smelling each other. This may sound a little vulgar. However, any of us who have used perfume knows that the sense of smell is important to how we are perceived. Many a potentially intimate relationship has been aborted or remained distant because of bad odors or scents. See what happens as you break your taboos against smelling, and let yourself tell and be told about your smells.

By this time, as you made contact with your eyes, ears, skins, and sharing one another's inner space activities, you may already have a heightened appreciation of each other. It is equally possible that as you first looked, memories of old hurts were so strong that that was all you could see. I call this riding the garbage train. As long as you look now but see yesterday, the barriers will only get higher. If you encounter the garbage train, say so and dump it.

What is so important to remember is to look at one another in the present, in the here and now. Believe it or not, I have met hundreds of family pairs who have not touched each other except in rage or sex, and who have never looked at one another except in fantasy or out of the corners of their eyes. Eyes clouded with regret for the past, or fear for the future, limit vision and offer little chance for growth or change.

The next exercises are concerned with physical positions and how they affect communication.

Turn your chairs around back to back, about eighteen inches apart, and sit down. Talk to each other. Very quickly you will notice some changes. You become physically uncomfortable, your sense of enjoyment of the other decreases, and it's hard to hear.

Add another dimension to the exercise: move your chairs about fifteen feet apart, remaining back to back. Notice the drastic changes in your communication. It is even possible to "lose" your partner entirely.

One of my first discoveries after beginning the study of families in operation was how much of their communication was carried on in precisely this way. The context is as follows: The husband is watching TV; the wife is behind the newspaper. Each pays attention elsewhere, yet they are talking about something important. "I hope you made the mortgage payment today," says one. The other grunts. Two weeks later the eviction notice arrives. You can probably think of many similar examples of your own.

Don't be fooled by thinking that to be polite requires great physical distance between people. I think having more than three feet between people puts a great strain on their relationship.

Now let's try something else. *Decide which of you will be A and which B. In the first round, A stands and B sits on the floor directly in front of A. Talk about how this feels. Stop after one minute. Share how it feels to talk in this position. Then change places and share again.*

At one time we were all in the on-the-floor position in relation to the adults around us. It is the position of any young children in your family right now.

Still in these positions, let yourselves become aware of how your bodies feel. The sitter has to look up. Within thirty seconds, neck and shoulders will begin to ache, eyes and eye muscles will become strained, and the head will probably begin to ache. The stander will have to arch his or her back to look down, and back and neck muscles will begin to ache. It will probably become difficult to see as the strain grows.

(Give yourself just thirty seconds in these positions so you'll know what I'm talking about. They become really horrible by sixty seconds.)

The physical discomfort engendered by these positions negatively influences the feeling tone of any interaction.

This feeling tone is subliminal and therefore not conscious.

Everyone was born small and each of us spends ten to fifteen years (sometimes longer) being shorter than our parents. Considering the fact that most of our communication takes place in the positions described above, there is little wonder so many people feel so small all their lives. Understanding this, we can also understand why so many grow up with distorted views about themselves and their parents as people.

Try these same positions again, only this time using adult characters. Starting off with a male and female, for instance, visualize which of your parents was above and which was on the bottom.

Let's look at this exercise from a slightly different perspective. *Again, in the position of the last exercise, both of you look straight ahead and notice the scenery. From the floor you see knees and legs; and if you look down, you see feet and very big feet. Look up and you see all the protrusions: genitals, bellies, breasts, chins, and noses. Everything is out of perspective.*

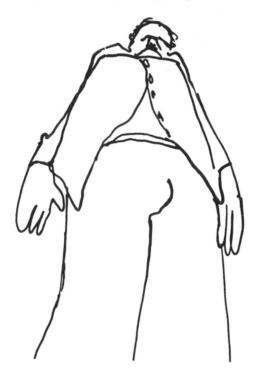

So often I have heard reports from people about their parents' mean looks, huge breasts, bellies, huge genitals, and chins, and so on. Then when I met the parents I often saw quite the opposite. The child had formed this menacing picture from an out-of-perspective position.

The parent sees the child out of perspective as well and might always envision the child as small. Images formed early in childhood can become the bases on which later experiences rest. These may *never* change.

Try this variation. Taking in the same up-and-down positions, make hand contact. The one on the floor holds a hand and arm up; the one standing has an arm down. Thirty seconds is enough time for the upraised arm to get numb.

Inasmuch as the adult enjoys a more comfortable position, with the arm down, it might be difficult to realize the discomfort being inflicted on the child. The child might struggle to get away and the adult could become irritated at this "negative behavior." All the poor kid wants is to get comfortable. The result is unintentional abuse.

How many times have you seen a child, both arms up, being virtually dragged along between parents? Or a hurrying parent dragging along his or her offspring by one arm on the bias?

Get into your standing and sitting positions for thirty seconds again. Then break eye contact and notice how quickly this change in positions relieves your neck, eyes, shoulders, and back.

Again, imagine how easy it would be for an adult to interpret this action on the part of a child as disrespectful. On the other hand, the child trying to contact her parent could interpret his glancing away as indifference or even rejection.

It would be natural for a child to tug at his parent for attention. This might annoy the parent to the extent that he or she slapped the pesky child. All of this would be humiliating, and the child could get hurt. This whole interaction is fertile breeding ground for engineering feelings of fear and hate in the child and rejection on the part of the adult. The sad part is that the causes are largely outside an individual's awareness. If you have young children or children smaller than you in your home now, conduct a little research to learn how contact is now being made with them.

Suppose the parent responds to the tugging by delivering a supposedly reassuring pat on the child's head but doesn't gauge the force very well?

You, the stander, give the sitter a rather obvious pat on the head. Is it experienced as comforting or as a cranial explosion?

The significance of eye contact can be seen in this last set of exercises. For people to contact one another successfully, they need to be at eye level and facing one another. When images and expectations of one another are being formed, eye-level contact is essential between adults and children. First experiences have a great impact, and unless something happens to change them, those experiences will be the reference points for the future.

If you have young children, work it out so you contact them at eye level. Most of the time this means that adults will have to squat or, as an alternative, build eye-level furniture so the child can stand on his/her own feet to be at eye level with you.

Now I would like to undertake some exercises that will help deepen understanding and make meaning between two people. Good human relations depend on people understanding one another's meaning, whatever words they happen to use. Since our brains work so much faster than our mouths, we often use a kind of shorthand, which might have an entirely different meaning for the other person than it does for us.

We learned from the picture-taking exercise that although we thought we were seeing, we were actually making up much of what we saw. This same kind of thing is possible with words. Let's try this exercise.

Make what you believe to be a true statement to your partner. That person then repeats it to you verbatim, mimicking your voice, tone, inflection, facial expression, body position, movement. Check for accuracy, and if it fits, say so. If it doesn't, produce your evidence. Be explicit; don't make a guessing game out of this. Then reverse roles.

This exercise helps us focus on really listening to and really seeing another person. Listening and looking require one's full attention. We pay a heavy price for not seeing and not hearing accurately: we end up by making assumptions and treating them as facts.

A person can look either with attention or without attention. Whoever is being looked at may not know the difference and assume he's being seen when he is not. And what the first person thinks she sees is what she reports. If she happens to be in a position of power—as a parent, teacher, or administrator—she can cause him personal pain.

Let's consider words a moment. When someone is talking to you, do those words make sense? Do you believe them? Are they strange, or do they sound like nonsense? Do you have feelings about the other person and yourself? Do you feel stupid because you don't understand? Puzzled because you can't make sense? If so, can you say so and ask questions? If you can't, do you just guess? Do you not ask questions for fear you'll be thought stupid, and thus you remain stupid? What about the feeling of *having* to be quiet?

These kinds of inner questions are natural and occasionally point to areas of specific concern. If you concentrate on these kinds of questions, you stop listening. I say it this way: "To the degree that you are involved with internal dialogue, you stop listening."

As you try to hear the other person, you are, at the very least, in a three-ring circus. You are paying attention to the sound of the other person's voice, experiencing past and future fears concerning you both, becoming aware of your own freedom to say what you are feeling, and finally concentrating on efforts to get the meaning from your partner's words. This is the complicated inner space activity each person has, out of which communication develops and on which interaction between any two people depends.

Let's go back to the exercises. *Can you begin to feel how it is to use yourself fully to get the other person's meaning? Do you know that words and meaning are not always the same? Do you know the difference between full listening and half listening? When you were imitating, did you find that your attention wandered and you made more errors in seeing?*

My hope is that you can learn to engage yourself fully while listening. If you don't want to or can't listen, don't pretend. Just say, "I can't be present right now." You'll make fewer mistakes that way. This is true of every interaction, but particularly true between adults and children. To listen freely requires the following:

1. The listener is giving full attention to the speaker and is fully present.
2. The listener puts aside any preconceived ideas of what the speaker is going to say.
3. The listener interprets what is going on descriptively and not judgmentally.
4. The listener is alert for any confusion and asks questions to get clarity.
5. The listener lets the speaker know that the speaker has been heard and also the content of what was communicated.

Now let's go to the next part of the meaning exercises. *Sit face to face with your partner, as before. Now one of you makes a statement you believe to be true. The other responds with, "Do you mean . . ." to indicate whether or not she or he has understood. The aim is to get three yeses. For example:*

"I think it's hot in here."

"Do you mean that you're uncomfortable?"

"Yes."

"Do you mean that I should be hot, too?"

"No."

"Do you mean that you want me to bring you a glass of water?"

"No."

"Do you mean that you want me to know that you are uncomfortable?"

"Yes."

"Do you mean that you want me to do something about it?"

"Yes."

At this juncture at least the listener has understood the speaker's meaning. If the listener was not able to get any yeses, the speaker would simply have to explain what was meant.

Try this several times with the same statement, changing partners each time. Then try a question. Remember you are trying to get the meaning of the question, not to answer it. Do several rounds.

You are probably discovering how easy it is to misunderstand someone by making assumptions about what was meant. This can have serious results, as we've indicated, but they can also be funny.

I remember a young mother who was eager to clue into her son's sexual questions. Her opportunity came one day when he asked her, "Mommy, how did I get here?" Believe me, she made the most of her opportunity. When she finished, her son, looking extremely puzzled, said, "I meant, did we come by train or by airplane?" (The family had moved some months previously.)

As you were doing the meaning exercises, were you able to become fully aware of the trust and enjoyment that can come from engaging in a deliberate effort to understand? It is probably becoming more clear that everyone has different images for the same words. Learning about those images is called understanding.

Has the following ever happened at your house? You and your spouse meet at the end of the day. One of you says, "So, how was your day?" The other answers, "Oh, nothing special."

What meanings are evident in this exchange? One woman who went through this fairly frequently said this was her husband's way of turning her off. Her husband told me this was the way his wife showed him she didn't care.

"So, how was your day?" can mean, "I had a tough day, and I'm glad you're here. I hope it will go better now."

It can mean, "You're usually a grouch. Are you still grouchy?"

It can mean, "I am interested in what happens to you. I would like to hear about anything exciting that happened to you."

"Oh, nothing special" can mean, "Are you really interested? I'd like that."

It can mean, "What are you trying to trap me in now? I'll watch my step."

How about some examples from your family?

Many people assume everyone else already knows everything about them. This is a very common communication trap. Another is the *hint method,* in which people use one-word answers. Remember this old story? An inquiring reporter visited a rather plush old people's home. As the director proudly escorted him around, the reporter heard someone call out "31" from a nearby room. Great laughter ensued. This procedure went on with several other numbers, all of which got the same response. Finally someone called out, "Number 11!" There was a dead silence. The reporter asked what was going on, and the director replied that these folks had been there so long they know all each other's jokes. To save energy they had given each joke a number. "I understand that," said the reporter. "But what about Number 11?" The director responded, "That poor guy never could tell a joke well."

Another communication trap is the assumption that no matter what one actually says, everyone else should understand one. This is the *mind-reading method.*

I am reminded of a young man whose mother was accusing him of violating an agreement to tell her when he was going out. He insisted he had told her. As evidence he said, "You saw me ironing a shirt that day, and you know I never iron a shirt for myself unless I am going out."

I think we've established that human communications involves mutual picture-taking, and that people may not share common pictures, the meanings they give the pictures, nor the feelings the pictures arouse. They then guess at each other's meanings; the tragedy is that they may also treat these guesses as facts. To cope with this, develop the habit of immediately checking with the other person to determine whether your meanings match theirs.

Our guesses about one another are anything but 100 percent accurate. I believe this guessing procedure is responsible for a great deal of unnecessary estrangement between people. Part of the problem is that we are such sloppy talkers! We use words such as *it, that,* and *this* without clarifying them. This is particularly difficult for a child, who has fewer clues from experience. Any listener in this situation is in an impossible bind if the rules require that he act as though he understood.

Thousands of times I've heard one person say to another, "Stop that!" What is *that?* The second person may have no idea. Just because I see you doing something I want you to stop doing doesn't mean you know what I'm talking about. Many harmful reactions can be avoided simply by remembering to describe what you are seeing and hearing—being specific about what you are saying.

This brings us to what I consider one of the most impossible hurdles in human relationships: the assumption that *you* always know what *I* mean. The premise appears as follows: If we love each other, we also can and should read each other's minds.

The most frequent complaint I have heard people make about their family members is, "I don't know how he feels." Not knowing results in a feeling of being left out. This puts tremendous strain on any relationship, particularly a family one. People tell me they feel in a kind of no-man's land as they try to make some kind of a bridge to a family member who doesn't show or describe feelings.

Many people who are accused of this are often feeling very strongly, however. They may not realize they aren't showing it. They believe themselves to be as transparent to others as they are to themselves. They reason, "She knows me. Therefore, she knows what I feel."

I have a little experiment that I use to help people develop an awareness of this condition. I ask two people to discuss something, and I videotape their interchange. Then I play back the tape and ask these same two to respond to what they see in comparison to what they remember feeling as it happened. Many people are astonished because they see things of which they were not even in the remotest way aware when the tape was being made.

I remember a terrible ruckus in a family because the father sent his son to the lumber yard for a board. The child was obedient, wanted to please his dad, and thought he knew what was expected. He dutifully went and came back with a board that was three feet too short. His father, disappointed, became angry and accused his son of being stupid and inattentive.

The father knew how long a board he wanted, but it apparently had not occurred to him that his son wouldn't know also. He had never thought of this and did not see it until we discussed it in the session. Then he was clear that he had not requested a specific length.

Here is another example. A sixteen-year- old son says at 5:30 P.M. on a Friday, "What are you doing tonight, Dad?"

Ted, his father, replies, "You can have it!"

Tom, the son, answers, "I don't want it now."

With irritation Ted snaps, "Why did you ask?"

Tom responds angrily, "What's the use?"

What are they talking about? Tom wanted to find out if his father was planning to watch him play basketball that night. Tom didn't ask his father directly because he was afraid Ted might say no; so he used the hint method.

Ted got the message that Tom was hinting, all right, but he thought it was a request for the family car. Tom thought his dad was putting him off. Ted then thought his son was ungrateful. These interactions ended with both father and son being angry and each feeling the other didn't care. I believe these kinds of exchanges are all too frequent among people.

Sometimes people have become so used to saying certain things in certain situations that their responses become automatic. If a person feels bad and is asked how she feels, she will answer, "Fine," because she's told herself so many times in the past that she *should* feel fine. Besides, she probably concludes, no one is really interested anyway, so why not pick the expected answer? She has programmed herself to have only one string on her violin; and she has to use that one string with everything, whether or not it applies. The music is hardly enticing.

People can check out their mental pictures by depicting what they see or hear—by using *descriptive,* not judgmental language. Many people intend to describe, but they distort their pictures by including judgmental words. For example, my camera picture is that you have a dirt smudge on your face. If I use descriptive words, I would say, "I see a dirt smudge on your face." The judgmental approach ("Your face is a mess") makes you feel defensive. With the descriptive statement, perhaps you feel only a little uncomfortable.

Two traps are implicit here: *I read you in my terms* and *I hang a label on you.* For example, you are a man, and I see tears in your eyes. Since I think men should never cry because that shows weakness, I conclude that you are weak, and I treat you accordingly. (Personally, I happen to feel just the opposite).

If I tell you what meaning I make of a given picture, avoid being judgmental, and tell you what I feel about it—and you do the same with me—at least we are straight with each other. We might not like the meaning we discover, but at least we understand.

I think you are ready now to try the ultimate risk with your partner. *This time assign yourself the task of confronting your partner with three statements you believe to be true about him or her and three you believe to be true about yourself. You'll probably be aware that these are your truths as of now; they may change in the future. To keep focused on telling your truths, try beginning with the following words: "At this time, I believe such and such to be true about you." If you have a negative truth, see if you can put words to that. In my opinion, no relationship can be a nurturing one unless all states and aspects can be commented on openly and freely.*

I used to tell my students they had it made when they could say straight to someone that he or she had a bad smell in such a way that the information was received as a gift. It is painful at the outset but definitely useful in the long run. Many people have reported to me that, contrary to their expectations, relationships stood on firmer, more nurturing and trusting ground when they found they could be straight with negative as well as positive content. Remember, one does not have to approach something negative, negatively. One can do it positively. Maybe the chief difference is being descriptive.

On the other hand, many people never put words to their appreciation. They just assume the others know of it. When one voices objections only, without acknowledging satisfaction as well, estrangement and resentment arise.

Who doesn't like (and need!) a pat on the back from time to time? This "pat" could be as simple as the statement, "I appreciate you."

I recommend that families do the educational exercise I just described at least once a week. After all, the first and basic learning about communication comes in the family. Sharing your inner space activity with one another accomplishes two important things: becoming really acquainted with the other person and thus changing strangeness to something familiar, and also making it possible to use your communication to develop nurturing relationships—something we all continue to need.

You could now be more aware that every time two people are together, each has an experience that affects him or her in some way. The experience can serve to reinforce what was expected, either positively or negatively. It may create doubts about the other's worth and thus create distrust; or it may deepen and strengthen the worth of each, and the trust and closeness between them. Every interaction between two people has a powerful impact on the respective worth of each and what happens between them. This includes the tasks they share in common, such as child rearing.

If encounters between a couple become doubt-producing, the individuals involved begin to feel bad about themselves and defend themselves against each other. They begin to look elsewhere—to work, to children, to other sexual partners—for their nurturing. If a husband and wife begin to have sterile and lifeless encounters, they eventually become bored with one another. Boredom leads to indifference, which is probably one of the worst human feelings and, incidentally, one of the real causes of divorce. I am convinced that anything exciting, even dangerous, is preferable to boredom. Fighting is better than being bored. You might get killed from it, but at least you feel alive while it goes on.

When communication between any pair or in any group produces something new and interesting, then aliveness and/or new life comes into being. A deepening, fulfilling relationship develops, and each person feels better about him- or herself and the other.

I hope that now, after the many exercises you have experienced, my earlier words about the communication process will have more meaning: *Communication is the greatest single factor affecting a person's health and relationship to others.*

7
Patterns of Communication

After many years of listening to interactions among people, I gradually became aware of certain seemingly universal patterns in the way people communicate. Over and over again I observed four ways people had of handling the negative results of stress. These four patterns—which I call *placating, blaming, computing,* and *distracting*—occurred when one was reacting to stress and at the same time felt one's self-esteem was diminished—that "the pot got hooked." In addition, the "hooked" one could not say so.

As I began to understand these patterns more fully, I saw that self-esteem became easily hooked when one had not developed a solid, appreciative sense of self-worth. When one is doubtful about one's worth, it is easy to use another's actions and reactions to define oneself. For instance, if someone called us green, we would agree without checking and take the other's comment as fitting us. We are green because the other person said so.

It's easy for anyone with doubts about self-worth to fall into this trap. I recommend you treat everything that comes to you from the outside as something with which to cope, not as a way to define yourself.

Likewise, stress alone need not feel like an attack on self-worth. Feeling stress might be painful or annoying, but that isn't the same as doubting your own worth.

Do you know your internal feeling when your pot gets hooked? When mine does, my stomach gets knots, my muscles get tight, I find myself holding my breath, and I sometimes feel dizzy. While all this is going on, I find that my thoughts concern the dialogue I am having with myself. The words are variations of "Who cares about me? I am unlovable. I can never do anything right. I am a nothing." Descriptive words for this condition are embarrassed, anxious, incompetent, helpless, and fearful.

What I say at a point like this might be quite different from anything I am feeling or thinking. If I think that the only way out of my dilemma is to make things right with you—so you will think I am lovable, acceptable, and so on—I will say whatever I think would fit. It would not matter if it were true. What matters is my survival, and I have put that in your hands. When I do this, I give away my power.

Suppose, instead, I keep my survival and power in my hands. Then I can say straight out what I think and feel. I might feel some initial pain at exposing my weaknesses and taking any accompanying risk, but I avoid the greater pain of hurting myself physically, emotionally, intellectually, socially, and spiritually.

It's important to understand that every time you talk, all of you talks. Whenever you say words, your face, voice, body, breathing, and muscles are talking, too:

Verbal communication	— words
Body/sound communication— (with or without words)	facial expression
	body position
	muscle tone
	breathing tempo
	voice tone
	gestures

Discrepancies between verbal and nonverbal communication produce double messages. Your words are saying one thing, and the rest of you is saying something else.

Have you ever heard, "Oh, I really like this!" and wondered why the speaker's head was moving from side to side?

The troubled families I have known handled their communication through double messages. Double messages come through when a person holds the following views:

1. I have low self-esteem (low pot) and believe I am bad because I feel that way.
2. I am fearful about hurting the other person's feelings.
3. I worry about retaliation from the other.
4. I fear rupture of our relationship.
5. I do not want to impose.
6. I am unconscious of anything but myself and do not attach any significance to the other person or the interaction itself.

In nearly all of these instances, the person is unaware of giving double messages.

So the listener will be confronted by two messages, and the outcome of the communication will be greatly influenced by her or his response. In general, the possibilities are: pick up the words and ignore the rest; pick up the nonverbal part and ignore the words; ignore the whole message by changing the subject, leaving, or going to sleep; or commenting on the double nature of the message.

For example, if I have a smile on my face and the words "I feel terrible" come out of my mouth, I am giving a double message. What are your options? Picking up on the above possibilities, you might respond to the words and say, "That's too bad," to which I can respond, "I was just kidding." Your second choice is to respond to the smile and say, "You look great," in which case I can say, "How can you say that!" Your third choice is to ignore the whole thing and go back to your paper, in which case I would respond, "What's the matter? Don't you give a damn?" Another choice, the leveling response, is to comment on my double message: "I don't know what you're telling me. You're smiling, yet you tell me you're feeling bad. What gives?" I then have a chance to respond, "I didn't want to impose on you," and so on.

I feel terrible

I believe that unless any family communication leads to realness or a straight, single meaning it cannot possibly lead to the trust and love necessary to nourish family members.

What goes on in a moment between two people has many more levels than are visible on the surface. The surface represents only a small portion of what is going on, much in the way that only a very small part of an iceberg is visible.

Thus, in this interaction:

"Where were you last night?"
"You are always nagging me!"

something is happening to each person in relation to herself or to himself.

Something is happening to the perception by each of the other.

The relationship can go toward distrust, personal low pot, or frustration. On the other hand, this can be the beginning of new depth and trust. Outcomes depend on the responses one chooses.

Let's take a closer look at the four universal patterns people use to get around the threat of rejection. Feeling and reacting to the threat, the individual who doesn't want to reveal weakness attempts to conceal it in the following ways:

1. *Placate* so the other person doesn't get mad;
2. *Blame* so the other person will regard one as strong (if the person goes away, it will be her or his fault—not one's own);
3. *Compute* so that one deals with the threat as though it were harmless, and one's self-worth hides behind big words and intellectual concepts;
4. *Distract* so one ignores the threat, behaving as though it were not there (maybe if one does this long enough, it really will go away).

Our bodies have come to portray our feelings of self-worth whether we realize it or not. If our self-worth is in question, our bodies show it through some form of physical manifestation.

With this in mind I have devised certain physical stances to help people get in touch with parts of themselves that are obvious to other people but not always to themselves. I've exaggerated and expanded each facial and vocal message into the whole body so nobody can miss it.

To help clarify the responses (we will play out these roles in communication games in the next chapter), I have included a simple word-diagram with each descriptive section. Please note that these responses are used by men as well as women, by children as well as adults.

PLACATER

Words	agree	"Whatever you want is okay. I am just here to make you happy."
Body	appeases	"I am helpless"—shown in victim's posture.
Insides		"I feel like a nothing; without you I am dead. I am worthless."

The *placater* talks in an ingratiating way, trying to please, apologizing, and never disagreeing, no matter what. This is a "yes man" who talks as though he could do nothing for himself; he must always get someone's approval. You will find later that if you play this role for even five minutes, you feel nauseous and want to vomit.

A big help in doing a good placating job is to think of yourself as really worth nothing. You are lucky just to be allowed to eat. You owe everybody gratitude, and you really are responsible for everything that goes wrong. You know you could have stopped the rain if you used your brains, but you don't have any. Naturally you will agree with any criticism of you. You are grateful that anyone even talks to you, no matter what they say or how they say it. You would not think of asking anything for yourself. After all, who are you to ask? Besides, if you can just be good enough, it will come by itself.

Be the most syrupy, martyrish, boot-licking person you can be. Think of yourself as being physically down on one knee, wobbling a bit, and putting out one hand in a begging fashion. Keep your head up so your neck will hurt, your eyes will strain, and in no time at all your head will ache.

When you talk in this position, your voice will be whiny and squeaky because you don't have enough air to project a rich, full voice. You will be saying yes to everything, no matter what you feel or think. The placating stance is the body position that matches the placating response.

BLAMER

Words	disagree	"You never do anything right. What is the matter with you?"
Body	accuses	"I am the boss around here."
Insides		"I am lonely and unsuccessful."

The *blamer* is a fault-finder, a dictator, a boss who acts superior and seems to be saying, "If it weren't for you, everything would be all right." The internal feeling is one of tightness in the muscles and organs. Meanwhile the blood pressure increases. The voice is hard, tight, and often shrill and loud.

Good blaming requires you to be as loud and tyrannical as you can. Cut down everything and everyone. Think of yourself pointing your finger accusingly and starting your sentence with "You never do this," "You always do that," "Why do you always," "Why do you never," and so on. Don't bother about an answer; that is unimportant. The blamer is much more interested in throwing weight around than really finding out anything.

When you are blaming, you breathe in little tight spurts, or hold your breath altogether, keeping your throat muscles tight. Have you ever seen a really first-rate blamer whose eyes were bulging, neck muscles and nostrils standing out, skin getting red, and whose voice sounded like someone shoveling coal?

Think of yourself standing with one hand on your hip and the other arm extended with your index finger pointed straight out. Your face is screwed up, your lips curled, your nostrils flared as you yell, call names, and criticize everything under the sun. Your blaming stance looks like this:

You don't really feel you are worth anything, either. So if you can get someone to obey you, then you feel you count for something. Given their obedient behavior, you feel effective.

COMPUTER

Words	ultrareasonable	"If one were to observe careful-ly, one might notice the very workworn hands of someone present here."
Body	computes	"I'm calm, cool, and collected."
Insides		"I feel vulnerable."

The *computer* is very correct, very reasonable, and shows no semblance of feeling. The person seems calm, cool, and collected. She or he could be compared to an actual computer or a dictionary. The body feels dry, often cool, and detached. The voice is a dry monotone, and the words are likely to be abstract.

When you are a computer, use the longest words possible, even if you aren't sure of their meaning. You will at least sound intelligent. After one paragraph no one will be listening anyway. To get yourself really in the mood for this role, imagine that your spine is a long, heavy steel rod reaching from your buttocks to the nape of your neck, and a ten-inch-wide iron collar girds your neck. Keep yourself as motionless as possible, including your mouth. You will have to try hard to keep your hands from moving, but do it.

When you are computing, your voice will naturally go dead because you have no feeling from the cranium down. Your mind is bent on being careful not to move, and you are busy choosing the right words. After all, you should never make a mistake. The sad part of this role is that it seems to represent an ideal goal for many people. "Say the right words, show no feeling. Don't react."

Your computer position stance will look like this:

DISTRACTER

Words	irrelevant	The words make no sense or are about an unrelated subject.
Body	angular	"I'm off somewhere else."
Insides		"Nobody cares. There is no place for me here."

Whatever the *distracter* does or says is irrelevant to what anyone else is saying or doing. This person doesn't respond to the point. The internal feeling is one of dizziness. The voice can be singsong, often out of tune with the words, and can go up and down without reason because it is focused nowhere.

When you play the distracting role, it will help you to think of yourself as a kind of lopsided top, constantly spinning but never knowing where you are going, and not realizing it when you get there. You are too busy moving your mouth, your body, your arms, your legs. Make sure you are never on the point with your words. Ignore everyone's questions; maybe come back with one of your own on a different subject. Take a piece of imaginary lint off someone's garment, untie people's shoelaces, and so on.

Think of your body as going off in different directions at once. Put your knees together in an exaggerated knock-kneed fashion. This will bring your buttocks out, and make it easy for you to hunch your shoulders and have your arms and hands going in opposite directions.

At first this role seems like a relief, but after a few minutes of play, the terrible loneliness and purposelessness arise. If you can keep yourself moving fast enough, you won't notice it so much.

You will look like this:

As practice for yourself, take the four physical stances I have described, hold them for just sixty seconds, and see what happens to you. Since many people are unaccustomed to feeling their body reactions, you may find at first that you are so busy thinking you aren't

feeling. Keep at it, and you will begin to have the internal feelings you've experienced so many times before. Then, the moment you are on your own two feet and are freely relaxed and able to move, you find your internal feeling changes.

My hunch is that we learn these ways of communicating early in childhood. As children make their ways through the complicated and often threatening world in which they find themselves, they try out one or another of these communication patterns. After enough use the child can no longer distinguish response from feelings of worth.

Using any of these four responses bolsters an individual's feeling of low self-worth or low pot. These ways of communicating are reinforced by the way we learn about authority in families and by attitudes prevalent in our society:

"Don't impose; it's selfish to ask for things for yourself" reinforces placating.

"Don't let anyone put you down; don't be a coward" reinforces blaming.

"Don't be so stupid; you're too smart to make mistakes" reinforces computing.

"Don't be so serious. Live it up! Who cares?" reinforces distracting.

At this point you may well be wondering if these four crippling modes of communication are all we have. Of course not. There is another response that I have called *leveling* or flowing. In this response all parts of the message are going in the same direction: the voice's words match the facial expression, body position, and voice tone. Relationships are easy, free, and honest, and people feel few threats to self-esteem. This response relieves any need to placate, blame, retreat into a computer, or be in perpetual motion.

Of the five responses, only leveling has any chance to heal ruptures, break impasses, or build bridges between people. And lest leveling seem too unrealistic to you, let me assure you that you can still placate if you choose, blame if you like, be on a head trip, or be distracting. The difference is you know what you are doing and are prepared to take the consequences.

When you are leveling, you apologize when you realize you've done something you didn't intend. You are apologizing for an act rather than your existence. Likewise, you may criticize and evaluate in a leveling way, by evaluating an act, not blaming the person. Usually you'll be able to offer a new direction as well.

At times, you'll be talking about intellectual things, giving lectures, making explanations, or giving directions, when precise word meanings are essential. When you are leveling in this area, you are still showing your feelings and moving freely while you're explaining. You aren't coming off like a machine. (Many people who make their living with their brains—scientists, mathematicians, accountants, teachers, and therapists—are often motivated by a wish to be objective. They behave like machines and epitomize the computing response.) In addition, you will sometimes want to change the subject. In the leveling response you can say what you want to do instead of hopping all over the place.

The effect of leveling is congruence. When a leveler says, "I like you," the voice is warm and the person looks at you. If the words are, "I am mad as hell at you," the voice is harsh, and the face held tight. The message is single and straight.

The leveling response also represents a truth of the person at that moment. This is in contrast, for example, to a blaming response, in which the person is feeling helpless but is acting angry—or is hurting but is acting brave.

A third aspect of the leveling response is that it is whole, not partial. The body, thoughts, and feelings are all shown, in contrast to computing, for example, in which nothing moves but the mouth and that only slightly. People who are leveling show an integration, a flowing, an aliveness, an openness, and what I call a juiciness. Leveling makes it possible to live in a vibrant way, rather than a dead way. You trust these people; you know where you stand with them, and you feel good in their presence. Their position is one of wholeness and free movement.

Now, to help you distinguish these five different ways of expressing yourself, let me present five ways of apologizing. This can also serve as a demonstration before you play the games in the next chapter. Let's imagine that I have just bumped your arm.

PLACATING (*looking down, wringing hands*): Please forgive me. I am just a clumsy oaf.

BLAMING: Ye gods, I just hit your arm! Keep it in next time so I won't hit it!

COMPUTING: I wish to render an apology. I inadvertently struck your arm in passing. If there are any damages, please contact my attorney.

DISTRACTING (*looking at someone else*): Gee, some guy's mad. Must've got bumped.

LEVELING (*looking directly at person*): I bumped you. I'm sorry. Are you hurt?

Let's take another imaginary situation. I am your father, and there is something wrong in what you, my son, are doing.

PLACATING (*with a hushed voice, downcast face*): I'm—uh, uh—gosh, gee, Jim, I . . . am sorry—you feeling okay? You know—promise me you won't get mad. No, you're doing okay, it's just—maybe you could do a little better? Just a little, maybe? Hm?

BLAMING: What's the matter with you, don't you know anything, you dumb cluck?

COMPUTING: We are making a survey of our family efficiency. We find that in this department, namely with you, efficiency is beginning to go down. Would you have any comments to make?

DISTRACTING (*talking to his other son, standing next to Jim*): Say, Arnold, is your room about the same as Jim's? No, nothing wrong—I was just taking a walk through the house. Tell Jim to see his mother before he goes to bed.

LEVELING: Jim, your room is in bad shape. You haven't made your bed since yesterday. We need to stop, take a look, and see what's wrong.

It's anything but easy to break old habit patterns and become a leveler. One way you might help yourself achieve this goal is to learn what some of your fears are that keep you from leveling. To thwart the rejection we so fear, we tend to threaten ourselves in the following ways:

1. I might make a mistake.
2. Someone might not like it.
3. Someone will criticize me.
4. I might impose.
5. She will think I am no good.
6. People might think me imperfect.
7. He might leave.

When you can tell yourself the following answers to the foregoing statements, you will have achieved real growth:

1. I am sure to make mistakes if I take any action, especially new action.

2. I can be quite sure that there will be someone who doesn't like what I do. Not everyone likes the same things.

3. Yes, someone will criticize me. I really am not perfect. Some criticism is useful.

4. Sure! Every time I speak and interrupt in the presence of another person, I impose!

5. So maybe she will think I'm no good. Can I live through that? Maybe sometimes I'm not so hot. Sometimes the other person is "laying a trip on me." Can I tell the difference?

6. If I think of myself as needing to be perfect, chances are I will always be able to find imperfection.

7. So he leaves. Maybe he should leave, and anyway, I'll live through it.

These attitudes will give you a good opportunity to stand on your own two feet. It won't be easy and it won't be painless. If we can laugh at ourselves, the journey will be easier. You can grow and feel good about yourself. The outcome will be worth the effort.

With no intention of being flippant, I think most of the things we use to threaten ourselves and that affect our self-worth turn out to be tempests in teapots. This is an opportunity to see the joke in how we treat ourselves. Another way I helped myself through these threats was to ask myself if I would still be alive if all the imagined threats came true. If I could answer yes, then I was okay. I can answer yes to all of them now.

I will never forget the impact of discovering other people worried about these same silly threats. I had thought for years I was the only one, and I kept myself busy trying to outwit them, simultaneously doing my best to conceal my anxiety. My fear was, "What if somebody found out?" Well, what if somebody did? Now I know we all use these same kinds of things to threaten ourselves.

By now you realize this leveling response isn't some kind of magical recipe. It's a way of responding to real people in real situations that permits you to agree because you really do, not because you want to make points. Leveling allows you to use your brain freely but not at the expense of your feelings or your spirit. It also enables you to change course, not to get you off the hook but because you want to and need to.

The leveling response makes it possible for you to live as a whole person: real, in touch with your head, your heart, your feelings, and your body. Being a leveler enables you to have integrity, commitment, honesty, intimacy, competence, creativity, and the ability to work with real problems in a real way. The four other communication patterns result in doubtful integrity, commitment by bargain, dishonesty, loneliness, shoddy performance, strangulation by tradition, and dealing in a destructive way with fantasy problems.

It takes guts, courage, some new beliefs, and some new skills to become a leveling responder. You can't fake it.

People are hungry for straightness, honesty, and trust. When they become aware of it and are courageous enough to try it, they diminish their distance from other people.

I came to this awareness in a tough, trial-and-error way, trying to help people who had serious life problems. I found that people healed by finding their hearts, their feelings, their bodies, and their brains; this process once more brought them to their souls and thus their humanity. They could then express themselves as whole people, which in turn helped them to greater feelings of self-worth, nurturing relationships, and satisfying outcomes. None of these results is possible through the use of the four crippling ways of communication.

From what I have seen I've made some tentative conclusions about what to expect when I meet new groups of people. In general, 50 percent will say yes, no matter what they feel or think (placate); 30 percent will say no, no matter what they feel or think (blame); 15 percent will say neither yes nor no and will give no hint of their feelings

(compute); and 0.5 percent will behave as if yes, no, or any feeling did not exist (distract). That leaves only 4.5 percent who will be real, who will level. My colleagues tell me I am optimistic, saying the leveling response is probably found in only 1 percent of our population. (Again, this is not validated research. It is only a clinical hunch.)

In the vernacular, it would seem we are a bunch of emotional crooks, hiding ourselves, playing dangerous games with one another, and calling it society. If we want to make our bodies sick, become disconnected from other people, throw away our beautiful brainpower, and make ourselves mute, deaf, and blind, we can continue using only the four crippling ways of communication.

I feel very strongly as I write this. For me, isolation, helplessness, and feeling unloved, low-pot, or incompetent comprise the real human evils of this world. Certain kinds of communication perpetuate this, other kinds of communication can change it. If we can understand and recognize the leveling response, we can also learn to use it.

I would like to see each human being value and appreciate himself or herself, and feel whole, creative, competent, healthy, flexible, beautiful, and loving.

Despite my exaggerations of the first four ways of communication (they may even seem amusing) I am deadly serious about their killing nature. In the next chapter, when you play the games I have invented, you will experience exactly what these communication styles are like. You will quickly understand the toll they take on your body, the distrust that forms in your relationships, and the blah, disappointing, and many times disastrous outcomes that ensue.

8

Communication Games

Now we are ready to play the communication games. I'm going to spell them out in detail in the hope that you'll be challenged and curious enough to try them in earnest. Reading about something is far different from seeing and doing it. I'd like you to have all three experiences: reading about these games, doing them, and then interesting another group in doing them so you can watch. Each approach adds a new dimension to your learning.

You can read about swimming, you can watch others swim, but you don't really know what it's all about until you take the plunge yourself.

I have introduced these games to people all over the world, from preschool children (who call it "playing house") to various adult groups: businesspeople, clergy, hospital staffs and personnel, as well as families. I've never met anyone who couldn't play. I've met a few here and there who wouldn't, but I believe they were too scared to try and covered up by saying they couldn't.

It may seem strange, but the minute people start to play these games, they know the dialogue. For me this validates the fact that my games reflect actual experiences in families and in society. Regardless of economic status, race, age, sex, nationality, or religion, everybody knows the language and the gestures in these exercises.

I urge you to take the plunge into these games. You'll be surprised at what you learn about yourself, the other members of your family, and how you all function together. After playing, most people say the games opened new doors into greater understanding. I know that every time I play them I learn something new. They've been very useful to me in regaining my perspective when I temporarily lose it, and they certainly are a means of growing. You might have a similar experience. Go ahead!

Apart from the learning and growing, you can find a lot of fun in these games.

To begin, play with three people at a time—a triad—with the others watching. I start with a triad because that is the basic family unit (mother, father, and child). This is where we all learned our communication patterns. You can start with any three in your family, but I suggest you start with the oldest children first. Incidentally, the children will probably have to be at least three years old before they can enter in well.

The first triad could be husband, wife, and the first child. To really make the plunge in your efforts to understand the communication in your family, I suggest you play with all your possible triads, one triad at a time. If you are a family of five, your triads would be as follows:

Husband, wife, and first child

Husband, wife, and second child

Husband, wife, and third child

Father, first and second child

Father, second and third child

Father, first and third child

Mother, first and second child

Mother, second and third child

Mother, first and third child

First, second, and third child

This makes ten triads altogether, which will probably take three to four hours. Take your time. If some helpful material emerges, let it happen. Don't push.

If you have access to an audio or video tape recorder, use it. Later look at or listen to it, and be prepared for some surprises.

All right. Three of you have agreed to play the game. Invite the other members to watch you. They will have helpful feedback for you later. Seat yourselves in chairs near one another. Then each of you takes a name other than your own, including a different family name. Announce your new name out loud. It seems that more freedom to learn is possible when people use different names.

To do these games, each of you selects a way of communicating. (You may need to refer back to the previous chapter, in which I discussed placating, blaming, computing, distracting, and leveling.) For instance, one of you could blame, one could placate, and the third might also blame. The next time around, you can all pick different roles. Below are combinations I see frequently:

PERSON 1	PERSON 2	PERSON 3
Blaming	Placating	Blaming
Placating	Blaming	Placating
Blaming	Blaming	Placating
Computing	Blaming	Distracting
Blaming	Computing	Distracting
Computing	Computing	Blaming
Distracting	Computing	Placating
Computing	Distracting	Blaming
Placating	Placating	Distracting

As you play these, you may come upon a combination that seems familiar to you. If so, linger with it. Learn how it may work against you. Ask your onlookers to comment.

Now that you have decided who is going to do which kind of communication, tell each other out loud. Start by taking the physical position that matches your communication. Remember the communications stances that correspond to placating, computing,

blaming, and distracting? Here the stances are shown in combination with each other.

Hold your stances for one minute. While you are doing this,
allow yourself to be aware of how you feel about yourself and the
others. Then sit down and play these same communication styles by
using conversation. Here is an example of a possible interaction.

SAM   [father-husband] *(blaming)*: Why haven't you got
our vacation planned?

ELSA   [mother-wife] *(blaming)*: What are you yelling
about? You've got as much time as I have.

CARL   [son] *(blaming)*: Aw, shut up. You two are always
yelling. I'm not going on any vacation, anyway.

SAM   *(blaming)*: Says who? Besides, young man, keep your nose out of this.

      (Or, placating): Where would you like to go, dear?

ELSA *(computing)*: According to the last issue of *Woman's Day*, making a change of pace is a good way to plan a vacation.

SAM   *(placating)*: Whatever you would like to do, dear.

CARL *(placating)*: You always plan nice times, Mother.

ELSA *(computing)*: That's good. I will begin to make lists in the morning.

Set a timer for five minutes. If any particular conflict is brewing in your family, use this as your topic. If you do not have such a situation, then try to plan something together: a meal, a vacation, a garage clean-up, or anything your family might conceivably attempt. As you play, don't be afraid to exaggerate your communication. When the timer rings, stop, even if you are in the middle of a sentence. Immediately sit back, close your eyes, and let yourself become aware of your breathing, your thoughts, your feelings, how your body feels, and how you feel about your partners.

Try to imagine how it would be to live this way in your family all the time. It could be that your blood pressure may be rising; you might be sweating or experiencing aches of various kinds. Just let yourself relax, with your eyes still closed. Move about a bit to loosen tight muscles if you need to. Then mentally take off your role-playing name and quietly say your real name to yourself.

Gradually open your eyes, then, and tell your partners about your inner experiences as you were playing your role. What actually happened? What were your thoughts and feelings, and what parts of the past and present came to the fore? What was your body doing? Tell how you felt toward the other members in your group while you were enacting your role.

Possibly you are becoming aware that the outcome of any planning or conflict-solving is related to your communication. Using another kind of communication will produce a different outcome.

Some of the combinations in these games are similar to the communication patterns you actually use to interact with one another. You might find some of them painful. Playing the games can also bring back memories of what your life was like, perhaps some of the time, with your parents when you were a child. If this is the case, treat it as a discovery rather than as a club with which to punish yourself. Instead of telling yourself how bad or stupid you are or they are, use the discovery as a point from which to go forward.

Try again with a different set of communication stances. You could also experiment with changing roles. For example, the male who was father might now become a son or daughter.

At the end of each game, take as much time as you need to express your inner experience to your partners. Then put on your next role, set the timer, and keep going on to the next set of stances until you finish.

When you are sharing your inner experience, you may find yourself feeling uncomfortable. This will begin to ease as you put words to your discomfort. You may also find that you use a different voice when you are talking about your inner self. At this point you are close to using a leveling response.

When people first start playing these games, they are often revolted by being asked to do openly what they secretly fear they have been doing all along. Some, for instance, feel nauseous at the thought of placating because they want to be perceived as powerful. Others react strongly against blaming because they don't want people to judge them for it. You will learn a great deal, though, if you let yourself develop your roles fully. Remember, you can choose whether you let it rub off.

If you are a woman, worry about being a bitch, and handle it by never, never letting yourself be bitchy, you will be ruling yourself with an iron hand. That hand can get awfully heavy, and you will have to set it down sometimes. Then, bingo! Out comes the bitch. In contrast, you can choose behavior at any moment. Bitchiness properly nurtured turns into healthy assertion, which all people need.

This concept can be compared to keeping three hungry dogs who are always trying to get out of a cage, and three who are well fed and come quickly when called. If you forget to close the door, the hungry ones will get out and may even devour you. The well-fed dogs may run out and even run away, but they won't eat you.

So you have a tendency to be bitchy. Take it out, dress it up, and honor this tendency as part of yourself. Love it and give it a place with the rest of your feelings. You can do the same with all your tendencies. This way one tendency won't stomp all over the rest of you; it will come out and act nice at your bidding. It may turn out that you summon it less and less until, like a formal gown you have outgrown or that is no longer in style, you perhaps reshape it into a play gown for your young daughter, give it away, or use it to dust with.

If you try to hide or bridle your tendencies, however, you won't be able to do this very well. They will be waiting for the chance to escape and act up.

If you are a man and worry about appearing like Mr. Milquetoast, and handle it by being Mr. Big or Mr. Terrible, you are in the same spot. Your tendency is always ready to do you in. Nurtured and reshaped a little, however, that milquetoast quality becomes that tenderness that you, as a man, sorely need. It enables you to keep your body juicy and healthy, to make a loving connection with your wife and children, and to connect with your colleagues. Developing your tenderness does not have to eradicate your toughness. You need that, too. You can have both; you don't have to settle for only one.

Once people decide to look at all their parts, they can develop a sense of perspective and a sense of humor to help make better choices. They can also learn to neutralize any negative attitudes toward their tendencies and learn how to use these tendencies more positively.

Here is another useful experiment. After all the triads have had a turn, play a game with the whole family. By now you will all be familiar with the games and have some skill at playing them.

Each family member chooses a name and announces it. Each of you then privately chooses one of the four responses but doesn't tell the others which one. Once you are all in character, try planning something together. Again, use a tape recorder.

Set the timer for thirty minutes. When you start to have internal feelings of discomfort, change your roles. If you've been placating, change to another style—perhaps blaming. Use that until you again experience discomfort.

At the conclusion of the exercise, tell your partners as fully as you can what you were feeling and thinking about them and yourself as you were playing. You may have noticed that long before the thirty minutes passed and even though you switched roles, you felt uncomfortable and got relief only when you talked fully about your experience. Again, this will bring you closer to the leveling response.

As a result of thoroughly learning these games, people frequently realize they have more talent than they thought. Everyone can develop skill in playing the various roles. You'll find that instead of being stuck with one possibility, you have at least four and perhaps five. Realizing this enables you to be a chooser, and this brings up your level of self-respect.

Say to yourself, "I can be a placater, a blamer, a computer, a distracter, and a leveler. *I can choose.*" Personally, I prefer the leveling response. It has the best consequences; and it is, as you all must know by now, the hardest to learn. The only reason it is hard, however, is because we did not learn it as children.

To apologize without placating, to disagree without blaming, to be reasonable without being inhuman and boring, and to change the subject without distracting give me greater personal satisfaction, less internal pain, and more opportunities for growth and satisfactory relationships with others, to say nothing about increased competence. On the other hand, if I choose to use any of the other styles, I can take responsibility for the consequences and accept the pain that comes from crippling my communication.

Could you feel the wear and tear on your body while you were playing these games? Common aches and pains such as headaches and backaches, high and low blood pressure, and digestive difficulties are much more understandable when we look at them as natural results of the way we do or do not communicate. Can you also imagine how little chance we would have for growing closer to anyone or understanding that person if these patterns were all we had? The relationship would have to deteriorate!

As you begin to feel the internal stress, personal frustration, and hopelessness that accompany communication patterns, can you further imagine that, if you were stuck in these responses, you might be tempted to think about getting sick, having an extramarital affair, committing suicide, or even committing murder? Only a very strong rule on your part will stop you. And the chances are pretty good that if you put all your energy into keeping that rule, you would give yourself unnecessary trouble. I'll have more to say about rules in the next chapter.

You see, just about everyone I have found who has serious problems coping with life— school problems, alcoholism, adultery, whatever—was communicating in the first four crippling ways. If people exist who are successfully making it with these responses, I haven't seen them. I can hardly overemphasize that these four communication styles arise from low pot, low feelings of self-worth that we learned as children.

Now you can see clearly how your pot connects with your communication. You can also see how other people's actions grow out of their communications. It becomes like a merry-go-round: I have low self-esteem to begin with, I have poor communication with someone, I feel worse, my behavior reflects it, and around it goes.

Let's consider a common example. You woke up this morning grouchy and out of sorts. You have to go to work and face a boss who you think has something against you. You have a rule that no one should know about your fears. Your husband or wife notices your sour face and comments, "So what's the matter with you?"

"Nothing," you respond coldly, rushing out the door, slamming it without kissing him or her good-bye. You're not aware of the impact of your behavior.

Your spouse is upset and acts accordingly. When you come home, you find a note that she or he has gone out. After your partner does come home, your invitation to come to bed is ignored. And so it goes.

All four responses demonstrate that each person is making the other his or her choice-maker. We put our fate on someone or something else and don't live as though we are free to make our own choices about our own reactions. Then, of course, it is easy to complain about how badly we have been treated.

This scenario shows you that each person makes the other more of what he or she already is. The blamer makes the placater even more of a placater, and the placater makes the blamer even more blaming. This is the beginning of what I call a closed system, which I shall discuss later.

After this kind of communication has gone on for several years, you get to thinking of yourself as blighted and of the world as tainted and impossible. You stop growing and start dying prematurely.

It is important that we realize the power of these kinds of responses with other people.

The placating response can evoke guilt.

The blaming response can evoke fear.

The computing response can evoke envy.

The distracting response can evoke longing for fun.

So:

If I evoke your guilt, you might spare me.

If I evoke your fear, you might obey me.

If I evoke your envy, you might ally with me.

If I evoke your longing for fun, you might tolerate me.

In no case, though, can you love me or trust me. In the final analysis, this is what makes for a growth-producing relationship. All we can do is survive.

I think we need to discuss feeling a bit more at this point. I have met so many people who never openly share their insides—probably because they either don't know how or they are scared to. I hope you are finding out whether you can share your feelings. If you find that you have not been doing this, remember it is in the interest of your health that you start.

Successfully hiding your feelings, by the way, takes a kind of skill most people don't really have. So their efforts often turn out to be like the traditional ostrich with its head in the sand. It thinks it's safely hidden, but of course it is not. We who delude ourselves like the ostrich often feel misunderstood and betrayed by others.

Oh, there are ways to hide yourself successfully if you insist. You could keep your body in a big black box with only a small hole for your voice to come through. You will have to talk in a steady monotonous voice. You won't have much of a life, but you'll be hidden.

As we learned in our elementary exercises, you can mask your feelings by always talking to someone whose back is to you. You can't see and won't hear each other well, but your feelings won't show. If you get thirty or forty feet away from a person, your feelings can be hidden pretty successfully, particularly if you put something between you, such as other people or a big table. In many families, marital partners often try to achieve this by putting their children between them.

Be assured, however, that when someone tries to hide feelings—especially strong, intense ones—it usually shows somewhere on the body or face anyway. The net result is that the hider just appears more like a liar or a hypocrite than anything else.

As mentioned, the four responses you've been experimenting with are forms of hiding or concealing parts of yourself. You could have been doing it for so long you are no longer aware of your other parts. You may be consciously thinking that this is a way of getting along, or it could be that you just don't know any better.

In the placating response, you hide your own needs; in the blaming response, you hide your need for the other person; computing hides your emotional needs and your needs for others. These same needs are ignored in the distracter, who also ignores any relationship to time, space, or purpose.

These, then, are the shields people use to hide their feelings so they won't be hurt. The problem is to convince them that it is *safe* to express their feelings. This is 90 percent of a therapist's work and the biggest job an individual has—to know himself, and to feel safe to express feelings honestly.

My experience shows that people who either can't or don't show their feelings are very lonely, even though their behavior might not always indicate it. Most people like this have been terribly hurt and neglected over long periods in their childhoods. Not showing their feelings is a way to keep from being hurt again. It takes time, a loving, patient partner, and some new awareness to change. Even then it doesn't always work very well unless the person wants the change and understands the need for it.

On the other hand, personal privacy is an important part of any relationship. At times, you have no words or simply don't want to share your feelings. In that case, you can openly say, "I don't want to tell you," or "I don't have the words to tell you." Telling someone close to you that you don't want to reveal something could easily cause discomfort, though. Secrecy can hurt. However, if the two of you clearly understand you can give each other privacy, both internal and bathroom, then you can stand the discomfort. What is important is that you make it clear that you don't want to talk about your insides at that moment in time. This is being real and leveling. "I choose not to say what I am thinking and feeling now" is vastly different from using shields to hide your feelings.

Being expected to "spill your guts" all the time can also make you very uncomfortable. The key to leveling is that you can choose when and how to talk, and find a context in which this is possible. Having privacy is part of maintaining self-integrity.

What have you been accustomed to doing about your privacy? How well do you think it's working for you? How do you find out whether or not it's working?

As you look back over your experience in playing the games, if you played them seriously, you may have been surprised that your body, feelings, and thoughts got stirred up even though you knew you were only role-playing. Your response indicates how powerful these roles really are. They are also a tip-off to your vulnerable points.

Something else of which you're probably well aware by now is how tired you got playing these games. Suppose you knew of no other way to communicate except these four? You could feel tired and hopeless and unloved much of the time. Maybe the tiredness you regularly experience isn't only because you work so hard.

Remember how alone, helpless, and isolated you felt inside regardless of how you sounded and what you said? Did you notice how your sight, hearing, and thought processes were diminished?

I consider it tragic that I have found thousands of families who live out their lives in this way. They simply don't know anything else, and thus live miserable, isolated, and meaningless existences.

By now you have an idea of which communication patterns you follow with your family members when you are under stress. *Position yourself in your specific communication stances and see what happens.* My guess is that you are finding it isn't as easy as you might have thought to be fully honest and complete in your responses when given the opportunity. If this is the case, you may be getting in touch with some of the barriers between you and the rest of your family. This is helpful. Try the exercise of bringing yourself up to date with each other.

Whether or not you achieved the flowing, leveling response as fully as you would have liked, you are probably more aware now that you do have choices about how to respond. When you exercise these choices, you like yourself better.

Second, you probably realize you have been responding in ways of which you hadn't been aware. This realization may help you when other people react to you in ways you didn't expect.

Third, you probably realize you have been responding in ways you would never have used intentionally. Though painful at the outset, this realization can help you to a greater understanding of what has been happening to you. **Understanding is the first step to change.**

After a bit, you will find you can really have fun with these games. It may even turn out that you develop a little do-it-yourself drama group and, in the process, find yourself doing something pretty exciting and dynamic about increasing your sense of humor.

9

The Rules You Live By

Webster states that a *rule* is an established guide or regulation for action, conduct, method, or arrangement. In this chapter I intend to move away from this flat definition and show you that rules are actually a vital, dynamic, and extremely influential force in your family life. Helping you as individuals and as families to discover the rules by which you live is my goal. I think you're going to be very surprised to discover that you may be living by rules of which you're not even aware.

Rules have to do with the concept of should and should not. They form a kind of shorthand, which becomes important as soon as two or more people live together. The questions of who makes the rules, from what material are they made, what they do, and what happens when they are broken will be our concerns in this chapter.

When I talk with families about rules, the first ones they mention usually concern handling money, getting the chores done, planning for individual needs, and dealing with infractions. Rules exist for all the other contributing factors that make it possible for people to live together in the same house and grow or not grow.

To find out about the rules in your family, sit down with all family members present and ask yourselves, "What are our current rules?" Choose a time when you all will have two hours or so. Sit around a table or on the floor. Elect a secretary who will write the rules down on a piece of paper to help you keep track of them. Don't enter into any arguments at this point about whether the rules are right. Nor is this the time to find out whether they are being obeyed. You're not trying to catch anybody. This exercise takes place in the spirit of discovery, much in the manner of poking about in an old attic just to find out what's there.

Maybe you have a ten-year-old boy who thinks the rule is that he has to wash the dishes only when his eleven-year-old sister is justifiably occupied somewhere else. He figures he is a kind of backup dishwasher. His sister thinks the rule is that her brother washes the dishes when his father tells him to. Can you see the misunderstanding that can result? This may sound foolish, but don't kid yourself, it could be happening in your home.

For many families, simply sitting down and discovering their rules is something very new, and it often proves enlightening. This exercise can open some exciting new possibilities for more positive ways of living together. I've found that most people *assume* that everyone else knows what they know. Irate parents tell me, "She knows what the rules are!" When I pursue the matter, I often find this isn't the case. Assuming that people know the rules is not always warranted. Talking over your rule inventory with your family can clear the way to finding reasons for misunderstanding and behavior problems.

For example, how well are your rules understood? Were they fully spelled out, or did you think your family could read the rules in your mind? It is wise to determine the degree of understanding about rules before deciding somebody has disobeyed them. Perhaps as you look at your rules now, you may find that some of your rules are unfair or inappropriate.

After you have written down all the rules your family thinks exist and cleared up any misunderstanding about them, go on to this next phase. Try to discover which of your rules are still up to date and which are not. As fast as the world changes, it is easy to have out-of-date rules. Are you driving a modern car with Model T rules? Many families are doing just this. If you find that you are, can you bring your rules up to date and throw away the old ones? One characteristic of a nurturing family is the ability to keep its rules up to date.

Now ask yourself if your rules are helping or obstructing. What do you want them to accomplish? Good rules facilitate instead of limiting.

All right. We've seen that rules can be out of date, unfair, unclear, or inappropriate. What have you worked out for making changes in your rules? Who is allowed to ask for changes? Our legal system provides for appeals. Do the members of your family have a way to appeal?

Go a little farther in this family exploration. How are rules made in your family? Does just one of you make them? Is it the person who is the oldest, the nicest, the most handicapped, the most powerful? Do you get the rules from books? Neighbors? From the families in which the parents grew up? Where do your rules come from?

So far the rules we've been discussing are fairly obvious and easy to find. There is another set of rules, however, which is often submerged and much more difficult to get one's fingers on. These rules make up a powerful, invisible force that moves through the lives of all members of families.

I'm talking about the unwritten rules that govern the freedom to comment of various family members. What can you say in your family about what you feel, think, see, hear, smell, touch, and taste? Can you comment only on what should be rather than what is?

Four major areas are involved with this freedom to comment.

What can you say about what you're seeing and hearing? You have just seen two other family members quarrel bitterly. Can you express your fear, helplessness, anger, need for comfort, loneliness, tenderness, and aggression?

To whom can you say it? You are a child who has just heard Father swear. There is a family rule against swearing. Can you tell him?

How do you go about it if you disagree or disapprove of some-one or something?

If your fifteen-year-old daughter or son reeks of mari-juana, can you say so?

How do you question when you don't understand (or do you question)?

Do you feel free to ask for clarification if a family member is not clear?

Living in a family provides all kinds of seeing and hear-ing experiences. Some of these bring joy to the heart, some bring pain, and perhaps some bring a feeling of shame. If family members cannot recognize and comment on what-ever feelings are aroused, the feelings can go underground and gnaw away at the roots of the family's well-being.

Let's think about this for a moment. Are there some subjects that must never be raised in your family? The kinds of things I am referring to include: your oldest son was born without an arm, your grandfather is in jail, your father has a tic, your mother and father fight, or either parent was pre-viously married.

Perhaps the man in your family is shorter than the average man. The rule honored by all members of the fam-ily is that no one talks about his shortness: no one talks about the fact that they can't talk about his shortness, either.

How can you expect to behave as though these family facts simply don't exist? Family barriers against talking about what *is* or what *has been* provide a good breeding ground for troubles.

Let's consider another angle to this perplexing situa-tion. The family rule is that one can talk about only the good, the right, the appropriate, and the relevant. When this is the case, large parts of present reality can't be com-mented on. In my opinion, there are no adults and few chil-dren living in the family or anywhere else who are consistently good, appropriate, and relevant. What can they do when the rules say no one can comment on these kinds of things? As a result some children lie: some develop hatred for, and estrangement from, their parents. Worst of all, they develop low self-worth, which expresses itself as helplessness, hostility, stupidity, and loneliness.

The simple fact is that whatever a person sees or hears has an impact on that person. He or she automatically tries to make an internal explanation about it. As we've seen, if there is no opportunity to check out the explanation, then that explanation becomes the "fact." The "fact" may be accurate or inaccurate, but the individual will base her or his actions and opinions on it.

Forbidden to comment or question, many children grow up to be adults who see themselves as versions of saints

or devils instead of living, breathing human beings who *feel*.

All too often, family rules permit expressing feeling only if it is justified, not because it *is*. Thus, you hear expressions like "You shouldn't feel that way" or "How could you feel like that? I never would." The point here is to make a distinction between acting on your feelings and telling your feelings: to talk about feeling suicidal is not the same as killing yourself. This distinction makes it easier to give up the rule "Thou shalt have only justified feelings."

If your rules say that whatever feeling you have is human and therefore acceptable, your self can grow. This is not saying that all actions are acceptable. If the feeling is welcome, you have a good chance to develop different courses of action—and more appropriate action at that.

From birth to death, human beings continually experience a wide range of feelings—fear, pain, helplessness, anger, joy, jealousy, and love—not because they are right, but because they *are.* Giving yourself permission to get in touch with *all* parts of your family life could dramatically change things for the better. I believe that anything that exists can be talked about and understood in human terms.

Let's get into some real specifics. Take anger. Many people are not aware that anger is a necessary human emergency emotion. Because anger sometimes erupts into destructive actions, some people think anger itself is destructive. It isn't the anger, but the action taken as a result of the anger that can be destructive.

Let's consider an extreme example. Suppose I spit at you. For you that could be an emergency. You might feel you have been attacked and feel bad about yourself and angry at me. You might think of yourself as unlovable (why else would I have attacked you?) You feel hurt, low-pot, lonely, and perhaps unloved. Although you *act* angry, you are *feeling* hurt—of which you are only remotely aware. How would you show what you are feeling? What would you say? What would you do?

You have choices. You can spit back. You can hit me. You can cry and beg me not to do it again. You can thank me. You can run away. You can express yourself honestly and tell me how angry you feel. Then you'll probably be able to be in touch with your hurt, which you can tell me. *Then* you can ask me how I happened to spit at you.

Your rules will guide you in how to express your responses. If your rules permit questions, you can ask me and then understand. If your rules don't permit questions, you can guess, and maybe make a wrong guess. The spitting could represent many things. You could ask yourself, did she spit because she doesn't like me? Because she was angry with me? Because she is frustrated with herself? Because she has poor muscle control? Did she spit because she wanted me to notice her? These possibilities may seem farfetched, but think about them awhile. They aren't really so far-fetched at all.

Let's talk about anger some more because it's important. It's not a vice; it is a respectable human emotion that can be used in an emergency. Human beings can't live out their lives without encountering some emergencies, and we all will find ourselves in a state of anger at times.

If an individual wants to qualify as being a Good Person (and who doesn't?) she or he will try to hold in occasional feelings of anger. Nobody is fooled, though. Have you ever seen anyone who's obviously angry but trying to talk as if he or she were not? Muscles tighten, lips go tight, breathing gets choppy, skin color changes, eyelids tighten; sometimes the person will even puff up.

As time goes on, the person whose rule says anger is bad or dangerous begins to tighten up further inside. Muscles, digestive system, heart tissue, and artery and vein walls get tight, even though the outside looks calm, cool, and collected. Only an occasional steely look in the eye or a twitchy left foot will indicate what the person is really feeling. Soon all the physical manifestations of sickness that come from tight insides, such as constipation and high blood pressure, show up. After a while the person is no longer aware of the anger as such but only of the pain inside. He or she can then truthfully say, "I don't get angry. Only my gall bladder is acting up." This person's feelings have gone underground; they are still operating, but out of the range of awareness.

Some people don't go this far but instead develop a storage tank for anger. It fills up and explodes periodically at small things.

Many children are taught that fighting is bad, that it is bad to hurt other people. Anger causes fighting, therefore anger is bad. The philosophy with far too many of us is, "To make a child good, banish the anger." It is almost impossible to gauge how much this kind of teaching can harm a child.

If you permit yourself to believe that anger is a natural human emotion in specific situations, then you can respect and honor it, admit it freely as a part of yourself, and learn the many ways of using it. If you face your angry feelings and communicate them clearly and honestly to the person involved, you will drain off much of the "steam" and the need to act destructively. You are the chooser and, as such, can feel a sense of managing yourself. As a result, you can feel satisfied with yourself. Family rules about anger are basic to whether or not you grow with your anger or allow yourself to die from it, a little at a time.

Now let's consider another really important area in family life: affection among family members, how it is expressed, and the rules about affection.

I have found all too often that members of families cheat themselves in their affectional lives. Because they don't know how to make affections safe, they develop rules against all affection. This is the kind of thing I mean: fathers often feel that after their daughters reach the age of five, they are no longer supposed to cuddle them as it may be sexually stimulating. The same holds true, although to a lesser degree, with mothers and their sons. Too, many fathers refuse to show overt affection to their sons because affection between males might be taken as homosexual.

We need to rethink our definitions about affection, whatever sexes, ages, or relationships are involved. The main problem lies in the confusion many people experience between physical affection and sex. If we don't distinguish between the feeling and the action, then we have to inhibit the feeling. Let me put it bluntly. If you want problems in your family, play down affection and have lots of taboos about discussing or having sex.

Displays of affection can have many meanings. I've been hugged in such a way that I wanted to slug the hugger. Other times a hug is an invitation to sexual intercourse; an indication of simply being noticed and liked; or an expression of tenderness, a seeking to give comfort.

I wonder how much of the truly satisfying, nurturing potential of affection among family members is not enjoyed because family rules about affection get mixed up with taboos about sex.

Let's talk about that. If you had seen as much pain as I have that clearly resulted from inhuman and repressive attitudes about sex, you would turn yourselves inside out immediately to attain an attitude of open acceptance, pride, enjoyment, and appreciation of the spirituality of sex. Instead, I have found that most families employ the rule, *"Don't enjoy sex—yours or anyone else's—in any form."* The common beginning for this rule is the denial of the genitals

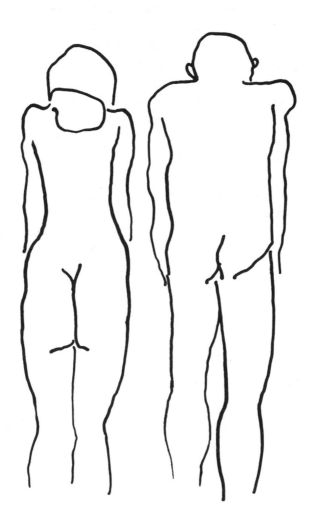

except as necessary nasty objects. "Keep them clean and out of sight and touch. Use them only when necessary and sparingly at that."

Without exception, every person I have seen with problems in sexual gratification in marriage, or who was arrested for any sexual crime, grew up with these kinds of taboos against sex. I'll go further. Everyone I have seen with *any* kind of coping problem or emotional illness also grew up with taboos about sex. These taboos apply to nudity, masturbation, sexual intercourse, pregnancy, birth, menstruation, erection, prostitution, all forms of sexual practice, erotic art, and pornography.

Our sex, our genitals, are integral parts of ourselves. Unless we openly acknowledge, understand, value, and enjoy our sexual side, we are literally paving the way for serious personal pain.

I once headed up a program for family life education in a high school of about eight hundred students. Part of the program concerned itself with sex education. I had a box into which young people could put questions they felt they couldn't ask openly. The box was usually full. I would then discuss these questions during the class period. Nearly all the students explained that they would not have been able to ask their parents these questions for at least three common reasons: their parents would become angry and accuse them of bad conduct; parents would feel humiliated and embarrassed and would probably lie; or they simply wouldn't know the answers. So the students were sparing themselves and their parents, but at the cost of remaining ignorant and seeking information somewhere else. These young people expressed gratitude for the course, and for my accepting, knowledgeable, and loving attitude; they also were feeling better about themselves. I remember two questions particularly: an eighteen-year-old asked, "What does it mean if I have lumps in my semen?" and a fifteen-year-old boy asked, "How can I tell if my mother is in the menopause? She seems awfully irritable now. If she is, then I can understand and will treat her nicely; otherwise I'm going to tell her how mean she is. Should I tell my father?"

How would you, as parents, feel about being asked these questions? If asked, what would you say?

In quite a nice follow-up to this course, the students asked if I'd run a similar course for their parents. I agreed. About a quarter of the parents came to it. I had the same box, and I got very similar questions.

In short, I think we can forgive ourselves for not always knowing the complexities of our sexual selves. But it is psychologically dangerous to go on in ignorance and cover up by a don't-talk-about-it attitude, implying that sexual knowledge is bad, criminal. Society and the individuals who make it up pay heavily for this kind of ignorance.

Fear on the part of family members has much to do with taboos and rules about secrets, even though adults may express the rules as "protection for the kids." This is like another taboo I find rampant in families: the adult mystique. Almost wholly invented by adults to "protect the children," this rule is usually expressed as, "You are too young to . . ." The implication is that the adult world is too complicated, too terrifying, too big, too evil, too pleasureful for you, the mere child, to discover. The child gets to feeling there must be some magic password and that when he or she comes of age, the doors will automatically open. I find adults in droves who haven't discovered the password.

At the same time, the "you-are-too-young-to" pattern implies that the child's world is inferior. "You are just a child; what do you know?" adults say, or, "That is childish." Since gaps obviously exist between what an individual child is ready to do and might like to do, I think the best preparation is to teach children how to make bridges for these gaps, rather than denying them the opportunity of bridging the gaps.

Another aspect of this business of family taboos concerns secrets. Common examples of family secrets are: that a child was conceived before the parents were married, that a mate conceived a child who was later adopted, or that a mate is hospitalized or jailed. These kinds of secrets are usually heavily shrouded in shame.

Some of the biggest secrets involve parents' behavior during their adolescent years—the rule being that, by definition, no parents ever did anything wrong; it is only "you kids" who ever misbehave. This kind of thing has happened so many times that if I hear a parent getting hysterical about something her or his child is doing, I look immediately to see whether the child's behavior has stirred up a secret in the parent's youth. The behavior of the child may not duplicate that of the parent, but it can come close. My job in this instance is to help the parent get rid of old shame so he or she doesn't have to lock a secret part away. Then the parent can deal rationally with the child.

Present secrets are also shrouded in shame. Many parents try to hide their goings-on from their children ("to protect them"). Examples of such present secrets that I have run across are that the father or mother (or both) has a lover, either or both drink, or they don't sleep together. Again, people tell themselves that if it isn't talked about, it doesn't exist. This simply does not work, ever, unless everyone you are "protecting" is mute, deaf, and blind.

Now let's take a look at what you might have discovered about your rules for commenting in three areas.

The human-inhuman sequence means that you ask yourself to live by a rule that is nearly impossible to keep: "No matter what happens, look happy."

In *the overt-covert sequence,* some rules are out in the open, and some are hidden yet obeyed: "Don't talk about it. Treat it as though it didn't exist."

Then there is *the constructive-destructive sequence.* An example of a constructive way of handling a situation is, "We've got a problem about a money shortage this month. Let's talk about it." An obstructing or destructive way of handling the same situation is, "Don't talk to me about your money troubles—that's your problem."

Let's summarize some of the things we've been discussing in this chapter. Any rule that prevents family members from commenting on what is and what has been is a likely source for developing a restricted, uncreative, and ignorant person, and a family situation to match.

If, on the other hand, you are able to get in touch with all parts of your family life, your family life could change dramatically for the better. The family whose rules allow for freedom to comment on everything, whether it be painful, joyous, or sinful, has the best chance of being a nurturing family. I believe that anything that *is* can be talked about and understood in human terms.

Almost everyone has skeletons in the closet. Don't you have at least one? In nurturing families these are simply reminders of human frailty, and they can be easily talked about and learned from. Other families hide them away and treat them as gruesome reminders of the badness of human beings, which must never be talked about. It may be difficult at the outset to talk about these touchy matters, but it can be done. Talking helps everyone in the family learn how to risk such difficulty and survive—even improve— the situation.

Rules are a very real part of the family's structure and functioning. If the rules can be changed, family interaction can be changed. Check into the kinds of rules by which you are living. Can you understand more now what is happening to you in your family? Can you allow yourself to be challenged into making some changes? New awareness, new courage, and new hope on your part can enable you to put some new rules into operation.

The courage will come from letting yourself accept new ideas. You can discard the old and unfitting ideas, and you can select from those you've already found useful. This is just plain logic. Nothing remains eternally the same. Think of your pantry, the refrigerator, a tool shed. These always need rearranging, replacing, and discarding of their old contents and the adding of the new.

By now, you've thought about your rules and examined them. Why not check out your rule inventory against the following questions?

What are your rules?

What are they accomplishing for you now?

What changes do you now see you need to make?

Which of your current rules fit?

Which do you want to discard?

What new ones do you want to make?

What do you think about your rules? Are they overt, human, up to date? Or are they covert, inhuman, and out of date? If your rules are mostly of the second variety, I think you realize you and your family have some important and necessary work to do. If your rules are of the first category, you are probably all having a ball.

10

Systems: Open or Closed?

In this chapter I want to discuss something that at first you might not think has much to do with your family and peoplemaking. Stay with me. The concept of *systems* was borrowed from the world of industry and commerce. It has become a way of understanding how human beings in groups work.

Any system consists of several individual parts. Each part is essential and related to each other part to attain a certain outcome; each acts as a stimulus to other parts. The system has an order and a sequence which is determined

through the actions, reactions, and interactions among the parts. This constant interplay governs how the system manifests itself. A system has life only now, when its component parts are present.

Sounds confusing? It isn't really. You put yeast, flour, water, and sugar together to make bread. The bread isn't like any one of its ingredients, yet it contains all of them.

Steam isn't like any of its parts, but it contains them all.

All human life is part of a system. We hear a lot about beating the system, which would seem to say that all systems are bad. Not so. Some are and some are not. The implications of systems thinking for personal, family, and societal behavior are evident everywhere today; in the early Seventies, when this book first came out, they were just beginning to be apparent.

An operating system consists of the following:

A purpose or goal. Why does this system exist in the first place? In families, the purpose is to grow new people and to further the growth of those already here.

Essential parts. In families, this means adults and children, males and females.

An order to the parts' working. In families, this refers to the various family members' self-esteem, rules, and communication.

Power to maintain energy in the system so the parts can work. In families, this power is derived from food, shelter, air, water, activity, and beliefs about the emotional, intellectual, physical, social, and spiritual lives of the family members and how they work together.

Ways of interacting with the outside. In families, this means relating to changing contents, the new and different.

There are two types of systems: closed and open. The main difference between them is the nature of their reactions to change, both from the inside and from the outside. In a closed system, the parts are rigidly connected or disconnected altogether. In either case, information does not flow between parts or from outside in and inside out. When parts are disconnected, they often appear as if they are operating: information leaks in and out but without any direction. There are no boundaries.

An open system is one in which the parts interconnect, are responsive and sensitive to one another, and allow information to flow between the internal and external environments.

If one were to deliberately design a closed family system, the first step would be to separate it as completely as possible from outside interference, and to rigidly fix all roles for all time. The fact is, I don't believe anyone would deliberately design a closed system. Closed family systems evolve from certain sets of beliefs:

> People are basically evil and must be continually controlled to be good.
>
> Relationships have to be regulated by force or by fear of punishment.
>
> There is one right way, and the person with most power has it.
>
> There is always someone who knows what is best for you.

These beliefs are powerful because they reflect the family's perception of reality. And the family then sets rules according to their beliefs. In other words, in closed systems:

> Self-worth is secondary to power and performance.
>
> Actions are subject to the whims of the boss.
>
> Change is resisted.

In open systems:

> Self-worth is primary; power and performance, secondary.

Actions represent one's beliefs.

Change is welcomed and considered normal and desirable.

Communication, the system, and the rules all relate to each other.

Most of our social systems are closed or very nearly so. A little change is allowed, which in my opinion is the reason we have been able to limp along as well as we have.

Now we come to an important philosophical question. Do you believe that all human life deserves the highest priority? *I believe this with all my being.* Therefore I unashamedly admit I will do everything I can to change closed systems into open ones. An open system can choose to be open or closed when it fits. The important word is choice.

I believe that human beings cannot flourish in a closed system; at best, they can only exist. Human beings want more than that. The task of the therapist is to see the light that shines in every person or family, and to uncoil the wrappings that shroud that light.

Right now you and I could point to countless examples of closed systems, including dictatorships in current society, schools, prisons, churches, and political groups. What about the system in your family? Is it open or closed? If your communication now is mostly growth-impeding and if your rules are inhuman, covert, and out of date, you probably have a closed family system. If your communication is growth-producing and your rules are human, overt, and up to date, you have an open one.

Let's return to an exercise we've done before and do it again with different goals and different reasons for doing it. Ask your family members or any other five people to work with you. They can be a family or coworkers or a board of directors. As before, ask them to take different names and to pick one of the growth-impeding communication styles (placating, blaming, computing, or distracting). Try planning something together for ten minutes.

Notice how quickly the nature of the system emerges. Before I was asking you to do this with three people to see what happened to you individually. This time you might begin to see how closed systems develop. In addition to your back hurting, your head aching, and not being able to see and hear well, you may begin to feel locked in. People look like strangers or burdens. They are not giving each other information, only grief.

Now try the same planning experiment with the leveling response. Can you see the beginnings of an open system? In contrast to your experience in the closed system, you may feel more loose, more lucid. Your body probably feels better and you may be breathing easier.

The following chart shows how the closed system applies to troubled families, and the open system to nurturing families.

CLOSED SYSTEM

SELF-ESTEEM	low
COMMUNICATION	indirect, unclear, unspecific, incongruent, growth-impeding
Styles	blaming placating computing distracting
RULES	covert, out-of-date, inhuman rules remain fixed; people change their needs to conform to established rules
	restrictions on commenting
OUTCOME	accidental, chaotic, destructive, inappropriate

Self-worth grows ever more doubtful and depends more and more heavily on other people.

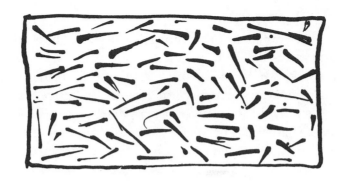

OPEN SYSTEM

SELF-ESTEEM	high
COMMUNICATION	direct, clear, specific, congruent, growth-producing
Style	leveling
RULES	overt, up-to-date, human rules; rules change when need arises
	full freedom to comment on anything
OUTCOME	related to reality; appropriate, constructive

Self-worth grows ever more reliable, confident, and draws increasingly more from the self.

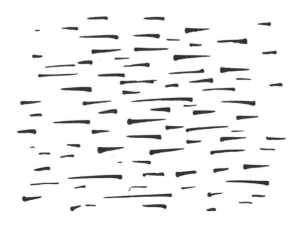

All right. When three or more people are related in any way and are joined in one common purpose, they will develop into a system. This happens in families, with friends, and at work. Once established, the system remains very much in operation, even when not in evidence. If it's a closed system, it will probably operate on a *life–death, right–wrong* basis; fear permeates the atmosphere. If open, it probably operates on the basis of *growth, intimacy,* and *choice.*

Put very simply, your self-worth, your communication, together with your rules and your beliefs, are the ingredients that make up your family system. Leveling communication and human rules characterize an open system and allow everyone in that system to flourish. Crippling communication and inhuman rules make a closed system, retarding and distorting growth.

Becoming aware of their system usually opens the way for family members to become searchers and to stop berating themselves and others when things go wrong. People can ask "how" questions instead of "why" questions. Generally speaking, "how" questions lead to information and understanding, and "whys" imply blame and so produce defensiveness. Anything contributing to defensiveness contributes to low pot and leads to potentially unsatisfying outcomes.

Another important part of any system is that it tends to perpetuate itself. Once established, a system will stay the same until it dies or something changes it: a part breaks down from lack of care or because of a defect; or a catastrophic event affects the system. Sometimes even a minor incident can overwhelm the system, which indicates that the system's designers behaved as though change would never happen.

Each member in a system is a most significant factor in keeping the system going as it is or changing it. Discovering your part in the system and seeing others' parts is an exciting, although sometimes painful, experience. And you can certainly see the importance of systems when you consider the very life of the family depends on its system to a very large degree.

Let's look at the family system in another way. Maybe another comparison would help at this point.

In a mobile all the pieces, no matter what size or shape, can be grouped together in balance by shortening or lengthening their strings, rearranging the distance between pieces, or changing their weight. So it is with a family. None of the family members is identical to any other; each is different and at a different level of growth. As in a mobile, you can't arrange one member without thinking of the others.

Try this. *Take objects—any objects—that are very different from one another and work out a balance for them. Take as many as there are different people in your family, and think of them as your family members. The more parts to your mobile and the greater the differences among them, the more variety and interest you will have.*

If you settle for the first balance you achieve, you'll be doing what so many people do: making the only way they know the "right" way. You resist other ways to bring balance to your family because you fear experimentation.

To avoid this bind, find at least two more ways to make the pieces balance. Many more ways exist, but I will have made my point if you find three. You now have three options, and you need not be stuck with only one.

The trick of making a vital family system is to enable each family member to have a truly individual place and to have fun in that place. Bringing off this trick entails your ability to change and to adjust the "strings" in your family mobile. The strings are your feelings, rules, and communication patterns. Are they immovable or flexible?

While you are working on your mobile, think of the parts of a family. They can be divided into two major categories: adults and children, then males and females. Even the most casual glance at this array shows a great diversity in what people have to give each other at any point in time.

No established rule says one person has to do all the giving and everyone else all the getting. Yet some families cripple themselves by appointing a specific person to be the giver, and nothing ever changes. Ordinary life is such that even if someone agreed to do so, he or she couldn't always give without great cost. One time it may be only the husband who is able to give; another time it may be only the wife or one child. Many families have rules that dictate who may give to whom:

Boys always give to the girls.

Mother always gives to the children.

Husband always gives to the wife.

Eventually, everyone gets cheated. However, if the ideal outcome of a family today is the growth of all its members, then the family job is to use all its parts to ensure this growth.

How can adults use themselves so the children can grow? How can the children use themselves so the adults can grow? How do the males make development possible for the females and the females for the males? How does everyone help everyone else—adult, child, male, and female alike? These are significant questions in families' efforts to become more nurturing.

Each of these groups has a world that members of the complementary group do not share. Talking about respective worlds, offering their variety and stimulation, not only adds interest but also expands our whole reality. No woman knows what it feels like to carry around a penis, and men don't know what it's like to carry babies. Far too many

adults have forgotten how to enjoy the simple pleasures children find in life. Simple sharing among groups can help greatly in these areas.

All families are in balance. The question is: What is the cost to each family member to maintain that balance?

I think the stakes are high regarding the nature of your family system. The family is the one place in the world where all of us can expect nurturing: soothing bruised souls, elevating self-worth, as well as getting things done.

The family is the obvious place to learn this nurturing and growing. To achieve these goals and become truly vital, there has to be continual observation and changing and re-shaping in the family. This can only take place in an open system.

11

The Couple:
Architects of the Family

Why did you get married? Why did you marry the person you did? Why did you marry when you did? Chances are, whatever you answer, your reasons for marrying represented an opportunity to add something to your life. Only the unusual person and for very unusual reasons would knowingly go into a marriage thinking it would make his or her life worse.

You had great hopes, I am sure, that things would be much better for you after you married. These dreams are part of the architecture of the family you set out to create. It is when something happens to these hopes that the stirrings for divorce begin. And they often continue unless the individual involved decides to resign herself or himself to duty or death—or change. This chapter talks about joy in relationships as well as the kinds of things that can threaten or even destroy the couple.

In our western culture I believe most of us would say we married for love. We probably also expected our lives would be enhanced by whatever we thought love would bring us: attention, sexual fulfillment, children, status, belongingness, being needed, material things, and so on.

I believe in love—in loving and in being loved. I think that love, including sexual love, is the most rewarding and fulfilling feeling any human being can experience. Without loving and being loved, the human soul and spirit curdle and die. But love cannot carry all the demands of life; intelligence, information, awareness, and competence are also vital.

Our feelings of self-worth have much to do with how we label what a love experience is and what we expect of it. The higher our self-esteem, the less we depend on continual concrete evidence from our spouse that we count. Conversely, the lower our sense of self, the more we tend to depend on continual assurances, which lead to mistaken notions about what love can do.

Truly loving means, "I put no strings on you, nor accept them from you." Each person's integrity is respected. I like the description of love and marriage as written by Khalil Gibran in *The Prophet:**

> But let there be spaces in your togetherness,
> And let the winds of the heavens dance
> between you.
> Love one another, but make not a bond of love:
> Let it rather be a moving sea between the shores
> of your souls.
> Fill each other's cup but drink not from one cup.
> Give one another of your bread but eat not from
> the same loaf.
> Sing and dance together and be joyous, but let
> each of you be alone,
> Even as the strings of a lute are alone though they
> quiver with the same music.
> Give your hearts, but not into each
> other's keeping.
> For only the hand of Life can contain your hearts.
> And stand together yet not too near together;
> For the pillars of the temple stand apart,
> And the oak tree and the cypress grow not in each
> other's shadow.

*From *The Prophet,* by Khalil Gibran. Copyright 1923 by Khalil Gibran; renewal copyright 1951 by Administrators C.T.A. of Khalil Gibran Estate and Mary G. Gibran. Reprinted by permission of Alfred A. Knopf, Inc.

Go back in time and try to remember what you hoped would be better for you when you got married. What were *your* hopes?

Let me review some hopes people have shared with me over the years. Women's hopes often center around having men who, of all people in the world, would love only them, would respect and value them, would talk to them in such a way as to make them glad to be women, would stand by them, would give them comfort, and sexual satisfaction, and who would be on their side in times of stress.

Men mostly have said they wanted women who would see that their needs were met, would enjoy their strength and their bodies, would regard them as wise leaders, and who would also be willing to help them when they expressed their needs. They spoke of wanting good food and good sex. As one man put it, he wanted someone "who is all for me. I want to feel needed, useful, respected and loved—a king in my own house."

Not too many women or men have seen these kinds of things materialize in their parents' relationships. Actually, few models exist. The hopes are those of the heart. We have been both awkward about and resistant to letting the heart be open about what it wants. Many people regard the heart as weak. They think only the head is strong. We forget that good architecture requires both: we can design relationships that function and that please us as well.

In the early years of my career, I was puzzled that so many people somehow could not get what they wanted, no matter how hard they worked. I have come to learn, sadly enough, that most failures are due largely to ignorance—ignorance that is due to naive and unrealistic expectations about what love can do, and the inability to communicate clearly.

To start with, people often marry partners they really do not know as people. Sexual attraction may bring people together, but it guarantees neither compatibility nor friendship. People who are congruent realize they can be sexually attracted to many people. Being able to make a satisfying, creative life with someone requires compatibility in many other areas. We spend relatively little time in bed. Lest I be misunderstood, I am saying that sexual responsiveness is important in intimate adult relationships. However, I am also saying that satisfying day-to-day relationships require much more than sexual attraction. It may even be that at some point, for various reasons, the sexual part is inactive. The relationship can still flourish.

I think few children grow up with healthy, satisfying sexual models as far as their own parents are concerned. What they saw going on between their parents as they were growing up probably did not come close to the romantic ideal publicized in our western culture today. I have heard adults express wonder that their parents ever got together in the first place. They had difficulty imagining their parents in bed together, much less ever having had a romance.

It's sad that children cannot know their parents when they were younger: when they were loving, courting, and being nice to one another. By the time children are old enough to observe, the romance has all too often faded or gone underground.

Without necessarily knowing it, parents are the architects of their childrens' romantic and sexual selves. Familiarity exerts a powerful pull. What we have observed and experienced day after day exerts a powerful influence. Most people will choose the familiar, even though uncomfortable, over the unfamiliar, because of that power. Haven't you seen women whose fathers were cruel end up with cruel husbands? And haven't you also seen men who had nagging mothers end up with nagging wives? People often work out marriages similar to those of their own parents'—not due to heredity; they are simply following a family pattern.

We're getting pretty close to talking about parenting, and I want to reserve that very important subject for a later chapter. Right now I want to focus on coupling.

Every couple has three parts: *you, me,* and *us;* two people, three parts, each significant, each having a life of its own. Each makes the other more possible. Thus, I make you more possible, you make me more possible, I make us more possible, you make us more possible, and we together make each other more possible.

Whether the initial love between a couple continues to flower depends on how the two people make the three parts work. How these three parts work is a part of what I call the *process,* which is crucially important in marriage. For example, couples need to reach decisions about things the two of them now do together that they once handled alone—such as money, food, fun, work, and religion. Love is the feeling that begins a marriage, but it is the day-to-day living—their process—that will determine how the marriage works.

I find that love can truly flourish only where there is room for all three parts, and no one part dominates. The single most crucial factor in love relationships is the feeling of worth each person has for self. In turn, this affects how each person expresses self-worth, what demands are made of each other, and how each acts toward the other as a result. I speak of this more fully in the chapter on positive pairing.

Love is a feeling. It cannot be legislated. It either exists, or it doesn't. It comes without reason. For it to continue and to grow, it has to be nourished. Love is like a seed that manages to germinate and poke its head above the ground. Without proper food, light, and moisture, it will die. The loving, caring feelings of courtship flower in marriage only if the couple understands that their love needs nurturing every single day.

All couples stumble and bumble at times. All have some pain, disappointment, and misunderstanding. Whether they grow beyond this again depends on the process that exists between them.

I have seen many couples who started out with love feelings but later became mixed up, angry, and helpless. Their love faded into the background. When they were helped to understand and change their processes, love again became evident. On the other hand, some couples have endured so much that they are dead to one another. Since I

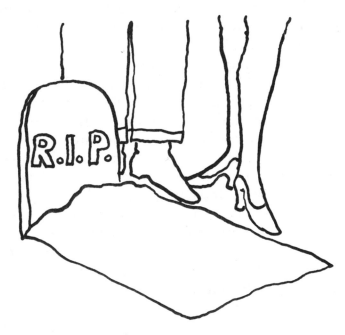

have not had much success in raising the dead, I think the best policy in these cases is to have a good funeral for the relationship and start over. If this has happened or is happening to you, use the experience as a learning and benefit.

The chances of spouses having things in common are about 100 percent. Likewise the chances are 100 percent that they will find differences from one another. Bringing up children highlights these kinds of differences. So does making decisions, which is a major part of any coupling process. For many couples, making decisions becomes a battle, either quiet or noisy, as to who has the right to tell whom what to do. When this is the case, each partner feels worse about the other as well as himself or herself every time a decision is made. Each begins to feel lonely, isolated, victimized, angry, betrayed, and depressed. Each lays his or her self-worth on the table every time a decision is pending. After enough battle experience, the feelings of loving and being loved are gone.

Sometimes couples try to avoid these problems by agreeing to let one partner be boss, and having the other go along with the decisions. Another out is to let a third person decide—an in-law, perhaps, or a child, or some trusted person from outside the family. Eventually all decisions get made. But how? And what happens as a result?

Let's pick up on some of the responses we talked about in the chapters on communication and apply them to how you and your spouse make decisions.

Do you do it by placating? Bullying? Lecturing? Distracting? Acting indifferent?

Who makes the decisions? How? Do you meet each decision squarely, realistically, and using everybody's talents?

Do you show you know the difference between competence in handling money and self-worth? (Writing a check is writing a check. It is not a way of showing love or not showing love.)

Using communication responses and stances, act out some of your recent and/or important decisions. Next, try to remember exactly how the decision was actually reached. Were there any similarities?

Here is an example. Before marriage, Manuel managed his money and Alicia managed hers. Now they are married, and they want to handle it together. This calls for a big decision, probably the first big one they make after the wedding.

Manuel says confidently, "Well, I am the man of the house, so I will handle the money. Besides, my father always did."

Alicia's response is slightly sarcastic. "Manuel, how can you? You're such a spendthrift! I naturally assumed I would do it. Besides, my mother always did it that way."

Manuel's answer is very quiet. "Well, if you want it that way, I suppose it's all right. I naturally thought that since I'm your husband, and you love me, you would want me to handle the money. After all, it's a man's place."

Alicia is a little frightened. "Oh, Mannie! Of course I love you! I wouldn't want to hurt your feelings. Let's not talk about it any more. Come on, give me a kiss."

What would you say about this decision-making process? Where do you think it will lead? Will it make for more or less love?

Five years later, Alicia says angrily to Manuel, "This company is threatening to sue us! You didn't pay the bill! I am tired of dodging bill collectors. I am going to take charge of the money, and I don't care what you think!"

Manuel snaps, "The hell with you! Go ahead, and see if you can do any better!"

Can you see their problem? They can't differentiate between their feelings of self-worth and the issue of coping with their finances.

Probably nothing is so vital to developing and maintaining a love relationship (or killing it) as the decision-making process. The difference between the issue in question, and the sense of self-worth around the issue, is worth learning.

Let's go into something a little different now. Let's consider some of the basic differences between courtship and marriage, and some of the problems implicit in those differences. During courtship, two prospective mates see each other by plan. They arrange their lives to make time for one another. Each knows the other has made being to gether a priority. This naturally gives each the feeling that the other sees him or her as a Very Important Person.

After marriage, this feeling is subject to drastic changes. In courtship it is easy to forget that the loved one has family, friends, work responsibilities, special interests, and other obligations. Courtship is a rather artificial situation as far as life is concerned. After marriage, these other life connections reappear and compete for attention. When one partner has felt he or she was everything to the other person and must now share with a lot of outside persons and responsibilities, trouble can begin. It is very hard to accept that you are not the center of someone else's life, as the courtship experience may have implied. Revelations such as "I didn't know you were so attached to your mother," or, "I

didn't think you liked to play bridge so much" are bound to occur and often lead to more serious disappointments. A good remedy for this is to sit down and talk about what is happening.

Frequently, one facet of a spouse is uppermost in the partner's attention. A man I know married a woman who always looked neat. In contrast, his mother always looked sloppy, which he hated. When his wife later looked sloppy at times for one reason or another, he began treating her with the same negative attitudes he had shown his mother. It is as though partners are not aware that they are married to people who do people things.

Many couples bank on the illusion that since they love each other, all things will happen automatically. Let's compare this situation to someone who, say, wants to build a bridge. An engineer isn't about to attempt this simply by liking or loving bridges. He or she has to know a good deal about the process before a real and successful bridge will be erected. The analogy applies to relationships.

Couples need to know about the process of relating as partners. Fortunately, many couples realize this today and are taking advantage of couple and family-life education classes which are becoming much more common. We need love *and* process in family architecture. Neither works by itself.

Let's carry our analogy a little further. The bridge builder who loves the work is going to endure the struggles and frustrations that are bound to occur in learning the job much more than one who is indifferent to bridge building or who doesn't expect problems. Even so, the devoted engineer still needs a sense of progress to persist in the job.

So it is with couples. If the "how" in their marriage doesn't fulfill their hopes and dreams, love goes away. Many people are aware that their love is disappearing without being aware in the slightest degree that it is their process—the "how" in their marriage—that is shoving love out.

Do you remember the love feeling you had for your spouse when you got married? Can you remember how you thought your life would be different? Do you also remember thinking certain problems would be solved by loving? Can you share together what some of these feelings and problems were and what has happened about them? Can you now form a new, more realistic basis for your relationship?

Marriage reveals much more about each partner than did the courtship. Lots of times sweethearts don't let themselves know too much about one another's defects, perhaps feeling that if they did, the marriage might not go through. Nevertheless some defects are obvious. Some sweethearts have plans for changing them; others accept them as part of being human and live happily with them.

It's impossible to live in close contact with another person without encountering less desirable traits eventually. This is the basis for cruel disappointment for many people. Disillusioned mates often say to me, "You certainly never know a person till you marry!"

Examples of faulty reasoning that lead to these kinds of post-wedding disappointments include a woman who tells herself, "He really drinks too much, but after we're married, I'll love him so much he won't drink." A man might say, "I really think she's a little ignorant, but after we're married, she'll go to school to please me." A man I knew said, "I can't stand the way she chews gum, but I love her so much I'll tolerate it."

Two people living together as one family unit is difficult at best. To do it successfully is very rewarding. An unsuccessful job can be dreadful. I often think of marriage as being similar to setting up a corporation: whether it succeeds depends on its organization, the "how" of its endeavors, its process.

I know plenty of people who loved their partners very deeply at the time of their courtship. However, they could not then make a marriage work because they couldn't get along with one another. Again, mutual attraction is not enough. How you get along with someone, what you expect from marriage, and how you communicate with each other are strong factors in what kind of marriage you create together.

One basic problem is that our society builds the marital relationship almost completely on love and then imposes demands on it that love alone can never fulfill:

"If you love me, you won't do anything without me."

"If you love me, you'll do what I say."

"If you love me, you'll give me what I want."

"If you love me, you'll know what I want before I ask."

These kinds of practices soon make love into a kind of blackmail that I call the *clutch*.

More specifically, if I do not feel I count for very much and if you and I have a relationship based only on love, then I can easily depend on your compliments, your attention, your agreement, your money, and so on, to make me feel good. If you are not eternally showing me that you live for me, then I feel like nothing. This practice can soon strangle the relationship.

Where are you now in your experience of loving and being loved? Facing this question squarely may help you reshape what you are doing and may well extend the life of your love. If you put both your questions and answers into words, your partner can see what's happening with you.

Another danger is practicing the *crystal ball* technique. In this one, you assume that because someone loves you or you love someone, each should know ahead of time what the other needs, wants, feels, or thinks, and act accordingly. Not doing so is the same as being unloved or unloving. The fact is that, no matter how much you and I may love each other, love doesn't tell me a thing about whether you like spinach or how you like it cooked.

I remember a couple who came to me because they felt very discontent in their marriage of about twenty years. As I talked with them, it became evident that each had tried to second-guess the other using the crystal ball theory: "If we truly love one another, we will always know what the other wants." Since this was their premise, they couldn't very well ask each other questions; that would cast aspersions on their love.

Their guessing had proved all right in a few areas but was now the crux of their being at odds with one another. They were not always guessing right. As we worked together, the couple accepted my invitation and encouragement to talk more openly. When we got to the part where I asked each of them to say openly what he or she resented about the other, the husband cried with a burst of emotion, "I wish you wouldn't always serve me that goddamned spinach!"

After his wife recovered from the shock, she answered, "I loathe spinach, but I thought you liked it. I just wanted to please you."

As we backtracked over the issue, it came out that, early in the marriage, the wife had asked her husband what he liked to eat. He told her whatever she fixed would be fine. She did considerable private research to find out what pleased him. Also, she once overheard him reprimand his young nephew for not eating his spinach; she interpreted this as a zest for spinach on her husband's part.

Her husband didn't recall this incident but did remember how sloppy he thought his sister-in-law was for not making her child eat right. Of course, I brought up the question of how come the husband made no comment and kept eating the spinach if he hated it. He said he hadn't wanted to hurt his wife's feelings. "Besides," he added, "if she liked it, I didn't want to deprive her of it."

He then turned to her. "But didn't you notice that I kept eating less and less?" "Oh," she said, "I thought you were reducing."

This episode gave rise to a slogan they used when they realized they were crystal-balling: "Remember the spinach!"

Probably no other couple in the world has had this particular experience, but my guess is nearly all of you have had something similar. Looking back, such an incident seems utterly absurd. And yet it happens again and again.

Another myth that corrupts and destroys love is the expectation that love means sameness. "You should think, feel, and act as I do all the time. If you don't, you don't love me." From this perspective, any difference can feel threatening.

Let's consider sameness and differentness a moment or two. I believe that two people are first interested in each other because of their sameness, but they remain interested over the years because of their ability to enjoy differences. To put it another way, if humans never find their sameness, they will never meet; if they never meet their differentness, they cannot be real or develop a truly human and zestful relationship with one another.

Differentness cannot be handled successfully until sameness is appreciated. Although each human is unique, everyone has certain qualities in common.

Each human being:

came into this world conceived through the union of sperm and egg, born from the body of a woman;

is encapsulated by skin which contains all the machinery for maintaining and growing;

has a predictable anatomy;

requires air, food, and water to survive;

has a brain capable of reason and the ability to see, hear, touch, taste, smell, speak, feel, think, move, and choose (except those born incomplete);

is able to respond; and

feels all through life.

Now as to differentness. Many have been taught to fear differentness because they saw it as the beginning of conflict or a fight. Fighting means anger; anger means death. So to live, avoid differentness.

A good, healthy fight does not have to mean death—it can bring closeness and trust. Yetta Bernhard and George Bach have done some excellent work on clean fighting,

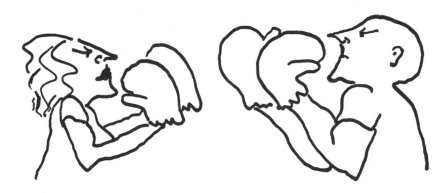

which every couple needs to be able to do when the occasion demands it. I put the emphasis on clean fighting. We all know about dirty fighting, and that *is* scary and can end in death.

We have in common those attributes previously named. We are also different from everyone else, and this is a natural consequence of being human. Over five billion people now live on this earth, and each one can be positively identified by her or his fingerprints. There are no duplicate sets; every human being is unique. So any two human beings, no matter what their similarities, are going to find differences. And *vive la difference!* Think how boring and sterile life would be if we were all the same. Difference brings us excitement, interest, and vitality. It also, of course, brings a few problems. The challenge is to find ways to deal with our differences constructively. How can we use differences as opportunities for learning instead of excuses for separation and war?

The wise couple will strive to learn about their differences early. They will try to see how they can make their differences work for them rather than against them. And as family architects, their example will exert unparalleled influence on their children.

If your self-esteem is high, you will have to come to know certain things:

No two persons are exactly alike; everyone is unique.

No two persons are going to have exactly the same timing, even in ways they are alike. Two people may like steak, but not necessarily fixed the same way; nor are they always hungry for it at the same time.

A further important learning is that you won't die because you're alone. Periodic aloneness is a natural outcome of being a separate person.

As I come to the end of this chapter, I am aware that I have talked a great deal about the complexity and potential pain involved in developing a satisfying, growing relationship between mates. I hope I have done it in such a way that new lights have come on for you to see new possibilities and accomplish them.

The ways of dealing with all this complexity generally fall in the following directions. The first has to do with one's beliefs about what people are like. Realizing that people seldom achieve perfection in their pursuits, and that few people behave destructively by design, can help you to see your mate as just an ordinary human being, like yourself.

The second direction has to do with becoming aware of yourself, getting in touch with yourself, and then being able to say where you are. This awareness helps you establish trust and confidence.

The third has to do with knowing within one's bones that each person has to stand on her or his own two feet. No one else can stand on your feet for you. This goes for the nitty-gritty as well as the juicy parts of life: no one person can carry another at length without both becoming cripples. In the coupling process, we have infinite opportunities for enjoying each other through our bodies, intellects, feelings, and interesting tasks.

Our challenge is to develop a sense of high self-worth, the willingness to risk, and the stimulation to create new possibilities. We will never run out of possibilities as long as we keep our eyes open and the rest of us ready.

12

Special Families

A great number of children today are being brought up by adults other than the ones who brought them into the world. I refer mainly to families in which parents have divorced, one or both parents have died, parents have never married, or parents can no longer take care of the children for whatever reason. An increasing number of children are also being brought up by same-sex couples, mostly women. When new families are created for these children, they are called step-, adopted-, or foster families. I call these reconstituted families *blended families*. When a family is not reconstituted, it is a *one-parent family*.

If you are in the process of building a blended family or developing a one-parent family, give yourself permission to know that it can be first-rate. Your family can become a wonderful place to be. All the possibilities and techniques exist to make it so. Think of the things you need to do as challenges, then become an enthusiastic detective and experimenter.

Families are more alike than they are different. All the factors I have presented so far—self-esteem, communication, and adults as family architects—apply to blended and one-parent families as well. While these families have additional aspects that sometimes make them seem different, other considerations are mere variations. All family forms can be first-rate, given the congruence and creativeness of the adults in charge.

The one-parent family offers special challenges. These families are presently of three sorts: one parent has left and the remaining parent does not remarry; a single person legally adopts a child; or an unmarried woman keeps a child. One-parent families, regardless of origin, are most commonly a female parent and her children. The challenge is, how can a family that includes only one adult be growth-producing for the children and the adult? Here we can see the effect of ghosts and shadows from the past. To form healthy families, the resentments and grief need to be put in place. In part this entails exploring why this is a one-parent family.

A big problem in the one-parent family is the presentation of a whole picture about males and females. It is easy for the remaining parent to give negative messages about the departed one, particularly if the departure was due to divorce, desertion, or something that caused great pain. A woman who remains with the children will have to work hard not to give them messages about the "badness" of the male. A male child who hears this will find it hard to believe that maleness is good. If he can't feel that maleness is good, how can he feel that *he* is good?

The female may be handicapped by having a skewed picture of what males are like. This is also a foundation for unhappiness with males later on. Meanwhile, it is all too easy for a mother to pull an older son into the role of husband, thus blurring his own role as son with his mother and his role as sibling with brothers and sisters.

In a growing number of families, fathers are the sole parent. Fathers who feel unable to handle all the needs of their children may bring in a housekeeper to help with the chores and supervision. Does the housekeeper then care for these children's intimacy needs? Much depends on the personality of the housekeeper, the attitude of the father, and the kids themselves. The situation is anything but easy; it takes great patience and understanding on everybody's part.

Finally, since children in a one-parent family do not experience an ongoing male-and-female relationship, they grow up without a full model of what that is like. This may be a factor in same-sex parenting as well.

These problems are not insurmountable. It is quite possible for a woman to have a healthy, accepting attitude toward males and be mature enough so that she does not have to give her children negative messages about males. She can be willing to provide and encourage relationships between children and adult males she knows and admires. These might be her own parents; they might be husbands of friends; they could be her own male friends. As far as putting one child on the spot by asking him to be a co-leader with her in the family, she can manage this by explaining the difference between competence at a given task and changing a full-time role. For instance, it is natural that if you are seventeen, you know more about putting up screen windows and are tall enough to do the job than if you were ten years old. Putting up screen windows or following through on any other job with which your mother needs help doesn't mean you also have to take on the role of coleader with your mother on a full-time basis.

Boys in a one-parent family probably face the greatest trap: being overmothered, and/or getting the picture that females dominate society, ending up with the feeling that the male is nothing. Very often the male's feeling of needing to nurture his mother's helplessness puts him into a position where he cannot himself take up his own independent life. Many boys react to this by remaining with their mothers and just not acting on their own heterosexual interests; or they rebel and leave home, feeling that women are enemies. They then alternately mistreat and worship women, all too often messing up the rest of their lives. A one-parent family is basically incomplete as far as live-in models are concerned. Adults who know this can do things to make completeness possible. This might even consist of periodically having children go to live with a loved and trusted family—a kind of informal foster-home arrangement.

The female child in a one-parent family also can get distorted learning about what male–female relationships are like. Her attitudes about being female can range all the way from being a servant—giving everything and receiving nothing—to feeling she has to do everything herself and be completely independent.

Now, let's turn to the blended family. Much is said and written about preparing people for marriage who have never been married before. Indeed, I have done so in this book. But I feel that perhaps this kind of preparation is even more important for people who have been married before and are now making another try—this time, with children. All blended families start out with great handicaps. I think that if these handicaps are understood, they can be overcome and used productively.

Blended families have certain things in common. They put together parts of previously existing families. There are basically three forms:

1. A woman with children who marries a man without children.
2. A man with children who marries a woman without children.
3. Both the woman and the man have children by previous partners.

In the first case, the blended family consists of the wife, the wife's children, husband, and wife's ex-husband. In the second case, the unit is husband, husband's children, wife, and husband's ex-wife. In the third case, the family consists of wife, wife's children, wife's ex-husband, husband, husband's children, and the husband's ex-wife.

Even though these people may or may not (and probably don't) all live under one roof, they are in each other's lives, for better or worse. Room has to be made for all of them. Each member is significant to the growth and success of the blended family. Many people in the blended families try to live as though other members didn't exist.

All of these people have authority in one way or another. Problems arise when they do not find time to talk openly with one another, are in disagreement, or, in some cases, are avowed enemies.

Picture the child who has a mother and stepfather in the home, and a father and stepmother living in another home; all four of these adults are taking some responsibility for him or her. Can you imagine what it would be like for that child to live in an atmosphere in which each adult is in some way asking something different, especially if the adults are unaware of this? Or if they are not on speaking terms with one another?

What is a child supposed to do with two conflicting directions? (At times there may be as many different instructions as there are parents.) For the child's sake, two things are necessary. First, the child needs to be encouraged by all concerned to tell what opposing directions have been given. Second, the adults need to have periodic meetings with the child or children so they can discover what each adult is doing and how they agree or disagree. The chances are that if the respective adults are open about what they are doing, the child can at least choose and won't have to be a secret- keeper for the adults—a problem that often arises between divorced parents who still regard one another as enemies and use their children as spies.

I remember a sixteen-year-old girl who was acting alternately crazy and depressed. It developed that she lived with her mother and stepfather, spent one weekend with her father and his fiancée, the next weekend with her mother and her new husband, and the third weekend with her maternal grandparents. Adults in each place asked her to tell what went on in the other places; they also made her promise not to tell what went on "here." The sad part was that all these adults really liked the girl and wanted to help her, but they inadvertently put the burden on her for their jealousy, rivalries, and resentments toward one another.

This same thing can go on in a natural family, with a husband and wife, if they can't be straight with each other. They unwittingly ask the child to deal with what they can't deal with themselves. Of course, the child cannot possibly do this in any constructive way, so the child often responds by becoming sick, bad, crazy, stupid, or all of these things.

Needless to say, in the session where I gathered everyone together with the sixteen-year-old girl, we had a few stormy hours until all the truth got put on the table. Headway was then made so the girl no longer had to be crazy or depressed. This didn't happen overnight, for she slowly had to learn to trust again.

A child benefits when all the adults around can be open with one another and take responsibility for what they think and feel. To be open with someone doesn't mean you have to love that person. Former marital partners cannot always be expected to continue loving one another, but they can be open and not foist their problems with each other on the child. This is probably the most crucial problem that challenges the blended family: to keep the child free of the adults' burdens.

The fact that a family is blended does not in and of itself deter developing a good family life. I have seen people develop blended families of all varieties very successfully. To do so, they need to be aware of many potential handicaps and deal with them in a loving, realistic, congruent manner.

Again, the process that goes on between people determines what happens in families.

Let's examine some of the problems in detail. For a divorced person who makes a new marriage, the experience of divorce itself was probably painful. Having to have a divorce involves disappointment, and the potential for developing mistrust is very much there, too. In a way, the second spouse has a harder row to hoe than the first one. There is often a subtle message that, "You need to be better than the one before you." People who remarry after divorce have been burned once, and they don't forget easily.

This is why it is so important for divorced individuals to work out for themselves the meaning of their respective divorces, understand it, and use whatever they discover to teach themselves something. This is greatly preferable to bemoaning their fate or carrying grudges or suffering extreme disappointment.

The woman with children who remarries is often inclined to treat her children as though they were her private property. This introduces a handicap for her new mate at the very beginning. She often believes that she does not want to impose on her new husband, feeling perhaps that he would not understand her children or the particular process she has with them. Sometimes she feels a misplaced loyalty to her former husband. Any or all of these modes add up to the fact that her new husband doesn't have a well-defined role as a helper. It also ignores the possibility that a man coming into a family has new perspectives and new ways of doing things that might be integrated in the new family.

One trap is that the woman may feel so much in need of a "father's firm hand" that she expects him to exert a power and an influence he has not had the chance to develop with her children. This is a pretty big order, particularly if she feels the children are out of hand. New husbands may be inclined to try to fulfill their wives' expectations and wishes, often doing a poor job of it. They may be the new head of the family but, as it is with new leaders in business or elsewhere, they have to feel their way into a new situation. If a new husband takes charge prematurely, he may be in for unnecessary trouble from the children. This is usually true with teenagers in particular.

Including a stepparent can be rocky in other ways. The natural parent and the children have spent years together, and things like in-jokes or family buzzwords can make a stepparent feel left out. Almost every family develops some kinds of rituals or traditions or specific ways of doing things. These customs have to be recognized and understood by everybody, or they can be a real source of trouble.

One of my suggestions when working with people who are preparing for a blended family life is that they constantly keep in mind that each had a life before and much of what goes on in the present life will have a reference point in the past. If one hears something and doesn't understand, freely asking questions is the way out. Many stepparents, rather than asking, handle the situation by thinking, "Well, maybe that's none of my business," or, "I shouldn't ask about it," or "Maybe I'm not supposed to know about it," or acting as though they do. This kind of message to oneself frequently gets translated directly into low self-esteem. Another frequent rationale is, "If she wanted me to know, she would have told me."

Another facet to this situation has to do with previous possessions, friends, and contacts that unintentionally impinge on the present marriage. Among these, of course, are the in-laws or grandparents and other relatives of the people who divorced. There are very few divorces in which the relatives don't have opinions (and oftentimes too much to say) about what did happen, what could have happened, or what should have happened. We need to take all these things into account. It is important that everybody is clear about what has happened and straight about his or her way of communicating it. Sounds easy. I know it is not. Nonetheless, we can't fall off the face of the earth, or destroy or get away

from all that we had yesterday. We need to include and integrate the things that belong to yesterday.

So far I have been talking about a spouse who has been divorced and remarried, and some of the strains and difficulties he or she faces. I'd like to remind you that the new spouse, too, had a previous life; and when he or she also has children, the same kinds of problems are possible. If the new husband's children live apart from him, he may spend more time with his stepchildren than his own kids, just by virtue of proximity. Frequently this makes for discomfort on his part; he may feel he is neglecting his own kids. Having his children come visit him in his new home can create a problem for his ex-wife, the children's mother, in that she shares parenting with another woman.

To do a successful job, adults who remarry must revamp their parenting styles. They need to parent their own children and their spouse's children without neglecting or cheating either. It is easy to see how complicated the blended family situation is. If both divorced parents and both remarried parents are mature, they can work things out together so that all their children gain instead of lose.

First, it is important to remember that the *adults* got married, divorced, or remarried. The children are either willing or unwilling followers. They need to be allowed to keep a place for their original parents, and be helped to find a way to add another parent. This takes time and patience, especially at first. I can hardly emphasize this point too strongly. The stepparent is a stranger, whom the child may even see as an interloper. This has little or nothing to do with innate goodness or lovableness.

For the moment, let yourself look through the eyes of the child who is part of the blended family. The child's questions will be, "How will I treat my new parent? What shall I call my new parent? How will my new parent feel about me and my relationship to my other parent?"

Perhaps the single most serious problem faced by a child in a blended family is that the child may not feel free to love whomever he or she wants to love. Loving the missing parent might get the child into trouble. Children in blended families need to be *convinced* they have that freedom.

Many adults want to preserve the value of the divorced parent in the eyes of their children. This can be tough. If you are the mother, what do you say to your children about your ex-spouse, an alcoholic who beat you and starved you during a marriage of many years? Now you're with a man who no longer does these things. Can you help your children value their father and, at the same time, help them receive the new man without sending out the message that the first one was no good? You can, if you separate the value of the self from the behavior.

Sometimes when the other parent has been sent to jail or a mental hospital, or has had a long history of irresponsibility—in any case, conditions that might make for a feeling of shame—the remaining parent tries to live as though the other person didn't exist. From where I sit, in the hundreds of cases I have seen, any time a child is asked to ignore and/or denounce either biological parent, she or he runs a great risk of developing low self-worth. How can you say, "I am good" if you feel you came from bad stock?

I certainly am not advising parents to say everything is good about a parent, whether or not it is true. That isn't the point. The important thing is to guide children to the awareness that people are made up of many parts, and that relationships sometimes bring two parts together that don't mesh well. Having such a part doesn't make someone a bad person. Nor does having problems make it a bad relationship: sometimes we know how to change things, to continue nurturing ourselves and each other; sometimes we don't know how to change things.

I have never found a human being who was all bad. For instance, a person whose partner has been violent toward him or her can gain something by seeing that the partner lashed out because of low self-esteem. Although an interaction between the two of them probably seemed to trigger the violence, the issue goes beyond blame, into communication and congruence.

Friction of any degree can remind us to relax. As a stepparent in a blended family, you can take it easy and not push. For the time being, you may be an interloper and a stranger in the child's life. Give yourself a chance, too.

Make room in your own mind for your stepchild's other parent. That person may live elsewhere, yet she or he is also a presence with your stepchild. You can't wish away the biological parent. Offer plenty of opportunities to let the child know that you are not trying to replace that parent. No one says you have to love automatically. You can, however, give the child the status of a human being, and leave room for trust and love to grow.

Important questions are: In what ways will the current spouse plan with the ex-spouse in relation to the child's welfare? How do you want to include the ex-spouse in the current family?

This brings us to the questions of visitation and support—difficult issues, particularly when minor children are involved. Answers depend almost completely on how each of the divorced partners has come to terms with the divorce. If strain still permeates the relationship, these questions are anything but easy to handle.

Shadows from the past are very real and must be dealt with by the new marital pair. The children are not exactly

out of these shadows, either. They may have been part of the old hurts; they often take sides. Their loyalties are torn. Frequently they are not living with the parent whose side they took. Their problems don't necessarily disappear simply because there has been a change in parents.

Bringing together children who do not know each other and who do not feel sure of their places can put tremendous strain on the marriage. These children do not necessarily reflect the joy of the new spouses. There are also blended families containing "your children," "my children," and "our children." This situation only increases the potential for problems, and the process for coping is just the same: the question is not whether there will be strains, but *what* are they going to be and how will they be coped with? This is a great creative challenge to the new marital team.

Time, patience, and the ability to stand not being loved (at least for a time) are terribly important. What reason is there, after all, for a child to automatically love the stepparent, any more than there is for the stepparent to love the child automatically?

One approach that has helped many families deal with this is that the new husband and wife are quite clear that their family faces big handicaps, and that they can be straight with each other and with the children. They don't ask the children to be phony with them; everyone is free to be honest. Again, this doesn't come easily. Few of us have learned how to be emotionally honest. We need to be patient with ourselves while we struggle with our learning.

As with adults, life after marriage for children is very different than it was during the courtship. Surprises abound. Life with Mama's boyfriend or Papa's girlfriend is just not the same when it comes to forging a family unit.

I remember a ten-year-old boy whose father and mother had divorced when he was five. His mother remarried when he was eight. About a year after the second marriage, the boy suddenly asked his mother, "Hey, Ma. Whatever happened to Harold?" Harold was a man who had come over fairly frequently for a period of time between the two marriages and stayed the night at his mother's home.

The stepfather immediately demanded, "Who's Harold?" Mother blushed and told her son to go to his room. He went and then overheard their quarrel. The husband essentially accused the wife of keeping things from him and ended up by calling her a slut, liar, and so on.

Apparently she had created a situation in which her second husband thought she had told him everything. It just so happened that Harold wasn't included in what she had told him. Her son's question had been innocent enough, but its effect was an unpleasant surprise.

Something else happens when the previous marriage has been particularly hurtful, especially as far as the mother is concerned. She may begin to see her children as symbols of that hurt. Every time she gets into any kind of negative thing with the children, it brings back memories of the hurtful times and all her fears about their terrible effects on her children.

I know one woman, married the second time, who went through this. Every time her four-year-old son said "no," she had visions of her husband. He had rebelled his whole life; eventually he went to prison for assaulting someone. So when her young son said "no" to her, her image was of a person already in prison, and she beat him unmercifully to keep him from becoming a criminal. This is a clear illustration of how this woman's attitude created more problems. Her expectations of this child and what his "no" meant belonged to her past, not to what was presently going on with her son.

Children have a lot of work to do to be clear about a father who is now married to another woman with whom he has other children. When things aren't straight between the children and their father, the situation can make for low-pot feelings, questions, jealousies, and so on. I have the impression that many of the children get deprived of their remarried fathers more than is necessary because these fathers and their second families aren't prepared to, nor do they really know how to, integrate previous children into the family.

How the current husband and wife got together has a great deal to do with how things go on in the present. Suppose they both were previously married, met each other while still married, carried on a courtship, divorced their respective mates, and made a new marriage of their own. Unless some very, very good and careful work has gone on, the previous spouses can easily sway the feelings of the children against acknowledging this new relationship.

The children's ages have a good deal to do with the difficulties inherited in a second marriage. If the children are young—perhaps under the ages of two or three—the possibilities for interference from the past life are not as great as for older children. If the children are grown, the new marriage may become irrelevant to them: it is a matter for the new marital partners to feel good about. When family matters involve children in money, property, business, or so forth, it is important to arrive at mutually acceptable agreements. I have known cases where older children fought the idea of new marriages by their parents because of the trouble they expected about money.

For purposes of bringing home some of these points about new partners and children in blended families, let's examine another hypothetical family. Jennifer and Jim are thirty-three and thirty-five years old, respectively. After ten years of marriage, they divorce. Three years later Jennifer meets Dave, with whom she feels she can make a better marriage. After a year-long courtship, she marries him.

Jim and Jennifer have three children. At the time of Jennifer's remarriage, Tom is twelve; Diana, ten; and Bill, eight. Jim has moved to a new town about two hundred miles away. According to the divorce settlement, Jim was to see his children once a month; but because he started a new business, he didn't always get there that often. He was, however, continuing to pay alimony and child support.

Before Jennifer's second marriage, she and the kids lived with her parents. Because Jennifer had to work, more and more of the parenting was turned over to her mother and father. Jennifer's job involved a lot of travel; in fact, it was on one of her trips that she met Dave. Much of the time she and Dave were together was time not shared with her three children. Dave had met them but only for short times. There had been nice feelings between him and the children, but in no way could Dave feel he really knew them.

Dave, by the way, had also been married before and had a daughter, Theresa, age twelve; she lived with her mother in a city some seven hundred miles away. His divorce agreement allowed him to have Theresa stay with him for summer vacations. Generally speaking, there was a good relationship between Theresa and her father.

After Jennifer and Dave married, Jennifer naturally wanted to set up a home for the children, which meant taking them away from Grandmother and Grandfather. Very much in love and without thinking too much about it, Jennifer and Dave just assumed they were going to be able to reconstitute the family very easily.

Let's consider some of the things that might have helped develop this blended family. First of all, there needs to be a clear recognition on everybody's part that when Jennifer's three children group together with their mother and her new husband, this will be a completely new family unit. Even though Jim doesn't visit very often, he does pay child support, and he too is part of the picture.

The question comes up immediately: What role will Dave have with the children? His role name is stepfather. But what does that really mean? Ordinarily a wife hopes her husband will participate with her in bringing up her children. And she may, without realizing it, assume that because her husband loves her and she loves him, he will know certain facts pertaining to the children.

Stepfathers rarely know these facts, though, and therefore should not expect to come into the lives of the children and be helpful immediately. Far too many stepparents expect this of themselves. Dave is a stranger, and he will be a stranger to Jennifer's children for some time. Jim's shadow is still very much there, and to some extent always will be.

Sometimes people feel their self-worth rests on how much change can be made right away. What we actually need when we come into a new situation is time—all the time that is necessary in any situation to become fully acquainted.

Back to Jennifer and Dave. What happened in the previous marriage between Jennifer and Jim may not have been totally acceptable to the children, which could form a barrier to their acceptance of their stepfather. Suppose the children perceive very subtle messages that they must be on their mother's side against their father, and they must take her new husband as their father. Jennifer may still be feeling much pain, bitterness, and disappointment—a legacy from her first marriage. Many women feel this way and expect their children to feel the same. Jennifer could say, with a very determined or blank look when Jim calls or writes for them to visit, "Well, it's your decision. You do it if you want to." Or, the message can be anything but subtle: "If you go to your father, just don't have anything more to do with me!" Subtle or direct, Jennifer or anyone else in her place is asking for trouble by expecting her children to reflect her own feelings about her first husband.

The legacy of pain from a first marriage is a source of trouble of another kind as well. People's expectations for a second marriage can be monumental— close, sometimes, to expecting Nirvana. Many adults in blended families expect magic. Because they got rid of the troubling spouse and now have a better one, "all the problems are solved." They forget that people will still relate to people, that there will still be the arsenic hour (the time when demands are far greater than any one person can meet), and the same kinds of things will go on, such as people being sassy with one another, or flip, angry, or stubborn.

It really comes down to the fact that people are people and will act like people whether in a natural family or in a blended one. For example, I remember a woman who had remarried when her oldest child was eleven. At fourteen he began giving his mother a lot of static. Her immediate conclusion was that it had been wrong for her to remarry; that if she hadn't remarried, her son wouldn't be the way he was. Certainly the communication that had gone on between her and the boy in relation to the stepfather had something to do with the situation, but so did the boy's experimenting with his mother, and his feeling on the outside of things. This could have occurred in a family where there was not a second marriage or a stepfather.

In short, anybody entering into marriage expects life to be better, and a second marriage is no exception. And further, it seems that the more you want out of life, the more you expect, and the greater your anticipation, the greater can be the disappointments.

Another variation of a blended family is when two people make a second marriage after one or both of the first spouses have died. There are different kinds of traps here.

Suppose a woman was married fifteen years and her husband died. Relatively soon afterward she met a man who had never been married. Let us say that her first husband died a tragic, accidental death. Their marriage was fair: not too exciting, on the dull side. But the impact of his death crowded out any memory of the boredom and dullness of that marriage and left this woman with an exaggerated feeling of how good the marriage had been. Then she marries a man who could provide for her, whom she cares about, and who may be more exciting than her former husband. But at times, when she feels disappointed or annoyed with her present husband, she could put into words how much better life had been with her former husband, leaving it open for the second husband to be compared unfavorably with him. Of course the same thing could happen with a man who marries again after his wife died.

I take the view that people are not angels, and every relationship has its difficulties. Because of our peculiar attitude toward death, we tend to elevate the departed one to the status of saint. And this is unreal. No human being can compete with a saint.

It is important for both the husband and wife to accept the fact that somebody did live before, was a person in her or his own right, and had a place. That place should be acknowledged. For instance, I know of several people who married again after their spouses died. The new spouse insisted that no pictures or belongings of the former man be allowed, almost as if he were asking his mate to rid herself of even the memory of him. Again, this is a low-pot response. It is almost as if the person is saying, "If you still acknowledge your first marriage, then you can't possibly acknowledge the second." I consider this a rather emotionally underdeveloped attitude. In short, nonsense!

Kids can have problems when adults either don't mention the person who has died or else deify him. It's pretty hard, if not impossible, for a child to relate to a ghost or a saint.

Another trap is when the new spouse is sensitive to comments about how things used to be. I've known some people who have come into families in which a spouse has died and who really wanted to and were willing to do everything they could, but upset the whole household by asking the family to behave quite differently from the way they were accustomed to. If such a person were to build bridges to the children and in a gradual way make room for new things, I think things would be much different. Again, one's self-esteem does not depend on how much change one can effect right away.

The foster family is another form of a blended family. It may include one foster child and no other children; one foster child and some "natural" children; or one natural child and several foster children. The composition of the family makes a difference in the kinds of handicaps to be overcome.

The foster child's former situation is also a factor. Generally speaking, a child becomes a foster child when, for whatever reason, his or her own parents can't be the caretakers. This may be because the child's behavior is such that the people in the family cannot stand to continue living with the child. Or a person in authority might decide the family system is harmful to the child, who would have a safer life in another family. Frequently the parents have been seriously neglectful—parents whose behavior was so punitive, punishing, or hurtful that somebody removed the child from the home.

Almost all foster children are placed in foster homes by reason of a court order, which brings another element into the picture, namely, the court. So the management of the child is now not only between the foster parents and the real parents, but also the court.

Sometimes both parents have died, leaving the child with no home. Relatives or guardians don't want to put the child in an orphanage, so they look for a foster family. For some reason the child may not be adoptable, which means the child will have no permanent status in the foster family. The child may live in a foster home a long time, taken in, in a sense, as a boarder.

In other instances, a child's sole parent has had to go to a mental hospital or jail. As far as the child was concerned, everything was fine up until the time this parent was taken away (let's say the other parent is dead or divorced). Now this child needs to live until his or her parent returns. This kind of placement is relatively temporary.

All these situations imply a message about the kind of a place the child will have in his foster family. The message answers the question in the minds of the foster family members: "How come you can't stay in your own family?" There is also a message about the message. This is what I mean: If the foster parents take a child who has been acting up at home, they might see their task as being super strict to prevent the child from acting up again. If the child comes because the parents have been abusive, the foster parents would probably feel sorry for her or him and bend over backward to be super loving. There is nothing like abusive parents to arouse the anger and protectiveness of foster parents. The trap here is that the foster parents might give the child negative messages about his or her own parents, in effect damaging the child's chances for developing an integrated self-concept. I can hardly express this thought too often: No one can feel high self-worth who feels she or he came from devils and bad people.

If the child has no living parents, foster parents have the job of feeling good about giving their all with someone who, after all, is not their child. On the other hand, foster parents are often wary of getting themselves too involved because, on the face of it, the child is with them only temporarily. (Foster placements range from overnight to twenty-one years.) One thing is certain: the child who comes into the foster home is having something done to him or her for his or her own good, and there is usually a strong message that somehow the child's own parents failed in some way.

Whether this "bad seed" psychology becomes a real handicap to the child depends a great deal on the emotional stability and development of the foster parents. If they can see themselves as offering not only time, but a bridge for this child toward some new growth, and they can freely involve themselves in a true family, parent–child manner, their foster family has a good chance to be successful and produce a well-balanced human being with good self-esteem.

Very often the child's natural parents are allowed visiting privileges or some kind of contact while the child is in the foster home. Whether or not the natural parents can become an integrated part of the child's ongoing life and participate in the child's growth depends on how the foster parents view the natural parents. In some ways this situation is not too different from integrating the divorced parent into a child's life. I have known some foster families who were revolted by what they learned about the behavior of the child's real parents and who found it very hard to treat the natural parents with any kind of acceptance when they visited.

So how can foster parents treat the child's natural parents as okay people if they know, for example, that the child has been badly beaten or burned by them? It is obviously destructive and irrational for an adult to burn or beat a child. Again, being aware that this behavior comes from a person who has a terribly low sense of self can help you be more understanding and not just ready to damn the parents. I wish that for every foster child placed, there were someone to help the natural parents grow and improve so that they could again become responsible, loving people who could do a good job of parenting. So often, if this happens at all, it comes about through the foster parents. I once saw a beautiful example of this. A pair of foster parents saw the parents of their three foster children as people who needed to grow. As opportunities presented themselves, they acted as parents to these parents in such a way as to help the natural parents grow, learn, change, and ultimately feel like okay people.

I want to say a word or two about another kind of family. This is the communal family, which has seen many variations over the years. In general, and for various reasons, a group of adults who have children live together either in the same building or the same complex. They share tasks and maybe even common property. They also share parenting among the many children; some of the adults even share sexual lives.

An advantage to this kind of family is that the child gets exposed to a variety of models. The one big problem, of course, is that a very good relationship must exist among all of the adults so that the mutual parenting can really offer something.

Israel's kibbutzim are one kind of communal living; but the major parenting goes on with an auxiliary parent, a woman. Biological parents are treated very much as visitors in that they don't participate fully in the decision-making.

They might have very little to do with the day-to-day living experience.

Families with live-in governesses or nurses are often informal kinds of foster families. Some of the same problems of distance are created between the child and the actual parents as we have been discussing in this chapter.

Many children have had a great variety of experiences in blended families. Through the course of life, a child may have belonged to a step-family, a one-parent, adoptive, and/or foster family. It's possible for a child, between birth and maturity, to have had fathering done by five different males. Suppose the child's biological father dies or leaves, and the child then spends time with a grandparent. The mother remarries, and a stepfather appears. It's possible that the stepfather may die, or perhaps the mother remarries, and the child has another stepfather. It is equally possible that the child has some kind of difficulty and goes to a foster home until coming of age. This kind of thing happens frequently. The same is true, although to a lesser extent, for the person who fills the mother slot. Many children have had a number of different adults filling the role of mother.

One thread runs through all of these family variations: the adults are trying to lend their resources to help children grow. Simultaneously, they are trying to manage their own growth—and in some way that will be compatible with their children's development. All of the things I mentioned that happen in the variations of the foster families I've described can also happen in natural families. Husbands and wives can be jealous of each other, children can feel left out or jealous of their sisters or brothers; they can all have experiences that make them feel isolated from other members of the family and feel low-pot.

The point is that the family's form is not the basic determinant of what happens in the family. Form presents different kinds of challenges to be met, but the process that goes on among the family members is what, in the end, determines how well the family gets along together; how well the adults grow, separately and with one another; and how well the children develop into creative, healthy human beings. For this, self-worth, communication, rules, and the system are the chief means of making a family work.

In this way, all families are alike.

13

Your Family Map

When I first started working with entire families, I was struck by the tremendous unrelated activity that went on in all directions: physically through bodily movement and psychologically through double messages, unfinished sentences, and so on. More than anything else I was reminded of the can of angleworms my father used to take as bait on fishing trips. The worms were all entangled, constantly writhing and moving. I couldn't tell where one ended and the other began. They really couldn't go anywhere except up, and down, around, and sideways, but they certainly gave the impression of aliveness and purpose. Had I been able to talk to one of those worms to see how he felt, it is my feeling that he would have told me the same kinds of things I have heard from family members over the years: *Where am I going? What am I doing? Who am I?*

The comparison between the way many families conduct themselves and the purposeless, tangled writhing of these worms seemed so apt that I termed the network that exists among family members a *can of worms.*

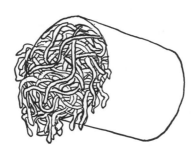

To show you what your family network is and how to map it will be the goal of this chapter. I think the best way to go about it is to take an imaginary family, the Lintons, and show you how their network works for and against them. No one can ever actually see this network, incidentally, but you can certainly feel it, as the exercises outlined in this and the following chapter will amply demonstrate to you.

All right. Here are the Lintons as individuals and as their family is today.

THE LINTON FAMILY NOW

ALICE
Adult Female
age 38

JOHN
Adult Male
age 40

JOE
Male Child
age 17

BOB
Male Child
age 16

TRUDY
Female Child
age 12

Tack a large sheet of paper to the wall where all of you can see it clearly. Begin the map of your family by drawing circles for each person, using a felt-tipped pen. Your family may now include a grandparent or other person as part of your household. If so, add a circle for that person on the row with the other adults.

If someone was once a part of your family but is gone now, represent her or him with a filled-in circle. If the husband or father is dead, has deserted the family or divorced his wife, and his wife has not remarried, your map would show it as follows:

If the woman has remarried, it would be shown thus:

If the second child died or was institutionalized, your map would look this way:

I believe that anyone who has ever been part of a family leaves a definite impact. A departed person is often very much alive in the memories of those left behind. Frequently, too, these memories play an important role—often a negative one—in what is going on in the present. This doesn't have to happen. If the departure has not been accepted, for whatever reason, the ghost is still very much around and often can disrupt the current scene. If, on the other hand, the departure has been accepted, then the present is clear as far as the departed one is concerned.

Each person is a separate self who can be described by name, physical characteristics, interests, tastes, talents, habits—all the qualities that relate to him or her as an individual.

So far our map shows the family members as islands, but anyone who has lived in a family knows that no one can remain an island for long. The various family members are connected by a whole network of ties. These links may be invisible, but they are there, as solid and firm as if they were woven of steel.

Let's add another strand to our network: pairs. Pairs have specific role names in a family. The illustration below shows the pairs in the Linton family with their *role names*.

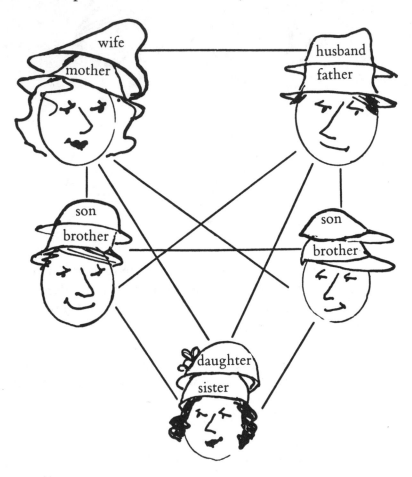

Roles and pairs in the family fall into three major categories: marital, having the labels of husband and wife; parental–filial, having the labels of father–daughter, mother–daughter, father–son and mother–son; and sibling, having the labels of brother–brother, sister–sister, and brother–sister. Family roles always mean pairs. You can't take the role of a wife without a husband, nor father or mother without a son or daughter, and so on.

Beliefs about what different roles mean can differ. Each role evokes different expectations. It's important to find out what the various roles mean to each family member.

When families come to me a little mixed up, one of the first things I do is ask for each member's ideas about what his or her role means. I remember one couple very vividly. She said, "I think being a wife means always having the meals on time, seeing that my husband's clothes are in order, and keeping the unpleasant things about the children and the day from him. I think the husband should provide a good living. He should not give the wife any trouble."

He said, "I think a husband means being the head of the house, providing income, and sharing his problems with his wife. I think a wife ought to tell her husband what's going on. She ought to be a pussycat in bed."

You can see that both were practicing what they thought the roles were; they didn't know how far apart they actually were in these important areas. Never having spoken about it, they had just assumed their views on their respective roles were the same. When they shared their ideas, some new understanding developed between them, and they achieved a much more satisfying relationship. I have seen this particular couple's experience over and over again in troubled families that come to me for help.

What about your family and your respective role expectations and definitions? Why not all sit down and share what you think your role is, and those of your spouse and your offspring as well? I think you'll be in for some surprises.

Now let's examine another facet of this role business. Alice Linton is a person who lives and breathes and wears a certain dress size. She is also a wife when she is with John, and a mother when she is with Joe, Bob, or Trudy. It might be helpful if we think of her roles as different hats she puts

on when the occasion demands. Aside from her self-role, which she wears all the time, Alice uses a particular hat only when she is with the person who corresponds to the role-hat. So she is constantly putting on and taking off hats as she goes through her day. If she or John were to wear all their role-hats at once, they would look like this, and it could get a little top-heavy.

Now add the network lines to your family map, linking every member with every other member. As you draw each line, think for a moment about that particular relationship. Imagine how each of those two people involved feels about that connection. All of the family should share in this exercise, so each can try to feel what the different relationships are like.

So far I have presented the Lintons to you as selves and pairs—five selves and ten pairs. If this were all there were to the map, living in a family would be quite an easy matter. When Joe arrived, however, a triangle came into being. Here the plot begins to thicken, for the triangle is the trap in which most families get caught. I'll talk more about triangles later, but first let's add the network of triangles to the Linton family map.

Now the Lintons' network looks like this. It's pretty hard to see any one part of it clearly, isn't it? You can see how the triangles obscure and complicate things. In families we don't live in pairs; we live in triangles.

When Joe was born, not one, but three triangles were formed. A triangle is always a pair plus one and, since only two people can relate at one time, someone in the triangle is always the odd one out. The whole nature of the triangle changes depending on who is odd one out, so what looks like one triangle actually is three (at different times).

The three triangles above consist of John, Alice, and Joe. In the first, John is the odd one, watching the relationship of his wife and son. In the second, Alice watches her husband and son together. In the third, little Joe watches his father and mother together. How troublesome any particular triangle is may depend on who is the odd one out at the moment and whether he or she feels bad about being left out.

There is truth to the old saying, "Two's company, three's a crowd." The odd person in a triangle always has a choice between breaking up the relationship between the other two, withdrawing from it, or supporting it by being an interested observer. The odd person's choice is crucial to the functioning of the whole family network.

All kinds of games go on among people in triangles. When a pair is talking, the third may interrupt or try to draw their attention. If the pair disagrees about something, one may invite the third to become an ally; this changes the triangle by making one of the original pair the odd one out.

Can you remember a time recently when you were with two other people? How did you handle that triangle? How did you feel? How are triangles handled in your family?

Families are full of triangles. The Linton family of five has thirty triangles:

John/his wife/his first son
John/his wife/his second son
John/his wife/his daughter
John/his first son/his second son
John/his first/son/ his daughter
John/his second son/his daughter
Alice/her husband/her first son
and so on.

Triangles are extremely important because the family's operation depends in large part on how triangles are handled.

The first step toward making a triangle bearable is to understand very clearly that no one can give equal attention to two people at the same time. Maybe the best idea is to approach the inevitable triangle as people do with Texas weather: stick around awhile, and it will change.

The second step, when you are the odd person, is to put your dilemma into words so that everyone can hear. The third step is to show by your own actions that being the odd one out isn't a cause for anger or hurt or shame. Problems arise when people feel that being on the outside means they are no good. Low self-worth!

To live comfortably in a triangle, it seems to me that one needs certain feelings about oneself. An individual has to feel good about him- or herself and be able to stand on two feet without leaning on someone else. He or she can be the odd one temporarily without feeling bad or rejected. She or he needs to be able to wait without feeling abused, talk straight and clearly, let the others know what she or he is feeling and thinking, and not brood or store up bad feelings.

If you glance again at the Lintons' family map and triangles, you can appreciate how complex family networks are. The concept of the can of worms may be more understandable to you, too.

Draw your family's can of worms by adding all the triangles to your family map. Using a different colored pencil or ink may help distinguish the triangles from the pairs. Again, as you draw, think of the relationship that each line represents. Among any three people you will be drawing only one triangle, although three actually exist. Think of how that triangle looks from each person's point of view.

The Lintons' network did not develop overnight. It took six years to gather the people now represented in the network—possibly eight years, if you consider the two years John and Alice courted. Some families take fifteen or twenty years to assemble their casts. Others take one or two years, and some never finish because the core (the couple in charge) keeps changing.

Whenever the Lintons are all together, forty-five different units are operating: five individuals, ten pairs, and thirty triangles. Similar elements exist in your family. Each person has his or her own mental picture of what each of these units is like. John may look very different to his wife Alice than to his son Bob. Alice may see her relationship to Bob one way; Bob would see it differently. John's picture is probably quite different from either of theirs. All these varying pictures are supposed to fit together in the family, whether or not the individuals are aware of them. In nurturing families, all of these elements and everyone's interpretation of them are out in the open and can easily be talked about. On the other hand, troubled families are either not aware of their family pictures or are unwilling or unable to talk about them.

Many families have told me they feel frustrated, physically tight, and uncomfortable when the whole family is assembled. Everyone feels constant movement, being pulled in many directions. If family members could be made aware of the can of worms in which they are trying to function, they wouldn't be so puzzled and uncomfortable.

When families see their network for the first time and fully realize how tremendously complicated family living really is, they often tell me they feel great relief. They realize they don't need to be on top of everything all the time. Who can keep track or control of forty-five units at once? Individual members can have a much easier time together because they didn't feel the necessity to control things; they became more interested in observing what is happening and in planning creative ways to make the family function better.

The challenge in family living is to find ways each individual can participate or be an observer of others without feeling he or she doesn't count. Meeting this challenge involves not being a victim of our old villain: low self-esteem.

A family's can of worms exerts tremendous push–pull pressures on the individual. It puts great demand on each one. In some families it is difficult to be an individual at all. The larger the family, the more units to be dealt with, the more difficult it is for each family member to get a share of the action. I certainly don't mean to imply that big families are always failures. On the contrary, some of the most nurturing families I know have large numbers of children.

Even so, the more children that come into the family, the more pressure on the marital relationship. A family of three has only three self–pair triangles; a family of four has twelve; a family of five has thirty; and a family of ten has 280 triangles! Each time a new person is added, the family's limited time and other resources have to be divided into smaller portions. A larger house and more money may be found, but the parents still have only two arms and two ears. And the airwaves can still carry only one set of words at a time without total bedlam.

What often happens is that the pressure of parenting gets so overwhelming that very little of the self of either parent finds expression, and the marital relationship grows weak with neglect. At this point many couples break up, give up, and run away. They have starved as individuals, failed as mates, and probably aren't doing very well as parents, either. Frustrated, turned off, emotionally dying adults don't make good family leaders.

Unless the marital relationship is protected and given a chance to flower and unless each partner has a chance to develop the family system becomes crooked and the children are bound to be lopsided in their growth.

Being good, balanced parents is not impossible. It is just that parents must be particularly skillful and aware to maintain their selfhood and keep their marriage partnership alive when the can of worms is so full. Such parents will be in charge of nurturing families. They are living examples of the kind of family functioning that channels pressures in the family network into creative, growth-producing directions.

14

The Can of Worms in Action

So far we've talked about the lines on the family map as if they were TV channels along which messages and feelings could pass. This is true, as far as it goes, but these lines are also family *ties*. These lines tie all the individuals together so that each one is affected by every other one. Any one person can be in the middle of many pulls at the same time. And again, the issue is not how to avoid these pulls (because that's impossible) but how to live with the pulls creatively. That is precisely what I want to deal with in this chapter.

Incidentally, some of the exercises I am going to ask you to do in this chapter may seem silly, possibly too time-consuming, or too much bother. I urge you to undertake them anyway. What can be revealed to you in something as artless and simple as these games will absolutely astound you. Surely it is worth an investment of some of your time and effort: the reward could be deeper understanding and a more fully functioning and creative family life.

We'll start with the Lintons. John comes home from work. Alice would like to have his company. Joe, Bob, and Trudy might also like to have his attention. If they all want to have his attention at once John will be in this position:

You can imagine how pulled he feels. You can do better than imagining by experiencing these kinds of pulls yourself.

Let's start with your "John." He should stand in the middle of the floor, straight and balanced. Then ask "Alice" to take his right hand. Ask your first-born to take "John's" left hand; ask the second-born, "Bob," to grasp "John" around the waist from the front; ask "Trudy" to put her arms around his waist from the back. If you have a fourth, have him or her grasp the right knee; a fifth, the left knee. Just keep going until all members of the family have their hands on "John." Now, everyone pull gently, slowly, but firmly toward themselves until everyone feels the pull. Then freeze. After a few seconds "John" will begin to feel stretched, uneasy, uncomfortable, and miserable. He may even fear he will lose his balance.

John's feelings in this exercise are very similar to his actual feelings when too many demands are made on him. He cannot stay in this position forever. He has to do something. Several choices of action are open. He can decide to endure it and get increasingly more numb until he no longer feels anything. Once he's numb, he can wait indefinitely. Finally people will just let go, left with the feeling that "Daddy doesn't care." Or John can decide to bully his way out by using brute force. Some of the family members might accidentally get slugged or knocked over. Then, as John looks at his family, he can see he has hurt them. He may feel guilty and blame himself for not being able to do what they want, or he may blame them for putting burdens on him. The others are likely to feel that Daddy is mean, unloving, and hurtful.

Something else John can do is collapse when he feels the pressure. He drops to the floor, which represents his solution of becoming sick or helpless. When this happens, his family could feel they are bad because they have hurt Daddy. And John could feel angry at them for making him feel weak.

Another choice open to John is to start making deals by bribing and making promises he probably can't keep but which provide a way out of his misery. In this case John asks each person's price for letting go, and the sky's the limit. Whatever they ask for, John will have to say yes; but since his promises aren't sincere, they probably won't be kept. Distrust grows out of this maneuver, as well as all the other feelings one directs at a promise-breaker.

John has still another choice. At the point of his discomfort he can yell for help—to his mother, his therapist, his pastor, the neighbors, or a visiting friend. "Come get me out of this mess!" And if the one he calls is skillful, powerful, or convincing enough, John can be freed. The entrance of an outside party, however, brings new chances for rifts within the family. Many secret relationships outside the family—lovers, and so on—develop and end this way.

One more choice is open to John. He can be aware that he is an important person to all of those who are asking things of him. He realizes that all those pulling on him are not feeling the same as he is. He can tell all the other family members how he's feeling and have the confidence to ask *them* for relief. He can ask for it directly—no hints.

John should now role-play all these ways of getting out of his bind. Then all members of the family can talk about how they felt as this was going on. I think all of you will learn something. Then go through the same procedure with each person having a turn in the center, being pulled.

I would like to underscore the fact that any time you are in a group, you subject yourself to getting into binds like this. I know of only three ways to avoid these binds completely: become a hermit; plan your family contacts so that no one approaches anyone else without a previous plan and permission ("You can see me at 5 P.M. for five minutes on Tuesday"); or simply don't care about anyone else. If there are other ways, I haven't found them.

None of these ways of avoiding binds is particularly satisfying. As a matter of fact, people who practice them complain about them. The real skill, as mentioned, is not in avoiding binds but in knowing how to resolve them. It is a fact, however, that most people use one of the approaches we had "John" enact in the last exercise: the martyr approach (enduring), bullying (fighting out), the poor-me approach (collapsing), the con artist (promises, promises), or passing the buck (calling for outside help). Few talk straight to the other family members and give them directions to help change the situation. I have found people usually respond when asked directly and honestly for help.

Obviously there are times when one has to endure pain, do battle, admit fatigue, or ask for help. There is nothing wrong with these states. They become destructive only when they are used to avoid binds.

We've been talking about John, but the same situation holds true for all members of the family. Every wife and mother knows how Alice feels when John is waiting for his dinner, Joe has just cut his knee, Bob is late for his clarinet lesson, and Trudy is yelling, "Mama!" from the top of the stairs. Alice has a headache.

Now Alice is the one in the bind. She has the same choices that John had. Which will she take? *Practice all of them to see how they feel.*

Joe is going out on his first date. Alice is giving him instructions on how to behave. John is warning him about staying out too late. Bob is teasing him about shaving, and Trudy is pouting because she'd hoped Joe would take her to the movies that night.

He, too, has the same choices. Which will he take? *Have your Joe practice the bind-breaking approaches his parents did.*

Bob has just cut his knee. Alice is scolding him for being careless. John is telling him to be brave, that men don't cry. Joe is calling him clumsy. Trudy is crying. Bob, too, has the same choices. Which one will he take?

Trudy got two low marks on her report card. Alice is consoling her; John is scolding her, telling her she'll have to spend two hours doing homework under his supervision every night until the next report card period. Joe is winking at her, and Bob is calling her a dummy. Which of the same choices open to her will Trudy take?

You are the center of this bind now. What kind of pressure are other family members putting on you? Try to feel them, then describe them to the people involved. Each of you take a turn. Then try to imagine what pressures you may be putting on others.

As I said, you do break binds by commenting on them. What is significant is what happens afterwards: the choice a person makes has after-effects, determines her or his reputation, and guides the ways the others treat him or her.

Now we're going to do an exercise that will make your family network come alive for you. Wholehearted participation can give you a good boost toward becoming a more vital and nurturing family.

Cut a piece of heavy twine or clothesline into twenty-foot lengths, four for each of you (in a family of five). In addition, cut five three-foot lengths, and tie one of these short pieces around each person's waist (some of you might prefer putting it around each other's necks, but I prefer the waistline). Next, have each person tie his four longer ropes to his waistline rope. Now each of you literally has a line available to each of your family members.

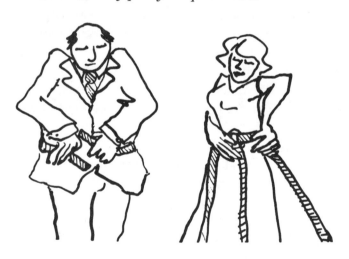

Now hand each of your ropes to the person who belongs on the other end. For example, John would hand his husband rope to his wife; she will hand her wife rope to him. When everybody has an-

other person at the end of each rope, you will be ready. And, you should excuse the expression, you have your hands full, don't you?

Tie the ropes you have received to your waist rope (many people do this immediately, almost without being aware of it). You'll look like the picture below.

Keep the lines tied while you do the following experiments.

Begin by having chairs placed in a circle no more than three feet from the center of the circle. Sit down. Now you'll hardly notice your lines. Everyone is in a chair; you can talk to each other, read, or do other quiet activities.

All right. Now imagine that the telephone is ringing, and your oldest child jumps up to answer it. It's probably thirty feet away. See what happens to the rest of you. You're all shook up! Individuals may feel invaded, pushed, or angry. You'll probably be aware that whatever your feelings are, they are feelings you have experienced before. ("Joe, why do you make so much noise?" "Why do you move so fast?") If the caller is a teenaged pal of Joe's settle in for at least ten minutes.

What is happening to the rest of you while Joe's talking? Maybe some of you will start to pull on Joe so you can be more comfortable. "Hurry up on the phone, Joe! You've got three minutes!"

Joe starts to yell, "Leave me alone!" He may get breathless and raise his voice.

Let yourselves see and feel what happens to you as you live with this.

Now go back to your chairs, and we'll do another scene. Mother, it's your turn. You remember something cooking on the stove fifteen feet away, and it may be burning. See what happens to everybody else as you rush to the stove. Then come back and get your balance.

This time, John, you are getting tired or bored, and you want to get up and take a walk. As you are headed for the door, you feel tugs and pulls. "My God, can't a man even take a walk without everyone getting on his back?" What happens to all the rest of you? How do you feel about yourselves and your family members?

Now, Trudy, you are tired and want to go to bed. Go over and put your head on your mother's lap. See what happens now.

Bob, you decide you want to have a little fun with Joe and start wrestling with him. Now what happens to everyone?

All right. Come back and get your balance. This time let's make an extreme plot for our little play. Joe, you answer the telephone; Alice, see about the cooking; John, try to take a walk; Trudy, you're sleepy and head toward your mother's lap; Bob, you start something with Joe. Do this all at the same time.

Along about now, you are probably all mixed up with one another and feeling angry and frustrated. Some of you have possibly tripped and are on the floor. The food is burning; the telephone is still ringing; Bob is struggling with Joe, who is still trying to get to the phone; Trudy caught her mother's foot as she turned; and John, you didn't even have a chance, did you? (Won't it be nice to get back to work tomorrow?)

The feelings elicited by this experiment probably seem familiar to you. Of course you don't run around every day with ropes attached to you, but I'm sure it often feels as if they were there. Perhaps next time you'll be aware of how easily family members can get in each other's way without meaning to.

Look on these lines as representing the love-care-duty-comfort relationships that exist among people in a family. It's easy to see how, without ever intending to, someone can upset the whole family applecart. What we should learn here is that we need to recognize each other's self-life, too.

Now let's try that last experiment again. Only this time when you feel the pull, say what you are feeling, and say what you are noticing. Then you'll have a chance to get your lines back from the others and to untie them so you are free. This is straight, clear, and full communication to the rescue.

You may have noticed that only five people are present, but there are twenty lines. And pulling a string between husband and wife affects the lines between each parent and the offspring.

Here is another experiment you can do while you're still all tied up. *John, you and Alice start pulling against one another. See what happens to the others. If you pull quietly and lightly, maybe your children won't notice (after all, they shouldn't see you two fighting, should they?). If your pull is light enough, maybe neither of you will notice it either. But if you pull as if you mean it, the lines to the children get taut, which draws the attention of your children and starts the triangles moving.*

Now John, you and Alice draw close together and embrace. See what happens with the children: they'll have to move. Try the same thing with each pair becoming active and see what happens.

Ready for another experiment? *The time comes when members of the family decide to leave it. This is Joe's wedding day. What happens to your ties now? Do you, John, give Joe your end of the rope and let him go? Do you just untie your end and tuck it in, symbolizing memories of fathering him? He's a grown man now.*

Joe, what do you do? It isn't enough for your parents to let go; you have to, too. Bob and Trudy have to do something about their ropes, and Joe has to do something about his ropes to them. Joe needs to untie his old lines and develop new ones as he prepares for the making of his own family.

For a final experiment, *think of some important event about to occur in your family or perhaps some everyday situation that frequently causes problems. Act it out with your ropes, and see what happens to the ties among the various family members. Where is the pull? What might you do to relieve it?*

One of the very real challenges of the family map is to keep it up to date. Compare the Lintons of today to where they were twelve years ago, when John was twenty-eight and Alice twenty-six. Joe was five; Bob, four; and Trudy, an infant. The only constant from that point to the current one is the number in the family. The needs, wishes, and individual forms have changed drastically. If the family map doesn't register these changes, you may feel disoriented, as though you're using a 1920 map of Chicago to locate a current address.

Is your map up to date? Are you still calling a six-foot, four-inch son whose name is William, "Willikens," or something equally absurd? "My baby," I hear a mother describe her twenty-one-year-old daughter; I notice the daughter cringe.

Another common happening in families is that several members may go through drastic changes simultaneously. This creates what I call a *normal developmental crisis cluster.* In short, things bunch up. It is not uncommon, for example, for the wife-mother to be pregnant with her third child when the first child is just entering kindergarten, the second child barely talking, and the husband-father just recently returned from military service.

Let's take the Lintons one year from now. Joe will be eighteen and probably taking a big step on his own. Trudy might be starting her active dating life, Alice might be approaching menopause, and John might be reassessing his dreams. As they all go through these deep, yet normal crises, the stresses become greater. When there is a cluster of such crises, someone in the family falls apart for a while. Everyone else feels squeezed, and the family can temporarily be as strangers, which is scary.

This is fertile ground for developing the generation gap, as well as a marital gap. For example, I know a young woman whose son, Joel, age six, became very interested in small garter snakes. For Joel the snakes were a source of interest and delight. For his mother they were frightening and horrid. In another instance, a man I'll call Josh one day announced to his wife that he had decided to have a vacation by himself. He wanted the chance to be totally outside any family demands. This fits *his* internal state, but to his wife it meant rejection.

Suppose Alice Linton decided to take a job to add variety and interest to her life, or to help with the income. This meant growth to her, but to John it meant she was dissatisfied with his ability to provide. There are countless illustrations of this kind of thing.

Although these kinds of situations generally reflect individual growth needs, they are often not understood that way. What action will be taken depends on the consequences that arise when family members' roles collide. Will Joel get to keep the snakes without giving his mother a nervous breakdown? Will Josh be able to take his vacation alone without rupturing his relationship with his wife? Will Alice get to keep her job without losing John?

I would like to describe the major, natural steps a family undergoes as its members grow. All of these steps mean crisis and temporary anxiety and require an adjustment period and a new integration.

The first crisis is the conception, pregnancy, and birth of a child.

The second crisis comes when the child starts to use intelligible speech. Few people realize how much adjustment this takes.

The third crisis comes when the child makes an official connection outside the home, namely, school. This brings the school world into the family, and brings in a foreign element for the parents and children alike. Teachers are generally parental extensions; and even if you welcome this, it requires adjustment.

The fourth crisis, which is a great big one, comes when the child goes into adolescence.

The fifth is when the child has grown to adulthood and is leaving home to seek independence. There are often heavy loss feelings here.

The sixth crisis comes when the young adult marries, and the in-laws become foreign elements to be accepted in the family.

The seventh is the advent of menopause in the woman.

The eighth, called the climacteric, involves a reduced level of sexual activity by the male. This is not a physical problem; his crisis seems to be more connected to his feelings that he is losing his potency.

The ninth comes, then, with grandparenting, which is chock full of privileges and traps.

Finally, the tenth comes when death comes to one of the spouses, and then to the other.

The family is the only social group I know that accommodates so many changing differentnesses in so little space and in such a short time. When three or four of these crises occur at once, life can get really intense and more "worriable" than usual. Chances are good, though, that if you understand what is happening, you can relax a little. In turn, you can clearly see what directions to take to make changes. I want to emphasize that these are normal, natural stresses;

they are predictable for most people. Don't make the mistake of regarding them as abnormal.

There is a positive side to all this. Usually, no one in a family has lived exactly the same number of years as anyone else. No one has had the exact kind of experience, and each has a wealth of experience to share with others. The Lintons, for example, have a total of 123 years of human experience from which to draw, and that is a whale of a lot of experience. Few families that I know of have looked at their accumulated ages in this way.

Change and differentness are constant, normal, healthy factors present in every family. If family members do not expect change or prepare themselves for emerging differentness, they run the risk of falling on their faces; they expect homogeneity when it doesn't exist. People get born, grow big, work, marry, become parents, grow old, and die. This is the human condition.

Becoming aware of one's family network helps shed light on the squeezes and stresses in family life. So does fully understanding roles in family life. Describing a family by its role names alone—husbands, wives, fathers, mothers, sons, daughters, sisters, and brothers—leaves out the human beings who live out these roles and give them life. As far as I am concerned, a role name describes only one part of a relationship. I think roles also set boundaries for that relationship. Thirdly, roles indicate the expectation that an affectionate, positive tie exists between people: that the husband loves the wife and vice versa, mother loves daughter/son, father loves son/daughter, children love the parents, and so on.

If I say that my feeling toward you is as toward a father, I am saying that I feel you as protective and do not see you as a sexual partner. The same is true if I see you as a brother, a son, or a daughter: I indicate a closeness but rule you out as a sexual partner.

Two forms of what I call the *role-function discrepancy* appear frequently in families. As we saw in the chapter on special families, one is where the son gets into a head-of-the-family role, commonly that of his father. This could be because the father is dead, divorced, has deserted, is incapacitated, incompetent, or neglectful. In the other form, a daughter gets into the mother role, presumably because her mother is unavailable for similar reasons.

The child in this condition usually ends up with all the responsibilities and none of the privileges of the new role. To take on a new role, the child leaves a real role behind; and this becomes a very lonely and unsure place to be. For example, suppose Joe Linton at the age of eighteen becomes the main support of the family as his father has become chronically ill. As the primary wage-earner, he could feel he has a right to decide how to spend the money; he could therefore come into contact with his mother over this issue as a husband might. His mother might turn to him as she would to a husband and ask him to help her discipline the younger children. Joe can't fully be a husband, a son, *or* a brother.

First children seem to get into this bind most frequently. They are neither fish nor fowl as far as their family positions are concerned. The way a role is lived out in the family seriously affects the self-worth of the individuals involved.

I see nothing wrong with anybody doing whatever he or she can to help with whatever is necessary. The problem lies in the messages surrounding the behavior.

Look at your family map again. Are there any people who have one role name but really are performing another?

Unfortunately, for a variety of reasons, many families have men who do not actively father. They're away because of work demands, they've been divorced, or incapacitated, or have emotionally resigned from fathering. As a result, their sons carry impossible burdens. If the father is unavailable, it is a great temptation for a woman to begin to use a son as a substitute husband. This usually works to the detriment of the son.

If I have made it as clear to you as it is in my own head, then some things must have struck you about your family map. Let me briefly describe what strikes me.

Every family member has to have a place, simply because each one is a human being and is present. For every family and for every family member, it is crucial that each person's place is fully recognized, accepted, and understood.

Every family member is related to every other family member. The importance here, again, is that these relationships be clearly understood.

Every family member affects and is affected by every other family member. Therefore, everyone matters and everyone contributes to what is going on with any one person and has a part in helping that person change.

Every family member is potentially the focus of many pulls simply because each has so many relationships. It is normal and natural. What is crucial is not to avoid the pulls but to deal with them comfortably.

Since the family develops over time, it is always building on what it has already developed. We stand on top of what was built before. Therefore, to understand what is going on in the present, one needs a perspective of the past. I would add that seeing one's past in terms of experience and resultant learning will usually illuminate the present. Never mind about labeling it right or wrong.

Every family member wears at least three role-hats in family living. What is important is that you are wearing the role-hat that matches what you are saying and doing. You need to develop a facility for being a quick-change artist so you can wear the right hat at the right time.

15

The Family Blueprint

Two big questions present themselves to every parent in one form or another: "What kind of a human being do I want my child to become?" and "How can I go about making that happen?" From the answers to these questions, the family blueprint develops. Since there are two parents, each may come up with different ideas. How you, as parents, handle those differences is a model in itself for your child. If the relationship with your partner is good, you can deal with these differences without putting an unnecessary burden on the child. Your answers to the above questions and your modeling are your design, your blueprint, for people-making. Every parent has some kind of answer to these questions. The answers may be clear, vague, or uncertain, but they are there.

Under the best of circumstances, the parenting job is anything but easy. Parents teach in the toughest school in the world: The School for Making People. You are the board of education, the principal, the classroom teacher, and the janitor, all rolled into two. You are expected to be experts on all subjects pertaining to life and living. The list keeps growing as your family grows. Further, there are few schools to train you for your job, and there is no general agreement on the curriculum. You have to make it up yourself. Your school has no holidays, vacations, unions, automatic promotions, or pay raises. You are on duty, or at least on call, 24 hours a day, 365 days a year, for at least 18 years for each child you have. Besides that, you have to contend with an administration that has two leaders or bosses, whichever the case may be.

Within this context you carry on your peoplemaking. I regard this as the hardest, most complicated, anxiety-ridden, sweat-and-blood-producing job in the world. Succeeding requires the ultimate in patience, common sense, commitment, humor, tact, love, wisdom, awareness, and knowledge. At the same time, it holds the possibility for the most rewarding, joyous experience of a lifetime, namely, that of being successful guides to a new and unique human being. What parent has not felt the juices flow when a child says, with eyes full of lights and twinkles, "Gee, Mom—Dad—you're great."

Peoplemaking includes a generous measure of trial-and-error experience. You learn most through your on-the-job training. Previous preparation helps, of course. Parenting courses and seminars that include role-playing and other experimental exercises are also quite helpful. The role-playing particularly helps give you a sense of options and choices.

I am reminded of the story of an unmarried psychologist who wrote his thesis on how to bring up children. He titled it "Twelve Requirements for How to Bring Up Children." Then he married, had one child, and changed the title to "Twelve Suggestions for How To Bring Up Children." After the next child, his title changed to "Twelve Hints on How to Bring Up Children." In the wake of the third child, he stopped giving the lectures. All this is to say there are no hard-and-fast rules for bringing up children. There are only guides that need to be modified for each child and each parent.

I think most parents would describe the kind of person they want their child to become in pretty much the same way: honest, self-respecting, competent, ambitious, clean, strong, healthy, bright, kind, good-looking, loving, humorous, and able to get along well with others. "I want to be proud of my child," a parent will say. *Do these qualities fit into your picture of a desirable person? What would you add or delete?*

The question is how parents can lead a teaching process that will achieve what they want. Here again, congruence on the part of parents is a most useful skill.

The combination of the "what" and the "how" is what I am focusing on in this and the next chapter. To go further, I will deal with the goals and values parents hope their children will have, and the ways they can achieve this. Blueprints vary from family to family. I believe some blueprints result in nurturing families, some result in troubled ones. It is important that you have a clear picture of what the differences might be.

Perhaps as you read this, you can let yourself be aware of what kind of blueprint you are using. Maybe you can look critically at how your plan is working for you and your family, now, at this point. I hope you will get some ideas about how you can change whatever isn't working too well right now. You may also find support for what you are already doing and you may notice ways to extend and enrich your current practices.

Many families are started by adults who are in the position of having to teach their children what they have not yet learned themselves. For example, a parent who has not learned how to control her or his temper cannot very well teach a child how to do this. There is nothing like raising a child to show up adult learning gaps. When such a gap appears, wise parents become students along with the children and they learn together.

The best preparation for parenthood that I know is for the parents to develop an openness to new things, a sense of humor, an awareness of themselves, and a freedom to be honest. When adults enter into making a family before they have achieved their own maturity, the process is infinitely more complicated and hazardous—not impossible, just rough. It can also be great fun. Who is perfect anyway?

Fortunately, changes can be made at any point in any person's life, if one is willing to risk doing it. Please remember to start your change from a perspective of knowing you are always doing the best you can. Through hindsight, we always see how we could have done better. That is the nature of learning. Knowing you're doing your best will help you create the confidence to go beyond where you are now.

You may have been anywhere in your own development when you became a parent. There is no point in berating and blaming yourself now if you think with hindsight that you were not where you "should have been" when you got married, became a parent, and so on. The important questions are: where are you now, what is happening now, and where do you want to go from here? Spending time on any kind of blame just makes you ineffective and limits your energy for change. Blame is an expensive, useless, and destructive way to use your energy.

Most parents want their children to have lives at least as good as or better than they had. They hope they can be the means by which this happens. This makes parents feel useful and proud.

If you liked the way your father and mother brought you up and felt good about the way they treated each other, they can be quite acceptable models for your blueprint. You say, "I will do it the way they did it" and therefore also feel empowered to add whatever else seems to fit.

If you don't like what happened as you grew up, you'll probably want to change what you do. Unfortunately, deciding what not to do is only part of the story. We get very little direction from "what not to do." You have to decide what you are going to do differently, and how you are going to do it. This is where the trouble starts: you are in a kind of no-man's-land when you have no models to follow. You have to make up new ones. Where will you find them? What will you put into your new models?

Changing the models derived from one's early past is often difficult. It is like breaking a long established habit. What we experienced in our childhood, day in and day out for years, is now a basic part of our life, whether it was comfortable or uncomfortable. I have heard parents lament, "I did not want to be like my mother and father, but I am turning out exactly like them." This is an effect of modeling. What you experienced as a child became familiar. The power of the familiar is very strong, often stronger than the wish to change. Strong interventions, lots of patience, and continual awareness help us challenge the power of the familiar.

Most people probably want their parenting to be different from the way they were parented. "I'm certainly going to bring up my kids different from the way I was brought up!" is a frequent refrain. It could mean anything from being more strict to less strict, being closer to one's children to less close, doing more work or less work, and so on.

Now take a minute to remind yourself about those parts of what you saw and experienced in your growing up that you want to change with your children. What have you tried to do instead?

How well is it working? Give yourself permission to find ways to make your changes work. Write down five family experiences that

were helpful to you. See if you can figure out what was helpful about them. Then find five experiences you felt were destructive and analyze them the same way. Have your spouse do the same thing.

Discuss and write down how you want to do things differently with your children. Share with your children what you want to have happen, and ask them to help you out. Remember how really wise you were as a child.

To go back to your family experience, you might, for example, remember how helpful it was when your mother told you directly and clearly what she wanted you to do rather than telling you indirectly. Maybe you remember how she looked directly at you, how she gently placed her hand on your shoulder, and how she spoke in a clear tone that was both firm and kind. "I want you to mow the lawn by five today." This helped you feel good about mowing the lawn. By contrast, your father may have come home after work and yelled, "Why don't you ever do anything around here? You're going to get your allowance cut if you don't watch out!" This made you afraid. You felt defensive.

You may remember that Grandma wasn't very helpful because she always said "yes" no matter what you asked. Somehow you got to feeling too obliged to her. It wasn't easy to be honest with Grandmother. Perhaps this memory will inspire you to teach your children to be honest in their responses.

You may have decided that Dad was very helpful when you took a problem to him. He would listen and then patiently help you struggle through finding a decision. This may have been in contrast to your uncle, who always solved your problems for you. Your uncle delayed your learning about finding your own two feet to stand on. Father was obviously more helpful to you.

You may have decided that neither parent was very helpful to you because whenever you interrupted them, they always stopped and put all their attention on you. This made you feel impossibly important. Later you felt hurt and confused when others didn't treat you the same way. You had temper tantrums when you did not get what you wanted. Life was painful. You had not developed patience and an understanding that sometimes you have to wait your turn.

A destructive experience for you might have been when you said a "dirty" word, and your mother washed out your mouth with soap or put you in the closet. Your body ached from fear, and then you plotted revenge. Later you cried because you felt so unloved and abandoned.

When you have made your list, go another step and decide how you can use what you are learning in ways to fit your situation.

Take your "destructive list" and try to figure out what your parents may have been trying to teach you. With your adult eyes you might be able to see what you couldn't see then. Chances are that you will want to teach your child some of the same things, only now you might be able to find a more constructive way to do it. For instance, is there a better way to respond to a child's use of a dirty word than washing his mouth out with soap or sticking him in a closet? Can you find it?

You may discover that some of the things your parents taught you turned out to be factually wrong. For example, before Columbus proved otherwise, parents taught their kids that the world was flat. When we learned the world was round, this was no longer accurate information. Another example might be the idea that masturbating will make you crazy. There actually was a time when even physicians believed that masturbation led to insanity. Almost everyone today knows this is not so. Thoughts about masturbating may disturb some people, but the act itself is harmless.

In the 1940s parents were advised to feed babies on a strict schedule with no deviations. We now know this was injurious to the child. The important point is to become aware of these kinds of untruths and learn the current truth. This is not always easy either, as there are so many "truths" around. We need to develop ways to judge what is truth and what isn't. Advertising and propaganda work on our emotions and sometimes conceal facts.

New parents have much to learn. For instance, many adults are ignorant as to how the human body grows. Many people are unfamiliar with the whole psychology of emotions and how emotions affect behavior and intelligence. Learning about how children develop is important information. Good information helps give you a sense of security.

Somehow or other, we have been a long time seeing that knowledge is an important tool for peoplemaking. We see it in the raising of pigs; however, it has been slow in relation to raising children. In some way, we got the idea that raising families was all instinct and intent. We behave as if anyone could be an effective parent simply by wanting to be, or because she and he just happened to go through the acts of conception and birth. Parenting is the most complicated job in the world. It is true that all of us are equipped with an inner wisdom. However, to be helpful, that knowledge has to be tapped.

We also need to accept coaching. Parents need all the help, knowledge, and support that is available. I think every community could benefit by having a parenting center that

met these needs. Maybe one of the readers of this book will want to start such a service. It might include a cuddle room for parents, where they could get a lot of TLC. So much is asked of parents, and so little is given.

Guiding a baby to full humanness involves knowing special things. Let's examine the beginning of a family. This starts when a couple has a baby. Now there are three where two once were.

The coming of the child, even though wanted, requires major adjustments in the couple's life. Shifts and changes in regard to time and presence with each other are essential to accommodate the immediacy of the infant's needs. People who have already worked out a healthy balance in their relationship can handle this adjustment more easily. For parents who are not at that place, these changes may appear as maladjustments and take the form of physical or emotional stress, or both.

When these stresses appear, I have the following suggestions for the parenting pair.

1. Get someone you trust to look after your infant and find a cozy, neutral place outside your home where you can talk frankly and forthrightly with each other. Spend time sharing what each of you is feeling, including your resentments and disappointments, and your feelings of helplessness and fear. Chances are that when this situation has arisen, the dream you have had with each other seems to be fading. The baby has taken over. This time can be especially hard for fathers, who don't have all a mother's obvious linkage to the child. Fathers need to know they are needed, wanted, and are essential. Women have the psychological authority to grant this place to the fathers.

2. Put words to what you mean to each other, and what your hopes are for and with each other. This will enable you to renew your self-worth enough to join your energies and cope more positively with each other and your child.

   Out of this frank talk, you may commit yourself to some connecting time each day, and also something special for the two of you each week. Keeping your connection and making it a priority are basic steps toward fulfillment as parents. This needs to be a firm commitment and needs to be adhered to consciously.

   What may further emerge is a fear of losing autonomy. "Where is some time for me?" is often an unspoken question. Couples need consciously to arrange time for each self. To make this work, verbalize your need and then ask for the cooperation of your partner (and, later, of other family members). Chances are good that something can be worked out, but you have to ask for and plan it.

3. Center yourself enough to tap into your own internal wisdom and see if you are working at cross-purposes with yourself or each other. If so, pinpoint where the difficulty seems to be. Your internal wisdom is also a good resource for new ideas about coping.

Most people will get farther by thinking of this crisis as a challenge, rather than a failure of some sort. I recommend approaching this in much the same way as a puzzle. How can two people who care about each other use their energy to team up and make things work in the interest of themselves, each other, and their child or children?

It is wise to remember that we have intelligence. Our intelligence works best when we are centered emotionally.

If none of the above work, I urge you to seek professional help.

All too often parenting becomes weighty and demanding, and life as a couple fades into the background. If this happens and goes unattended, the child will pay a heavy price. The child may be used as a reason for the couple to stay together; or the couple may project their difficulties on the child, overtly or covertly: "If it had not been for you, things would be better."

This can also be a time when one partner develops an emotional attachment with someone outside the marriage. This is often true of fathers who feel replaced by the child in the mother's affections.

Stop a moment and take stock. Is this happening with you? With your spouse? What effect is this having on all the family members? What are you willing to do or change now? Remember, the reason you got married and became a parent was to extend the joy in your life.

People often get discouraged because so much of what they have tried hasn't worked. Your willingness to admit this frankly could be a turning point for you. You can learn to do things differently, no matter how long things have been going wrong. We are only as far away from change as we are from really changing our minds and giving ourselves permission to go in new directions.

First, you have to find out what is happening and what you have to learn. Then search for a way to learn it. Someone whose name I have forgotten said, "Life is your current view of things." Change your view, and you change your life. I heard about a man who always complained that everywhere he went, it was dark. This all changed one day when he lost his balance; in falling, his glasses flew off. Lo and behold, it was light! He hadn't known he'd been wearing dark glasses.

How many of us are wearing the dark glasses of ignorance without knowing it? Sometimes it takes a crisis to discover this. If we can get introduced to our ignorance, isn't that something worth celebrating?

If you discover something going wrong in your family, treat it as you would when a red light in your car indicates that something isn't working right. Stop, investigate, share your observations, and see what can be done. If you can't change it, find someone you can trust who can. Whatever you do, don't waste your time moaning about "poor me" and "bad you."

Do what we talked about in the chapter on systems. Turn the family into a "research team" instead of a "blame society." Can you see how different things might be for your family if you take the negative, hurtful things that happen as signals for attention? There is no need to blame and tear your hair out. Keep your hair and be glad you finally got the signal, whatever it is. It may not be especially pleasant, but it is honest and real, and something can be done about it. Don't wait.

I remember a family I treated once. The father came with his wife and twenty-two-year-old son, who was quite ill psychologically. The red light had been on for some time before they took action. When the treatment was finished, the father, with tears in his eyes, put his hand on the son's shoulder and said, "Thank you, son, for getting sick, so I could get well." I still get goose bumps when I think about that one.

We can get into some traps unconsciously by using how we were parented as a guide to how we parent. One of these traps involves giving the child what the parent did not have growing up. The parent's efforts can come out very well, but they can also end in terrible disappointment.

I once saw a vivid example of this. It was just after Christmas, when a young mother whom I will call Elaine came to see me. She was in a rage at her six-year-old daughter, Pam. Elaine had scrimped and saved many months to buy Pam a very fancy doll. Pam reacted with indifference; Elaine felt crushed and disappointed. Outside, she acted angry.

With my help, she soon realized that this doll really was the doll she had yearned for as a youngster and had never had. She was giving her daughter what was really her own unfulfilled dream doll. She expected Pam to react as she, Elaine, would have reacted when she was six. She had overlooked that her daughter already had several dolls. Pam would much rather have had a sled so she could go sliding with her brothers.

The doll was really Elaine's. I suggested that she claim her own doll and experience her own fulfillment, which she did. This particular yearning from her childhood was satisfied directly, and she did not have to do it through her child. Instead, she bought Pam a sled.

Is there any good reason why adults cannot openly fulfill, in adulthood, some of the unfulfilled yearnings of their childhood? Oftentimes, if they don't, they pass off these old needs on their kids. Children rarely appreciate passed-off satisfaction (unless they have learned how to act like yes-persons). Nor do they like parental strings on their gifts. I am thinking of fathers who buy trains for sons or daughters and then play with the toys all the time, setting out strict conditions under which the children can use their own trains. How much more honest it would be for the father to buy the train for himself. It would be his train, and he then might or might not allow his children to play with it.

What lingers from the parent's individual past, unresolved or incomplete, often becomes part of her or his irrational parenting. I refer to this as the *contaminating shadows of the past,* of which many parents are totally ignorant. Another trap is when parents start out with a dream about what they want their child to be. This dream often involves wanting the child to do what they personally could not do, as in, "I want him to be a musician. I always loved music." Many children have pinioned themselves on an altar of sacrifice so their parents would not be disappointed.

It is easy for parents, without knowing it, to make plans for their child to be what would fit the parents but not necessarily the child. I once heard the late Abraham Maslow say that having these kinds of hopes and plans for your children is like putting them into invisible straitjackets.

I see the results of this in adults who say they wanted to be something else but did not know how to deal with pressures from their parents. After all, it takes a lot of guts and know-how on the part of the child to defy parents successfully, especially when a lot of love is present.

There is another hurdle if you, as a parent, are shackled to your own parents. You may not feel free to parent your own child differently for fear of being criticized by your parents. This could easily result in your dealing "crookedly" with your child. Some quite insidious situations can develop. I refer to this as *fettered parental hands.*

For instance, I know a thirty-four-year-old father, Jack, who won't chastise his child directly because his father would take the child's side. Then Jack and his father would argue. He is still afraid to argue with his father, because he fears his father's rejection. The effect, of course, is that Jack deals inappropriately with his child. The ideas in his blueprint don't match what he does. Were he to give a lecture on the best way to raise kids, his speech would be far different from what he practices.

I want to talk now about something I call the *parental cloak* (parental role). As I use the term, it refers to that part of the adult that lives out the role of a parent. To my mind, the parental cloak has a use only as long as the children are unable to do for themselves and need parental guidance. One of the problems is that the cloak may get stuck on the person, never changing, and stay forever. Once a mother, always a mother, even if the kids are already adults.

A major factor in one's blueprint is the kind of parental cloak you wear, and whether you feel you have to wear it all the time. Can you take it off when you are not parenting? After all, sometimes you may want to "spouse" or "self" and you would then look peculiar wearing the parental cloak.

The parental cloak has three major linings: the "boss" lining, the "leader and guide" lining, and the "pal" lining. For some people, the cloak has no lining at all: there is no evidence of any kind of parenting. I think there are far fewer of these cloaks than the others.

The boss has three main faces. First is the tyrant, who flaunts power, knows everything, and parades as a paragon of virtue ("I am the authority; you do what I say"). This parent comes off as a blamer and controls through fear. The boss's second face is the martyr, who wants absolutely nothing except to serve others. The martyr goes to great lengths to appear of little value and comes off as a placater. Control is managed through guilt ("Never mind me, just be happy"). The third is the great stone face who lectures incessantly, impassively, on all the right things ("This is the right way"). This person comes off as a computer. Control is managed through erudition and the consequent implication that someone is stupid, and it probably is "you."

The pal is the playmate who indulges and excuses regardless of the consequences. This parent usually comes off irrelevantly ("I couldn't help it—I didn't mean to"). Children need pals for parents like they need the proverbial hole in their heads. Irresponsibility in children is a frequent outgrowth of this kind of parental cloak lining.

I think we pay a heavy price for some of the ways parents use their power, their cloak linings. To me, one very destructive lining is that of the tyrant, who insists on creating obedient and conforming human beings. In every case, I have found that such behavior was primarily the result of an adult who tried to hide uncertainty by getting immediate obedience from a child even if it were inappropriate. How else would the uncertain parents know they were effective?

Many parents might occasionally entertain a momentary wish to knock in their kid's head, but few do it. Many children feel similarly toward their parents, but only a few act on those feelings. These feelings represent the ultimate in frustration.

It is rare that children who grow up on the obedience frame become other than tyrants, or victims, unless some unusual intervention occurs in their lives. The obedience theme is, roughly, "There is only one right way to do anything. Naturally, it is my way." It is beyond me how anyone can think that good judgment can be taught through "obey me" techniques. If we need any one thing in the world, it is people with judgment. The person who cannot use common sense is the person who feels he or she must do what somebody else wants or expects.

I heard about "the right way" so much that I investigated how many ways there were to wash dishes. I found 247, all of them going from dishes in the state of being dirty to that of becoming clean. The differences were related to the kind of equipment available, and so on. Do you know anybody who swears by a certain detergent? Or swears that dishes must always be rinsed before being washed? After you have been around a person who insists on the "right" way all the time, you probably want to kill him or her. Maybe it's no accident that over 80 percent of all murders are of family members. (I did not say that 80 percent of families murder each other.)

People who are around a tyrant—someone who says, "You do it because I say so," or "It is so because I say so"—suffer personal insult constantly. It is as though the other person were saying, "You are a dummy. I know best." Such statements have long-range crippling effects on morale.

In none of these parental cloaks can parents develop a trusting atmosphere with their children. Effective learning cannot occur in an atmosphere of distrust, fear, indifference, or intimidation.

My recommendation is that parents strive to be empowering leaders. This means being kind, firm, inspiring, understanding people who direct from a position of reality and love rather than negative use of power.

People play cruel tricks on themselves when they become parents. Suddenly now they must "do their duty," be serious, and give up lightness and joy. They can no longer indulge themselves or even have fun. I happen to believe just the opposite. People who believe that family members can be enjoyed and appreciated as real also see normal, everyday difficulties in families in quite a different light.

I remember a pair of young parents, Laurie and Josh, who told me their first priority was to enjoy their child. They were obviously already enjoying each other. Through enjoying their child, they were teaching their child to enjoy them. The enjoyment still goes on today, fifteen years and two other children later. I feel good every time I am around this family. Growth is obvious, and each takes pride in accomplishment and has good feelings about each other. These are not indulgent parents, nor is the family without secure and clearly set limits. Clear "no's" as well as "yes's" are considered healthy words in this family and are used honestly and appropriately.

Part of the art of enjoyment is being flexible, curious, and having a sense of humor. An episode of a five-year-old spilling milk can be a different experience depending on

what family the child lives in and how such matters are approached. There is no universal way of treating that.

My friends Laurie and Josh would probably say to Davis, their child, "Whoops! You let your glass be your boss instead of your hand! You will have to talk with your hand. Let's skip out to the kitchen and get a sponge and soak it up." Literally, then, Laurie or Josh would skip out to the kitchen with Davis and maybe even sing a song on the way back.

I can hear Josh saying, "Gee, Davis, I remember when that happened to me. I felt I had done something awful, and I felt terrible. How do you feel?" To which Davis would answer, "I feel bad, too. Now there's more work to do to clean up the mess. I didn't mean to do it." It would be a normal feeling of apology and not an assault on self-worth.

I can imagine the same episode with another set of parents, Al and Ethel. Ethel grabs Davis, shakes him, and demands that he leave the table, saying to Al as he leaves, "I don't know what I'm going to do with that kid. He's going to grow up to be a slob."

Another pair I know, Edith and Henry, would have still another scene. When the milk is spilled, Henry looks at Edith, raises his eyebrows, and goes on eating in stony silence. Edith quietly gets a sponge and wipes up the milk, giving Davis a reproving look when she catches his eye.

I believe Laurie and Josh approached the happening in a way that benefits everyone. The other two examples do not. *What do you think? Can you imagine basing your response to negative situations on the premise that what is happening is happening between people who have good will and love toward each other? And that therefore education and good humor, not punishment, are needed? How do you approach these kinds of events in your family?*

Do people in your family have times when they obviously enjoy each other as individuals? If you think not, see if you can find out how to change that. People who cannot enjoy each other probably have put obstacles in the way of loving each other as well.

A big part of a child's joy in him- or herself is learned from being encouraged to enjoy parts of the body, the feel of skin, touching, colors, and sounds—especially the sound of the child's own voice, together with the pleasure of looking. Parents show the way through their joy in the child. Laughter and love are catching.

Enjoyment is also a matter of aesthetics. Relatively speaking, we do very little in our customary child-rearing practices to help children consciously learn to enjoy themselves. I see many families whose whole idea of raising children and being parents is a grim experience full of labored work, hysteria, and burden. I've noticed that once adults lose their blocks against enjoying themselves, life seems easier on all fronts. They are lighter and more flexible with their children and themselves. I don't know if you are aware of how much heaviness and grimness exist among adults. I am not surprised to hear numbers of children tell me they don't really want to grow up because being an adult is no fun.

I don't think having fun or using humor takes away from being competent or responsible. As a matter of fact, I think real competence includes enjoying oneself, one's working partners, and what one is doing. At a recent conference, I learned that a large, successful corporation has three new criteria for selecting personnel: they are looking for candidates who are kind, fun to be around, and competent. Since these qualities are appreciated by everyone, let us make them goals for our child-rearing and for our own lives.

Learning how to laugh at yourself and see a joke on yourself is very important. Having these attributes may make the difference, in the future, in whether you get hired. Our learning and practice of this skill come from the family. If we have to take everything Father says and Mother says (or does) as though it were the ultimate wisdom and power, we have little opportunity to develop the fun side of things. I've been in some homes where the grimness and the seriousness hung like an impending storm in the air—where politeness was so thick that I had the feeling only ghosts lived there, not people. In other homes everything was so clean and so orderly that I felt as if I should be an especially sterilized towel from the laundry. I would not expect enjoyment of people to develop in either of these atmospheres.

What kind of an atmosphere do you have in your family? Can you believe that laughter and fun nurture the body?

We are just beginning to understand and hold seminars on how laughter and humor provide healing and nurture for the body. We have known for a long time how worry, fear, resentment, and other negative emotions have destructive results. Laughter and love are good medicine. They cost nothing but awareness. I believe that I do my most definitive and serious work when the atmosphere is light. And

Josh and Laurie's treatment of their child's milk spilling helped him learn more than those approaches that involved punishment and disapproval.

What can you put into your blueprint to encourage laughter, enjoyment, and humor?

Like enjoyment, loving is a very important part of life. Did you ever stop to realize what a feeling of loving is like? When I feel loving, my body feels light, my energy flow seems freer, I feel exhilarated, open, unafraid, trusting, and safe. I feel an increased sense of my own worth and desirability. I have a heightened awareness of the needs and wishes of the person toward whom I direct these feelings. My desire goes toward a joining of those needs and wishes with my own. I don't want to injure or impose on the one I love. I want to join with her or him, to share ideas, to touch and be touched, to look and be looked at, and to enjoy and be enjoyed. I like the feeling of loving. I consider it the highest form of expressing my humanness.

I find the manifestation of love a scarce commodity in many families. I hear much about the pain, frustration, disappointment, and anger that family members feel for one another. When people give so much attention to these negative feelings, their other positive feelings shrivel from being unnoticed.

I am in no way proposing that life does not have its hazards and corresponding negative actions and feelings. I am saying that if those are all we focus on, we miss opportunities to see what else is there. Hope and love are what keep us going forward. If we spend too much time focusing on doing the "right" things and getting the work done, we often have little time for loving and enjoying one another. We discover this at funerals or when it is too late.

All right. We've talked about some of the challenges of parenting. Perhaps you are beginning to see more ways to help you draft a stronger, more vital blueprint for your family.

I am reminded at this point of a classic Robert Benchley story. When Benchley was a college student, one of his final examinations was to write an essay on fish hatcheries.

He hadn't cracked a book all semester. Undaunted, he started his final something like this: "Much wordage has been devoted to fish hatcheries. No one, however, has ever covered this subject from the point of view of the fish." And thus he proceeded to create what is probably the most entertaining final in Harvard's history.

Having devoted all these pages to parenting, we are now going to take a look at the family situation from the point of view of the baby.

I am going to imagine being inside a baby called Joe, somewhere around the age of two weeks.

"I feel my body hurting me from time to time. My back hurts when I am tucked in too tight, and I have to lie too long in one position. My stomach gets tight when I am hungry or hurts when I get too full. When the light shines directly in my eyes, it hurts them because I can't move my head yet to turn away.

"Sometimes I am in the sun, and I am burning. My skin is hot sometimes from too many clothes and sometimes cold from too few clothes. Sometimes my eyes ache and I get bored from looking at a blank wall. My arm goes to sleep when it is tucked under my body too long. Sometimes my buttocks and my crotch get sore from being wet too long. Sometimes my stomach cramps when I am constipated. When I am in the wind too long, it makes my skin prickle.

"Sometimes everything is so still that my body feels dry and uncomfortable. My body hurts when my bath water is too cold or too hot.

"I get touched by many hands. I hurt if those hands are gripping tightly. I feel clutched and squeezed. Sometimes those hands feel like needles. Sometimes they are so limp that I feel I am going to fall. These hands do all kinds of things: push me, pull me, support me. These hands feel very good when they seem to know what I feel like. They feel strong, gentle, and loving.

"It is really painful when I get picked up by one arm, or when my ankles are held together too tightly when my diaper is changed. Sometimes I feel that I am suffocating when I am held so close to another person that I can't breathe.

"One terrible thing is when someone comes to my crib and suddenly puts that big face over mine. I feel that a giant

is going to stamp me out. All my muscles get tight, and I hurt. Whenever I hurt, I cry. That is all I have to let anyone know that I am hurting. People don't always know what I mean.

"Sometimes the sounds around me make me feel good. Sometimes they hurt my ears and give me a headache. I cry then, too. Sometimes my nose smells such lovely things, and sometimes smells make me sick. That makes me cry.

"Much of the time my mother or father notice me when I cry. It is so good when they know I am hurting and they find out what hurts me. They think of pins sticking me, my stomach needing food, or that I am constipated or lonely. They pick me up, rock me, feed me, jiggle me. I know they want me to feel better.

"It is hard because we don't speak the same language. Sometimes I get the impression that they just want to shut me up and get on with something else. They jiggle me for a short time as if I were a bag of groceries, and then leave me. I feel worse than before. I guess they have other things to do. Sometimes I guess I must annoy them. I really do not mean to do that. I don't have any good ways to tell them what is wrong.

"My body hurts seem to go away when people touch me as if they like me. They seem to feel good about themselves, and I know they are really trying to understand me. I try to help as much as I can. I try to make my cries sound different. It also feels good when someone's voice is full, soft, musical. It feels good when my mother and father really look at me, especially into my eyes.

"I don't think that my mother knows when her hands are painful to me and her voice so harsh. I think if she knew, she would try to change. She seems so distracted at those times. When my mother's hands feel painful many times in a row and her voice stays unpleasant, I begin to get afraid of her. When she comes around, I stiffen and pull back. She then looks hurt or sometimes angry. She thinks I don't like her, but I am really afraid of her. Sometimes my father is gentler and I feel warm and safe with him. When my father feels good, I feel relaxed.

"Sometimes I think my mother doesn't know that my body reacts just like hers. I wish I could tell her. Some of the things she says about me and the rest of the family when I am in my crib and she is with her friends, I don't think she would say if she knew that I have perfectly good ears. I remember once hearing her say, 'Joe will probably be like Uncle Jim,' and she started to cry. There were other similar things that happened, and I began to feel that something terrible was wrong with me."

[Years later, I find out that Uncle Jim was my mother's favorite brother and must have been a great guy. I have often heard my mother say how much I looked like him. She cried because he died in an automobile accident in which she was driving. That put a whole different light on things for me; however, I did not know this for years. I think if she had told me about her love feelings for Jim and how bad she felt about his death, particularly since I seemed to be like him in ways, I would have not felt so bad! I would have understood that when she looked at me and started to cry, she was remembering him.]

It is important for adults to tell children, no matter how young or old, what they are thinking and feeling. It is so easy for a child to read the wrong message.

"Since being born, I have spent most of my time on my back, so I've gotten acquainted with people from this position. I know more about my mother's and father's chins from underneath than almost anything else. When I am on my back, I see things that are mostly up and above me; and of course, I see them from underneath. This is how things are in the world."

Now I'll imagine Joe's perspective as he grows:

"I was very surprised to see how much things had changed when I learned to sit up. When I began to crawl, I saw things underneath me, and I really got acquainted with feet and ankles. When I started to stand up, I began to know a lot about knees. When I first learned to stand up, I was only about two feet tall. When I looked up, I saw my mother's chin differently. Her hands looked so big. In fact, a lot of times when I stood up between my mother and father, they really seemed far away and sometimes very dangerous, and I felt very, very little.

"After I had learned to walk, I remember going to the grocery store with my mother. She was in a hurry. She had hold of one of my arms. She walked so fast that my feet hardly touched the ground. My arm began to hurt. I started to cry. She got angry with me. I don't think she ever knew why I was crying. Her arm was hanging down, and she was walking on two feet; my arm was pulled up, and I was hardly on one foot. I kept losing my balance. I feel uncomfortable and sometimes dizzy when I lose my balance.

"I remember how tired my arms used to get when I would walk with my mother and father when each had hold of one arm. My father was taller than my mother. I had to reach higher for his hand. So I was kind of lopsided. Half the time I did not have my feet on the ground. The steps that my father took were very big. When my feet were on the ground, I tried to keep up with him. Finally, when I couldn't stand it anymore, I begged for my father to carry me. He did. I guess he thought I was just tired. He didn't know that I was contorted so badly that my breathing was even getting hard. There were very nice times, but somehow the bad times stayed with me longer.

"My mother and father must have gone to a seminar some place because they changed. Whenever they wanted to talk to me after that, they would always stand me on something so they could look at me at eye level and then they would gently touch me. That was so much better."

I try to contact all children at eye level. That usually means that I have to squat when I contact them, or have them stand on something to equalize our heights.

Since first impressions make such an impact, I've wondered whether that first picture the infant has of an adult isn't one of giantness, which automatically means great power and strength. This can feel like a great comfort and support, and also like a great danger compared to the littleness and helplessness of the child.

I've mentioned this before, but it's important enough to bear a little repetition. When an adult first gets acquainted with her or his child, the child is, indeed, little and helpless. This could account for parents' image of their child as little and helpless, which can continue far beyond the time

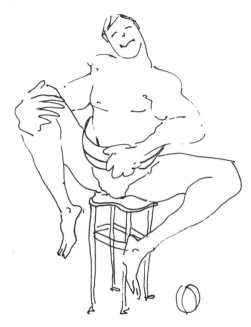

when the condition exists. That is, the son or daughter, even at eighteen, is still a "child," little and helpless in parents' eyes, no matter how grown-up, powerful, and competent the adult child really is. In much the same way, the adult child could hang onto the image of parents as all-powerful even when she or he becomes powerful in his or her own right.

I think parents who are aware of this possibility help their child discover his or her own power as quickly as possible. They freely use themselves to show their child how to become powerful and what limits exist for that power. Without this learning, a child could become an adult who is a parasite on other people, dominates them, or plays god to them, benignly or malevolently.

Infants have all the physical responses that adults have. Their senses are in working order at birth (as long as it takes to clean out the orifices); therefore it makes sense that the infant is capable of feeling whatever an adult feels. Infants' brains are working to interpret what they feel, even though they can't tell anyone what sense they are making. Taking this view, it becomes easy to treat children as persons.

The human brain is a marvelous computer, constantly working to put things together and make sense of what comes to it. If the brain cannot make sense, it makes non-sense. Like the computer, the brain doesn't know what it doesn't know; it can use only what is already there.

One of the things I do when I work with parents is the following exercise.

One adult is asked to become an infant in a crib, lying face up. Not yet old enough to speak, this person is asked to react only with sounds and simple movements. I then ask another pair of adults to bend over the baby, doing the things that babies need done for them, trying to follow the baby's clues. In turns, each adult becomes the baby. After about five minutes in this role-playing situation, I ask each adult to tell the other two what he or she was feeling as this was going on.

In another round, I announce some outside interference, such as the telephone or doorbell ringing. I choose the time when the baby is obviously fussy, then watch to see what happens to the two parents and the child. Again, I ask the role-players to tell each other what difference the interruption made to them. Try this yourself.

This is a simple way to help adults appreciate what a baby might experience and how the child uses this experience to build expectations of others.

The touch of a human hand, the sound of a human voice, and the smells in the home are the experiences by which a baby begins learning what the new world is all about. How a parent touches and sounds to the child form the basis for what the child learns. The baby must unscramble all the touches, faces, voices, and smells of surrounding grown-ups and make meaning of them. The newborn's world is a very confusing place.

I believe children already have some pretty clear expectations by the time they can feed themselves, walk, control their bowels and bladder, and talk. This is around the age of three. After that, children just develop variations. In this period, they learn how to treat themselves, how to treat others, what to expect from others, and how to treat the world of things around them. The family blueprint now becomes crucial: what do you teach and how do you teach it?

No learning is single-level. While children are learning to use their legs in walking, they're also learning something about how people perceive them and what is expected. From this, children learn about what to expect from others and how to deal with them. Babies also learn something about the world they are exploring and how to act in that world: "No, no! Don't touch," or "Touch this, doesn't this feel good?"

In the first year of life, a child must learn more major and different things than in all the rest of her or his life put together. Never again will the child be faced with learning so much, on so many fronts, in so short a time.

The impact of all this learning is much deeper than most parents realize. If parents understood this, they would better appreciate the link between what they do and the tremendous job their child has to do. We have focused too much attention on disciplinary methods and not enough on understanding, loving, and humor, and developing the beautiful manifestation of life that resides in every child.

Three other areas complicate carrying out the blueprint. They are in the iceberg, below the perceivable functioning of the family. The first is ignorance. You simply don't know something. Further, you may not know that you don't know, so you wouldn't be aware of the need to find out. Children can help a lot with this if the parent is open to children's comments. Be alert to children's hints for information.

The second is that your communication may be ineffective. You may be giving out messages you don't know about, or you think you're giving messages when you're not; so the goodies you have to offer your children do not get across. Watching for unexpected reactions from others can alert you to this.

Many parents are amazed at what their children have taken from their apparently innocent statements. For example, I know a white couple who wanted to teach their child racial tolerance. Along with some other children, a little black child was a guest in their home one day. Later the father asked his child, "What did you think of his very curly hair?" But he said this in a way that pointed out the differentness, thus forging the first ring of distance between the two children. If parents are alert to the possibility of this kind of thing happening, they can monitor themselves now and then to see what their child has picked up.

I am reminded of another story. A young mother went through a rather lengthy presentation of the facts of life to her six-year-old son, Alex. Several days later, she noticed Alex looking at her very quizzically. When asked about it, Alex said, "Mommy, don't you get awfully tired of standing on your head?" Completely baffled, she asked him to ex-

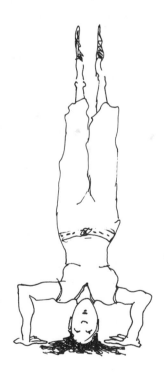

plain. He said, "Well, you know, when Daddy puts the seed in." His mother had neglected to embellish on the process of intercourse, so Alex filled in his own picture.

The third area in the iceberg has to do with your values. If you are uncertain of your own values, you can't very well teach your child anything definite. What are you supposed to teach if you don't know yourself? And, if you feel you can't be straight about your problem, this situation could easily turn into "Do what I say, rather than what I do," or, "It doesn't really matter," or, "Why ask me?" or, "Use your own judgment." Any of these responses could leave your child with feelings about your unjustness or phoniness.

Another inadvertent message from a parent is shown in the following story. I was visiting a young woman who had a four-year-old daughter. The telephone rang. My young friend said, "No, I can't come today. I'm not feeling well."

Her four-year-old asked, with some concern on her face, "Mama, are you sick?"

My friend replied, "No, I'm just fine."

The little girl attempted to deal with the apparent discrepancy: "But Mama, you told the lady on the telephone that you weren't feeling well."

Her mother's reply was, "Don't worry about it."

With this, the little girl went out to play in her sandbox. At lunchtime, her mother called her inside. The little girl replied, "I can't come, I am sick."

Mother's response was to go out to the sandbox, obviously angry, "I'll teach you to disobey me."

I intervened with the mother before she had a chance to chastise her child, and invited her to a private place to talk. I played back to her the chain of events, showing her that her child was simply imitating her. She saw the connection, to which she had been completely oblivious. She shuddered at how close she had come to misusing her child.

I suggested to the mother that a more useful way of coping with the original question might have been to say, "I am not sick. I told that woman that because I did not want to be with her and I did not want to hurt her feelings. It is hard for me to say 'no' to people. So I lie that way. I need to learn better ways of handling that. Maybe we can learn together."

The mother was not a monster and the child was not a disobedient brat. Yet in this scenario the child could have been punished for learning and using something her mother modeled. The child would have had the necessary experience to begin distrusting her mother, and neither would have known why.

As I said before, the main data that goes into our family blueprints comes from experiences in our own families and those other families with whom we had intimate contact. All the people we called by a parental name, or whom we were obliged to treat as if they were parents, supplied us with experience that we are using in some way in our own parenting. Some of this may have been helpful to us, and some not. All of it had its effect, however.

Those of us who are free enough to contact our Inner Wisdom have another wonderful resource. It takes courage to trust that wisdom. It means we are free of judging, blaming, and placating; we are willing not only to level but to take risks.

16

Some Essential Blueprint Ingredients

Every child born into this world comes into a different context and a different atmosphere from every other child, even when born to the same parents. *Atmospheric influences* refer to what is happening when the child is born and to the attitudes prevalent as she or he grows up. These influences are highly significant in the family blueprint.

The actual experience of conception, pregnancy, and birth often leaves shadows that get into the atmosphere surrounding a particular child. If conception came at the wrong time or under undesirable circumstances, the parents might feel angry, helpless, or frustrated about it. These feelings could get in the way of using the family blueprint.

The baby may become a symbol of a burden. Also, if the experience of pregnancy were accompanied with an extended period of sickness and continuing discomfort, and serious complications developed for either the mother or the child or both at birth, similar inhibiting effects might follow. As parents, you might develop unnecessary fears, which keep you from reacting normally to your baby, who might thus become a symbol of hurt or pity.

Some babies are born prematurely; some are born with physical parts missing or unusable, and some are born with internal and intellectual handicaps. When this happens, people can relate to the baby in terms of what is missing or unusable, out of proportion to the rest of the child. Again, the blueprint is affected. Often the child is treated not as a person but as some kind of cripple, which, of course, affects how he or she reacts and is reacted to.

Substantial numbers of children are also born to mothers when the fathers are away for long periods of time after the birth. These men may be in the service, prison, distant business ventures, or hospitals. This creates a difference for the infant from the beginning and lays a groundwork for skewing family relationships. When the father returns, he sometimes has a hard time finding as significant a place with his child as his wife has. Meeting your child at the age of two, you can hardly expect to be on a par with the adult who was there two years ahead of you.

If either spouse has died, deserted, or divorced at the time of the birth of a child, this can often result in an exaggerated relationship between the remaining parent and child, which eventually could hurt both of them. Dire consequences aren't automatic, but one needs to be actively alert and creative to avoid them.

Other unpleasant circumstances can affect how the infant gets started in the world, such as death, illness, unemployment, or serious trouble for some member of the family. The pressing nature of these kinds of problems frequently requires that parental attention gets focused elsewhere, and not on the newborn child who needs the attention. This can make for neglect and indifference—something the parents never really intended.

For example, I know a woman who already had two children, aged twenty-one months and ten months respectively, when a third child came along. She asked herself, "Where will I get enough arms and legs to take care of this one when I already have two babies?" A woman in tight financial circumstances was saying, "How am I going to feed this new child? I already have eight!" Or, "Good heavens, another girl, and we have three girls already!" Or, "Good heavens, another boy, and we already have five!" Perhaps a family hasn't had a child for fifteen years, and then along comes another one.

Each child comes into the parents' lives when many other things are going on. Adults are not always able to control the timing of a child's birth, and it may or may not be the best month or year for the parents. I have never taken the statistics, but I don't believe too many of us arrived at the best possible time. This doesn't make us rejected children, even though many of us could make a case for being "unwanted" if we so chose. The most important thing is that we got here.

Another possible atmospheric influence is trouble in the marital relationship when the baby comes. Marriage may not have turned out to be the satisfying experience hoped for by the marital partners. Very often this leads to the parents having difficulty being sensible and realistic with the child. I think marital harmony is directly related to successful peoplemaking. If the personal situation of one or both parents is not particularly happy, that person's self-worth will probably be low, and applying the blueprint enthusiastically and appropriately will be hard.

Bringing a first child into a family is a very big step. Existing circumstances change drastically for the couple. That first child is the means by which adults first find out what parenting is all about. The first child is always a testing ground and receives different treatment from any succeeding children. In many ways the first child forms the context for the children to follow. The first baby is truly a guinea pig, and I don't see how it could be otherwise.

I have described important factors that can affect how the family blueprint will be carried out. Briefly summarized, these atmospheric influences are: the actual experience of conception, pregnancy, and birth; individual circumstances in the family; the condition of the infant; and the relationship of the marital pair. Additional factors include the family's relationship to the grandparents, and the adults' level of knowledge, their ways of communicating, and their philosophy.

Within any atmosphere and blueprint, certain learnings are essential for every human being between birth and adulthood. They fall into four main categories which, when translated into family life, come out in the following questions:

What do I teach my child about herself or himself?

What do I teach about others?

What do I teach about the world?

And what do I teach about life and its source, about God?

The teaching process includes the following: a clear idea of what is to be taught, each parent's awareness of what she or he is modeling, a knowledge of how to interest the other parent in agreeing on a model, and the communication to make it work.

In the ideal family, adults show their own uniqueness; demonstrate their power; show their sexuality; demonstrate their ability to share through understanding, kindness, and affection; use their common sense; show their spiritual nature; and are realistic and responsible.

Have we said it's no disgrace to be an imperfect parent? There are no perfect parents! What's important is that you keep moving in the direction of good parenting. If you remain honest about where you are, your children's trust in you will increase. They care about truth, not perfection, and it is an impossible job for a human to play God. Yet many parents saddle themselves with this terrible responsibility.

I have never known any perfect families, any perfect children, or for that matter, any perfect people. Nor do I ever expect to meet any. The key words are unique, loving, powerful, sexual, sharing, sensible, spiritual, realistic, and responsible. *Can you describe yourself in these terms? Are you trying to teach your children to be what you are not? If you are, this realization may hurt; but if you use it as a signal, you may make a start on changing things in your family.*

Once someone achieves the essential learnings, a whole set of other things will follow: honesty, sincerity, creativity, love, interest, zest, competence, and constructive problem-solving. As human beings, we prize all of these. With them, we can also more easily teach the necessary information that all children need.

Once you as an adult grasp the notion that a human being is a *person* at any age—at birth, two weeks, fifteen years, thirty-five years, or eighty years—your job as a people-maker will be easier. You have more in common with your children than you thought. For example, disappointment is the same at any age, whether you are a grown man who loses a desired job or a four-year-old who loses a favorite toy. The effects of loss will have a greater impact on a child who is the brunt of a tirade from an angry mother; the nature of that emotion, though, is no different from the woman's feeling when she has been the brunt of a tirade from her angry husband, or vice versa.

A child feels very few things that the adult does not know something about from personal experience. Children seem to thrive on the knowledge that their world of hope, fear, mistakes, imperfection, and successes is a world also familiar to and shared by their parents. What adult is without occasional, if not frequent, feelings of hopelessness, fear, disappointment, poor judgment, and mistakes?

Yet many parents believe that they undermine their authority if they express these feelings. If you act on this, though, you come out looking phony to your children. If you do have this attitude, I hope you will experiment with changing it. Children have much more trust in humanness than they do in sainthood and perfection.

If you want to check this out, ask your children what they know about your feelings and hopes and disappointments. Ask them how they feel about talking to you about mistakes when you make them. And perhaps you could do it the other way around: tell your children your feelings about hopes and disappointments and mistakes that they make. Much can be cleared up in this way, with the result that new bonds form.

Once a child develops a feeling of distrust for parents, the feeling extends into personal isolation and general feelings of unsureness, personal imbalance, and rebellion. When adults do not acknowledge and express their own humanness and do not acknowledge the child's humanness, it is very scary to the child.

Now, to get back to the essential learnings, I think it isn't necessary to explain what I mean by *sensible, sharing,* and *realistic.* I use these words in the same way you do. But when it comes to *uniqueness, power,* and *sexuality,* I want to go into considerably more detail, not only because my use of the words may be different from yours, but also because understanding of these concepts is of primary importance in the family blueprint. *Spirituality* is discussed at length in chapter 22.

I believe that *uniqueness* is the key word to self-worth. As I discussed in the chapter on couples, we get together on the basis of our similarities, and we grow on the basis of our differences. We need both. It is this combination of sameness and differentness in a human being that I call uniqueness.

Very early you and your child are going to discover that she or he is different in some ways from you and other human beings, and vice versa. A frequently found example comes to mind. I know two boys in a family; one is fourteen, the other fifteen. The fifteen-year-old is interested in athletics and prefers to spend his time on that. The fourteen-year-old is more interested in the artistic side of life and prefers to devote his time to those interests. These boys have the same coloring and the same intelligence, but they have different interests. This is a very basic example of the kinds of differentness I am talking about. Fortunately for these boys, they have parents who respect their differences and help each boy evolve in his own way.

Genetically, each child is different even if he or she comes from the same parents. The equipment each child brings into the world, just from a genetic point of view, differs from every other child's. Each child, then, presents an opportunity to parents for unique adventure as he or she unfolds and develops.

By the same token, each husband and wife is different from one another. And they certainly don't stop unfolding just because they get married and have children. Helping a child to appreciate the differences between the two parents becomes an important part of learning. If parents try to present a facade of sameness, they bypass this very important opportunity. Mama likes to sleep late in the morning, and Papa likes to get up early, and that's okay. People don't have to be alike. Some differences make life a little more complicated, but most differences can be used constructively.

If infants don't have the opportunity to be treated as unique from the beginning of their lives, they develop habits that make it difficult to react to them as whole people. They will tend to react more as stereotypes of people—to stifle their differences for the sake of conformity—and can expect to be plagued with a variety of physical, emotional, social, and intellectual ills. They will be handicapped until they learn new ways of becoming whole people.

So how are you going to teach your child about the differentness that is his or hers? How are you going to teach children to distinguish between negative and positive differences? How are you going to teach them to judge which differences in others they should support and which ones they should influence for change? How can you teach them that they don't have to destroy people who are different, nor worship those associated with sameness? We all have these tendencies, you know.

Strangeness and differentness can be scary, but they contain the seeds for growth. Every time I come upon a new situation or a strange one (which is another way of describing differences), I have an opportunity to learn something I didn't know before. I don't expect all of it to be pleasant, but I can't help but learn something.

I've said this before, and it's important. Differentness can't be handled successfully unless sameness is appreciated. The samenesses of people are few in number but are basic and fundamental, predictable and always present, although not always obvious. Each human being experiences feeling all through life, from birth until death. Each can feel anger, sorrow, joy, humiliation, shame, fear, helplessness, hopelessness, and love. This is the basis on which we have a ready-made connection to all other human beings at any point in our lives or theirs.

Children feel.

Adults feel.

Men feel.

Women feel.

Black, brown, white, yellow, and red people feel.

Rich feel.

Poor feel.

Jews, Buddhists, Protestants, Moslems, Catholics, and Hindus feel.

People in power positions feel.

People in nonpower positions feel.

Every human being feels. It may not always show, but it's there. And the faith that it is there can make you act differently from the way you would if you reacted only to what shows. Being absolutely convinced that everyone feels makes parents and therapists effective.

Developing your sense of uniqueness, then, is basic to developing high self-worth. Without a sense of our own uniqueness, we are slaves, robots, computers, and despots—not human beings.

Now I think we're ready to talk about power. *Power is essential to every human being.* To be an effective person, everyone needs all her or his powers developed as fully as possible. *Power,* according to Webster, is from a word that means "to be able." It is defined as the ability to act, the ability to produce an effect, physical might, or the possession of control, authority, or influence over others.

Body power is the first power humans develop. Almost everyone greets evidence of the infant's lung power at birth with relief. The baby is alive. Later, physical coordination as shown in turning, sitting, walking, holding things; and toilet training is also greeted with joy. The child is growing as expected. Simply speaking, he or she is learning to manage body muscles, the end point of which is that one's body responds well to one's demands. Over the years I have noticed that parents have endless patience teaching their child body power and become joyful at the manifestations of every new successful effort.

I think this is also a suitable way to teach the other areas of power—to use patience and to respond to the expression of the child's newfound power with joy and approval. Other personal powers to be developed are emotional, social, intellectual, material, and spiritual.

A person shows intellectual power (thinking) in learning, concentration, problem-solving, and innovating. This is more difficult to teach, but can be met with the same kind of joy a parent expresses when the child, say, takes a first step. The parent can beam, "I've got a smart kid!"

A person's emotional power is shown in freedom to feel all emotions openly, clearly express them, and channel them into constructive action. This is oftentimes the scariest power to teach, so be sure to give yourself recognition and approval for trying.

A child's material power is demonstrated by the way she or he makes use of the environment for personal needs, while at the same time considering the needs of others. Unfortunately, this is all too often limited to the ability to work. You may want to think of other opportunities—playtime, naptime, or even picking flowers—for showing your child about material power.

An individual shows social power by the way he or she connects with other people, shares with them, and teams up with them for achieving joint goals, as well as how he or she can both lead and follow. This is an area rich in opportunities for parents to express joy in and approval of their children.

Spiritual power can be seen in a person's reverence for life—one's own and all others, including animals and nature, with a recognition of a universal life force referred to by many as God. Many people limit this part of their lives to an hour or so on Sunday. I think most of us know that all human beings have a spiritual side, a side involved with their souls. Right now we're having some pretty hard times with relationships among people of different races, economic groups, and generations. A great deal of this would be solved if we developed our spiritual power and were willing to put it into practice to a greater degree.

To meet life freely and openly, I think we need to develop our power in all of these areas.

I'm going to make adjectives out of the words Webster used to define power: able, active, effective, mighty, influential, controlling, and authoritative. These are the main faces of power. Few people would object to the first five adjectives, but the last two might bring up confused and/or negative messages. These are the words more related to negative use of power. Violence is even more extreme; it is the destructive use of power.

Control, responsibility, and *decision-making* are related to power. The questions arise over and over again of how much control I have over myself, over you, or over the situation I am in, and how I use this control. If I want to understand how action takes place between two people at a given point in time, there are three places I can look.

The first place is the self-worth level of each person (how I am feeling about myself at this moment in time). The second place is each individual's response to the other person (how I am looking and sounding, and what I am saying), and the third is each person's knowledge of the resources available at a given time (where I am, what time and what place this is, what situation I am in, who is here, what I want to happen, and what possibilities exist in this reality). Together, we come up with the following:

The self-esteem of person A and of person B

The response of A to B and the response of B to A

A's picture of what possibilities exist

B's picture of what possibilities exist

It's a good idea to separate those things over which you have control and those over which you have only influence. I have control over my choice of whether to act or not act and the course of action I take. For this, I am *responsible* to myself. I can't be responsible for what is presented to me, only for my response to it. I cannot hold myself responsible for the rain that falls as I am walking; I am responsible only for how I respond to it.

I cannot hold myself responsible for your tears. I can only be responsible for how I respond to them. The kind of response I make will influence your experience of crying but won't decide it. You have to do that. It may be that I exerted a powerful influence, to which you felt you had to respond by crying. Each of us, I think, bears the responsibility of being aware of what we give out to other persons. If I am twenty-eight and am your mother, and you are three, my responses to you will undoubtedly have a stronger influence with you than if you were also twenty-eight and a fellow employee. Some situations and some responses have a greater influence than others, and it is up to me to know about that, too. That means that I have an ethical and moral responsibility to treat you humanly.

I think there is a lot of murkiness about what responsibility is and how it can be exercised. I would like to tell you where I am in my practice of being responsible. First, I clearly own what comes out of me: my words, thoughts, body movement, and my deeds. I might have been influenced by you, but I accept that I made the decisions to act on that influence, so that part is my show completely.

Whatever comes out of you is your show and represents your decision to use whatever influence you used. I become responsible when I fully acknowledge this. I can use you to influence me, but only I can decide to act on that influence. The three exceptions to this are when a person is an infant, is unconscious, or is seriously physically ill. In addition, I only feel free to monitor your influence if I have a sense of high self-esteem.

If we do not know that we make the choices about how to use what influences us, then it is easy to feel insecure and to create relationships with others that are blaming and dissatisfying, leaving us helpless and even more insecure.

I want to point out here that an objective piece of reality doesn't necessarily change because of our choices. Let's take the objective reality of blindness. If your eyes don't see, they don't see—period. As long as you are busy blaming the world for your blindness, you will be spending your energies in hating the world and pitying yourself, and consequently shriveling as a human being. Of course, as long as you're doing this, you're not taking responsibility for acknowledging what *is*. The moment you do that, you can use your energies for creating and growing yourself.

Here is the same theme in a different example.

A husband shouts at his wife at 5:30 P.M., "You damned fool!" Whether he should have or wanted to or even whether he knew what he was saying is irrelevant to the fact that this is something the wife has to deal with at that point in time. She has choices, whether or not she knows it, about how she responds. It may not be any more pleasant than blindness, but she *does* have choices. You may remember the possibilities open to her from the chapter on communication.

"I'm sorry; you're right." (placating)

"Don't call me names, you idiot!" (blaming him back)

"I guess in marriage one has to expect times like this." (computing)

"Dr. Smith called and wants you to call him right back." (distracting)

"You sound all worn out," or, "I felt hurt when you said that"—either of which would be leveling. In the first instance, she'd be responding to his pain; in the second, responding to her own.

Each of these responses can influence her husband's response. Because they are different, there are apt to be different consequences; but again, how she responds doesn't necessarily determine how he responds.

In families, it is unfortunately true that control and authority are often assumed to be the primary province of the parent: "I [the parent] control you [my child]." In this way the child doesn't develop an appreciation for positive uses of power and could run into some sticky problems in adult life. There are two ways to use authority that seem to make a difference here. Does the parent speak as an empowering leader or as an autocratic one? If he or she speaks as an empowering leader, chances are that control can be used as a learning as well as an implementing tool. This can also serve as a model for learning about power.

Bossing a child, on the other hand, doesn't teach much about developing personal power constructively. The main result of bossing is that the child's self-esteem decreases, and

another example of the generation gap is well into the making.

What really scares parents, though, is the child's development of emotional power—the basic emotions of loneliness, hurt, love, joy, anger, fear, frustration, humiliation, and shame.

"Don't be angry."

"How can you love her? She's [Catholic, Jewish, black, or white]."

"Big boys are not afraid."

"Only babies complain."

"If you did what you were told, you wouldn't be lonely."

"You ought to be ashamed of yourself."

"Don't wear your heart on your sleeve."

"Keep a stiff upper lip."

These typical comments suggest the kind of teaching that goes on in families with regard to emotion. Our emotions are our experience of *feeling* human. Our emotions carry the energy of life. To be helpful to us, they need to be appreciated, acknowledged, and have appropriate ways of expression. There can be no valid argument about how one feels. One feels what one feels. The crucial mistake is to use feeling as a primary basis for behavior ("I am angry at you, so I hit you").

Unfortunately, few parents have developed their own emotional power enough so they can tolerate it, much less develop it, in their children. In fact, emotional power is apparently so scary that it is often actively squelched. Much of this fear is based on ignorance.

My own feeling is that if adults knew how to use their own emotional power constructively, they would become more willing to plan ways to develop it for their children.

What you have read so far, I hope, has shed some light on this subject for you.

This brings us to the essential learning about sexuality. The family teaches maleness and femaleness—*sex* in its broadest sense and in its more narrow genital sense. Babies can be clearly divided into two sexes at birth, but this says nothing about how each will grow up feeling about his or her sex, or whether each will find out how to live with what she or he has in common with the other sex. Men and women are different, but *how* different and different how? A great deal depends on what answers a parent gives to the child when asked these questions. Part of the child's learning comes from experiencing the parent as the parent answers these questions. How each parent tries to help each child establish sexual identity is a basic part of the blueprint.

Each parent represents one sex, and the child has a sexual model of what he or she can become. Did you know it takes a male and female both to develop the sexual identification of any individual child? Each person contains aspects of both sexes. Every man has some female potentials; every woman, some male potentials. I am convinced that the only real differences between men and women are physical and sexual. All other supposed differences are imposed by the culture and vary from culture to culture.

No woman can say how it feels to be a man, and no man can say how it feels to be a woman. This is immediately obvious when you realize that no woman knows what it's like to have and use a penis, or to have hair growing all over her face. Likewise, no man feels how it feels to menstruate, to be pregnant, or to give birth. In the course of life, most people make a union with the other sex, so this is important information to share. Each needs to teach the other what it is like to be that sex. The father teaches the little boy what it means to be a male, how a male views and interacts with a female; likewise with the mother and her little girl. Out of this teaching the child develops a picture of what a male is, and of what a female is, and how the two of them relate to one another. Clearly, confusion can set in if the parents don't understand this, don't value themselves as sexual people, or do not see each sex as having different but equal value.

If a child's father and mother do not have healthy ways of handling their differentnesses (including their bodies), the child gets an unclear idea of how to appreciate himself as a male, or herself as a female, and how to enjoy and appreciate the other gender. To make wholeness possible, the child needs to learn from adults of each gender. This takes greater effort in families with a single parent or same-sex parents. The point is that we owe our children a model of life in which they can experience their wholeness.

What is so sad is that many parents haven't achieved this for themselves. So how could they teach it to their children? The good news is that we can learn at any age. As we talked about in the chapter on rules, for many years sexual organs were considered dirty and shameful, which made an additional handicap to dealing openly with the whole male–female question. You can't really talk freely about maleness and femaleness without including talk about the genitals. Today, this information is readily available in books and magazines.

As a sexual being, the growing child learns much in the home by seeing the way the parents treat each other and how openly and frankly they can deal with male and female sexual matters. If you, as a woman, do not appreciate and find joy and pleasure in your husband and his body, how can you teach your daughter an appreciation of men? The same is true for the father. Somehow this veil of secrecy has to be lifted from the whole sexual subject so that adults who emerge from families are more fully whole.

Another learning that must take place is how males and females fit together, how they bring their separate selves to make a kind of new union—sexual, social, intellectual, and emotional. In the past it was very easy to pit males and females against one another—the old "battle of the sexes." This is unnecessary and uncomfortable. Many families train females to be subservient to males. The woman is told she has been put on this earth to serve the male. Still other families teach that males must always be the servants of the females: they must protect them, take care of them, think and feel for them, and never cause them any pain. Some children are taught that males and females are alike in every respect and deny the fact of difference. Still others are taught that they are sexually different but do have things in common and they can join together.

To use a rather homely comparison, when a plumber joins two pipes together, one part has to be smaller than the other. No plumber ever wasted time wondering whether one part is better than the other. He needs both to make a smooth fitting. So it is with males and females. Can there be

a flowing between the two as a result of their contact, without worrying about who is on top?

In the sexual stereotypes that determine much of the male–female teaching in families, the female is supposed to be soft, yielding, and tender, not tough and aggressive. The male is supposed to be tough and aggressive, not yielding and tender. I believe tenderness and toughness are qualities everyone needs. How can a male relate to a woman's tenderness if he hasn't developed it himself? How can a female relate to a man's toughness if she's had no experience with it in her existence? With these stereotypes as models, you can see how easy it is for men to regard women as weak, and for women to look at men as if they were cruel and beastly. How can anyone ever get together with anyone else on this basis?

Men live shorter lives than women, statistically, which I think is largely attributable to the fact that men strangle their soft feelings. Our soft feelings are the juice of our beings, but a man is not ever supposed to cry or be hurt. To accommodate this, he has to become insensitive. If he also has rules against being angry, he can't vent his aggressive feelings either, even in appropriate ways. These bottled-up feelings then go underground and play havoc on his body, and he ultimately gets high blood pressure and heart attacks. I have personally witnessed dramatic changes in those men who were able to get in touch with soft feelings. Almost all of them said they had been afraid of their violence; but having learned to honor their soft feelings, their aggressive feelings went into building energy instead of destruction.

Similarly, if women feel they can demonstrate soft feelings only, they feel in constant danger of being trampled. So they get men as protectors, paying for this by being in an emotional straitjacket. To keep any sense of security and feeling of safety, they turn into schemers.

When human beings are estranged from their soft feelings, they become dangerous robots. If they are estranged from their tough feelings, they become parasites or victims. The family is the place where all this is learned.

We've been talking a lot about teaching, but it is obviously not possible to teach a child what to do in every situation. We have to teach approaches and perspectives. Therefore the parent has to teach ways of approaching things: which way do you use what in this instance? Which way in that case? In other words, parents teach judgment when they use an empowering style of leadership.

I have a couple of stories that highlight this point. Epaminondos was a little boy of five who lived in a village far away. One day his mother needed some butter. She decided to send Epaminondos to the store for it. He was very glad to do something for his mother because he loved her very much and he knew she loved him. His mother's parting words were, "Mind how you bring the butter back."

Epaminondos skipped happily to the store, singing a tune as he went. After he bought the butter, he remembered his mother's words. He wanted to be very careful. He had never carried butter home before. He thought and thought and finally decided to put it on his head under his hat. The sun was very warm. By the time he got home, the butter had melted and was running down his face. His mother exclaimed disapprovingly, "Epaminondos, you haven't the sense you were born with! You should have carefully cooled the butter in the running brook, put it in a sack, and run home with it." Epaminondos felt very sad. He had disappointed his mother.

The next day she sent him to the store for a little puppy. Epaminondos was very happy. He knew just what to do. Very carefully and thoroughly he cooled the puppy in the brook, and when it was cold and stiff, put it in a bag. His mother was horrified. In a much sharper way she said, "You don't have the sense you were born with. You should have tied a string around his neck and led him home." He loved his mother very much and she loved him, but this terrible thing was happening. Now he knew exactly what to do.

The next day his mother decided to give him another chance. This time she sent him for a loaf of bread. Epaminondos gleefully tied a string around the loaf of bread and dragged it home through the dust. His mother just looked sternly at him and said nothing.

The next day she decided to go to the store herself. She had just baked a cherry pie. Before she left she said, "Mind how you step around that cherry pie." Epaminondos was very, very careful. He placed his foot right smack in the middle of that pie!

This folktale exemplifies the sad dilemma that frequently occurs between parents and children. Judgment is the decision of what to do when; no recipe covers all situations.

I am reminded of a near-tragic incident involving young parents, Bill and Harriet, and their four-year-old daughter, Alyce. Harriet was alternately rageful and frightened as she told me how Alyce had viciously attacked Ted, a mutual college friend of the parents who had come to visit. She had already whipped Alyce severely, mostly out of her embarrassment. Although Alyce had never behaved in this manner before, it was so dramatically different that Harriet wondered if the attack represented criminal tendencies or even psychosis. She remembered that her great-uncle had been some kind of a criminal.

Exploring the relevant facts, this picture emerged. In anticipation of Ted's visit, the parents had sent him a recent picture of Alyce but had neglected to introduce Alyce to Ted via a picture. When Ted arrived, Alyce was playing on the lawn. He knew her, but she didn't know him. He approached her in a rather boisterous fashion and tried to pick her up, to which Alyce responded by kicking and screaming and biting. Harriet and Bill were much embarrassed by this behavior, and Ted was angry and hurt.

When I pointed out that Ted knew Alyce, but Alyce did not know Ted, some light began to dawn. The final illumination came when I asked what Harriet and Bill had taught Alyce about responding to strange men. Some child-molesting had occurred in the neighborhood, and Harriet and Bill had made a big point of teaching Alyce that if a strange man tried to touch her, she should fight with all her might. Bill had even had her practice with him.

Bill got about halfway through telling me this part, stopped, and recoiled from his own words with shame and a terrible feeling in the pit of his stomach. Alyce had done

exactly what she had been asked to do. I shiver very much at the thought of how many more times this kind of thing happens and is never corrected. To Harriet and Bill, Ted was a friend; to Alyce, he was the strange man who was trying to touch her.

Now I would like to turn to a part of the blueprint that is an essential part of life but is rarely talked about: death. Some teachings about death are absolutely ridiculous: use this medicine or that perfume, think this way and not that way, and maybe you can cheat death. Impossible!

I know it is a hard subject for most of us to even talk about, let alone talk about frankly and openly. Yet living is meaningless unless we see dying as a natural, inevitable, and essential part of life. Death is not a disease or something that happens only to bad people. It happens to all of us.

I think a good goal would be to make it possible to prevent *premature* death. This is possible through better medical care, safety, better environmental conditions, better relationships among people, and a higher sense of self-worth. I happen to believe that life is extremely precious, and I would like to be productively alive as long as I can. I would like to help make this possible for other human beings as well, and I think the family is a good place to start.

What do your rules say about death? If you have valued a person who then dies, you suffer a loss and you grieve. Grieving is an important love act to perform for ourselves. Do you have rules about how to grieve, or how long to grieve?

Do you realize how much secrecy surrounds death? I know of adults who try to hide the evidence of death from their children. They prevent them from going to the funerals of their relatives. Then they compound the problem by dismissing the death with a statement like, "Grandma went to heaven," and never speaking of it again. I realize many adults think they are doing their children a favor by "protecting" them in this way, but I think they're doing them real harm.

Children who do not see evidence of the death of a loved one, and are not helped to grieve over the death and integrate it into their lives, can develop serious blocks in their emotional lives. I could fill this whole book with stories of adults who never really integrated their parents' deaths into their lives, particularly if the parents died when they were children. These people suffered severe psychological trauma.

Another distortion happens when the adults who survive elevate the departed one to some kind of saintly status. This completely skews the child's view of the one who died as a person.

I know of one youngster, Jim, who was ten when his father died. Every time Jim mentioned some negative experience with his dad, his mother sternly reprimanded him for speaking ill of the dead. Eventually this led to Jim's closing off all memories of his father. Then he developed a saintly picture of his father, whom he could neither relate to nor use as a model. Jim developed some serious problems coping with his life.

I know another situation in which whenever the child did anything wrong or questionable, her mother would tell her to be careful because her father was looking down from heaven and would punish her. Since the child believed this, she soon developed some paranoid ideas. Can you imagine what a helpless feeling it is to believe you have no privacy anywhere, that you are always watched?

At one time I was a staff member in a residential treatment center for girls. I was struck by how many of the children who had dead parents and had not participated actively in their deaths were troubled with serious self-esteem problems. Equally striking, this began to change when I showed these girls some evidence of their parents's deaths. I found obituary notices, went sleuthing for people who had been present at the funeral, or took the girls to cemeteries where their parents were buried. Then, with their help, I reconstructed their parents as people. Many times we role-played scenes from life before death, and the death itself.

Death is an inevitable part of life for all of us. I think the acceptance of death makes life a real and rewarding experience.

I have a hunch that until we accept mortality, we mistake a lot of other things for death and we mess up our lives. For instance, some people have so much fear of criticism that they avoid it at all costs. I don't think that criticism is pleasant, but it is necessary and often useful. To treat it as a death matter mixes it up. Did you ever know anyone who never tried anything for fear of getting criticized? The fear of making mistakes, or of being wrong–any fear, for that matter—can get tied up with death. I have heard it said that many people fear so much that they die a little every day. The rest of the time, they are trying to avoid dying, so they really die before they have ever had a chance to live.

Death is death. It happens only once in a lifetime. No other thing in life is like it. When you make this distinction, then everything except the act of death is life. To treat it any other way is a travesty on life.

The question of safety is related quite directly to death fears in the family. How are you going to teach a child how to be safe and at the same time allow the risks essential for expansion and growth? You don't want your child to die, so you teach caution.

Of course, nothing is 100 percent safe. I've met so many parents who, because of their fears, practically kept their kids chained to the front porch. I can understand wanting to protect the young. Yet we lived through it and are still around, so we should relax a little bit and give our kids the same opportunity to struggle with life's dangers as we had. I don't propose that we send three-year-olds across town alone, but that we look at what our children want to do, being real about the dangers rather than maximizing or minimizing them.

I know a twelve-year-old boy, Ralph, whose parents wouldn't let him ride his bike for three miles because he might get killed. Ralph was a good, careful bike rider and the bike was his only means of transportation. He felt his parents were unfair. So, by skillful lying, he worked out a deal with his friends so he could ride anyway. His wish to ride reflected his need to develop independence and self-reliance. Yet he had to do it at the expense of honesty and of being punished if he were caught.

I would like to see a parent ask each child at the close of the day, "What danger did you meet today? How did you meet it?" It would be an added bonus if the parent were able to share the same information.

Many times I quaked in my boots when my daughters were teenagers and I watched them meet dangers. When is our desire to protect them real, and when is it just a sneaky way to calm ourselves? Judging when a child is ready to take on new dangers is not easy but, as parents, we have to do it.

I remember when my second daughter took out the family car for the first time alone. She was only sixteen, just a baby, really, and my goodness, how was she going to manage in that heavy traffic? There were drunk drivers out there. She could be killed. Besides, we had only one car, and what if she wrecked it? What if I wasn't there to guide her? By the time I got through with my fantasy, the car was totaled and she was already stretched out in the morgue—in my mind. Actually, she had not yet gone out the door.

In another part of my reasoning, I knew she had had good driver training. I had ridden with her, and she drove well. We had insurance, and I trusted her. None of these realizations kept me from sweating as I watched her go out the door. I wasn't going to bug her with my fears, so I managed to say, weakly, "How do you feel about going off by yourself?"

She smiled and said, "Don't worry, Mother. I will be all right."

And, of course, she was. Later we had a chance to compare our "insides." She told me she knew I was worried, and that she was too. She said she was glad I hadn't burdened her with my fears, as they would have made her own worse.

Now, I want to end this chapter on something I touched on in the couples chapter, namely, dreams. Dreams and what we do about them—encouraging and keeping personal dreams alive—are essential elements of our blueprint, too. Dreams about what one will become are a big part of the lives of children. Our dreams stand as beacons beckoning us on to greater growth and accomplishments.

Your dreams are your hopes for yourself. When dreams are gone, "vegetablitis" sets in, with accompanying attitudes of indifference and resignation. You run the risk of becoming a robot and becoming old early. Sad but true, the family is often the place where dreams die. We learned this when discussing the couple: too often, individual hopes that flourished during courtship fall flat in the family.

Family members can give each other a great deal of inspiration and support for keeping their dreams alive. "Tell me your dream, and I'll tell you mine. Maybe then we can help each other achieve what we both want." I recommend that families sit down and talk openly about their dreams. This can be very important for children. How much better it is to say, "How can we all work together to make your dream come true?" than to say something like "Let me tell you why that isn't practical." Believe me, some exciting things can happen.

Don't take my word for it. Sit down with your family and openly discuss your dreams and their dreams. Find out about some of this excitement yourselves, first hand.

I remember a family who tried this. One of the parents asked one of the children, "What do you want to be when you grow up?" Tom, a four-year-old, said he wanted to be a fireman. After several interested questions, it turned out that Tom liked to put out fires; he also liked to light them. He enjoyed the bright, shiny red fire trucks and liked the looks of the sturdy men who rode on them.

The family decided Tommy didn't have to wait until he was grown up to become a fireman. He was given special instructions in laying and lighting fires in the fireplace. His dad took him to the fire station, where he had a chance to talk "man-to-man" with the firemen. They showed him different ways to put out fires. He had a chance to inspect the fire truck. Everyone in the family got something out of helping Tom with his dream. And his father, who also had his own dream, invited Tom to help him set up a chemistry lab at home. Could you do a similar thing?

What can you do to keep alive a spirit of curiosity and imagination, to stimulate a search for making new meaning, to find new uses for things already known, and to probe into the unknown for things not yet known? This is what makes for zest in life. The world is filled with much to wonder about, to be awestruck by, to explore, and to be challenged by.

Dreams occur in the present. Chances are pretty good that some part of almost any dream can be realized *now.* I recommend that people live out their current dreams as much as possible. Sometimes it takes help from other people, but they have to know about the dream first. Test out your dreams for possibilities. Realizing our little dreams helps us have faith in big dreams. The family is where it can happen.

In my lifetime, I have gone from crystal sets to color television; from a Ford crank-it-yourself car to today's slick, comfortable cars, which practically drive themselves; from walking three miles to a little country school to flying all over the world in a few short hours on a jet; and from cranking a telephone on the wall to call someone named Central to a pretty colored push-button phone that makes almost instantaneous connections. Not only have humans walked on the moon, many children use microcomputers in school and have a chance to make play out of this fantastic technical advancement.

During all of this, I was continually expanding my knowledge of the world and finding new things that awed, educated, and excited me. All these developments came out of someone's being willing to follow a dream. Unfortunately, we haven't yet had as many dreamers who know how to bring along the world of people at the same rate. My dream is to make families a place where people with high self-esteem can develop. I think that unless we get busy on dreams of this sort, our end is in sight. We need a world that is as good for human beings as it is for technology and nuclear energy. We have good tools. All we have to do is to dream up effective ways to use them.

I feel so sad about the number of adults that I meet in families who have turned their backs on their dreams. They are indifferent and resigned. "What difference does it make?" and "It doesn't really matter" are frequent statements.

I know some adults whose interest in their children's development led them to help with their children's dreams and thus become interested in reviving or developing their own. We, as human beings, use so little of our potential. I hope you don't let your dreams die. If you have, see if you can rekindle past cherished dreams or invent new ones. See what you can do to realize them by sitting and talking, sharing them with your other family members, and asking for their help.

17

Family Engineering

Things don't just happen by themselves, in a family or any-where else. In this chapter, we are going to talk about family engineering. It isn't too different from any other kind of en-gineering. In a family, like a business, getting the work done requires the management of time, space, equipment, energy, and people. To begin the engineering process, you find out what your resources are, match them with your needs, and then figure out the best way to get the results you want. Through this inventory, you will find out what you don't have; then you will need to figure out a way to get what is missing. It is this process that I am calling family engineering.

One of the most frequent complaints I hear is that fam-ily members have too many things to do, too many de-mands, and too little time. Some of this burden may be relieved when your family works out more efficient ways to carry out your family engineering requirements. Take a good look at how you are doing things.

Periodically find out about the specific resources that each member has to contribute. As persons grow older and learn more, they keep adding to their resources. Keep the family up to date by doing this inventory often. Get in the habit of asking each other, "What are we now capable of?" If this question is asked in a leveling way, it will usually get a real answer. Most people like to help. They just don't like to be bossed around.

Adults in particular forget that children can be of immense help. The more everyone participates, the more each feels an ownership in the family and the less any one person gets overburdened. If you are seven, you may be able to help Daddy in the garage. If you are five, you may be too little to do that, but you may be able to bring the silverware to the

table. On the other hand, maybe Johnnie, who is five, is more capable than Harry, who is seven. Some families limit help by such comments as "Women are not strong enough to . . . "Men don't . . . ." Very few jobs around the family are gender linked.

So many abilities of family members—especially the children—are wasted. Children are not supposed "to be able to," so their abilities are never really discovered. This not only makes the family tasks more burdensome, but deprives children of learning much-needed skills.

There would be far fewer harried fathers and mothers if children were not merely allowed but encouraged to use themselves more fully in the family and at an earlier age.

One of the most rewarding experiences for any human being is to be productive. You'll never find out how productive your kids are or can be unless you give them a chance to show what they can do.

How do you use four-year-old Paolo's ability to move fast? Maybe you can use him as an errand boy when you are working in the tool shed. How do you use seven-year-old Anna's ability at quick addition? Why not let her help you keep the household accounts straight? You can probably think of more ways in which your children can genuinely help you.

We all know that families live in different kinds of settings. Some live in big houses, some in little, some with lots of equipment, others with very little. Incomes can range from $100 a month to $50,000 a month, and the number of family members can vary from three to as high as seventeen or eighteen.

Given the same house, number of family members, income, and the same labor-saving devices, some people will feel their needs are met and some will not. Using one's resources at a moment in time is also related to what one knows about those resources, how one feels about oneself and those one lives with. Put another way, the fate of the engineering department depends just as much on the self-esteem of the individuals, the family rules, the communication, and the family system as it does on the engineering plans and the things to be engineered.

Let's look at the job situation first. Family jobs are frequently called chores. Although necessary, these jobs are often thought of as negative, a "somebody has to do it" kind of thing. It is still true that these chores form a major part of the family business and as such are important. The persons who do them can be given special attention.

I would like to propose something now that is similar to what you did in the Rules chapter. *Sit down together and make a list of all the jobs that have to be done to make your family function. Agree on a secretary, as before. In your list you will in-*

clude such things as laundry, ironing, cooking, shopping, cleaning, keeping accounts, paying bills, working at outside jobs, and so on. If you have pets or a garden or lawn, you will need to include these, too. If a family member needs special care, include that. These are the kinds of basic jobs that have to be undertaken regularly, if not every day.

Now consult your list and see how these tasks are being carried out by your family. You will learn something as you do this. Perhaps you have never sat down and looked at your whole family picture in this way.

Are you finding out that not all the necessary tasks are getting done? Maybe you'll discover that some things are done poorly or that too many tasks fall on one person and too few on others. If any of these things are true, someone in your family is being cheated and/or feeling frustrated.

Done about every three months, this simple exercise helps to keep a perspective in the family's engineering department. In business, this is where efficiency experts come in. Your list and what you do about it can become your guide to your own family efficiency.

Once you arrive at what needs to be done, choosing the best plan and the best person to get the job done is the next step and often the most difficult one. How do you decide who should or can do what and when? Most families find they have to use different methods at different times.

In what I call the *edict method,* a parent decides to use the authority of the leader and simply order what is to be done. "This is how it will be, and that is that!" I recommend that one use this method sparingly. When you do, take care to be congruent or you will have a rebellion on your hands.

Sometimes it is more fitting to use the *voting method,* the democratic way, in which the majority reaches the decision. "How many want to do it this way?"

Other times, what I call the *adventure method* works out the best. In this rather freewheeling approach, everyone states his or her views, and these are all tested against reality to see what's really possible.

Still other times seem to require the *expediency method*. We all know this one. Whoever is available gets stuck.

All these methods fit some situations. What is important is to choose the method that best fits the particular situation at a particular point in time. Expect that everyone will keep her or his promise. This is excellent training for learning responsibility.

The word to watch out for is *always*. Too many families *always* use edict, *always* vote, and so on. And if *always* is lurking around your family engineering, somebody's getting strangled. You will also find yourselves in the well-known, unenviable rut with open or covert rebellion in the wings.

Parents have to be able to say "yes" or "no" firmly. They also need the skill to ask, at times, "Well, what do you want to do?" Sometimes they'll need the insight to recognize a situation in which they'll say, "This is something you'll have to figure out for yourself."

I know some families, for instance, whose parents never decide anything—choices are always left "for the children." Still other families have no leadership at all. Everyone sits for long hours in judgment on everything—even as to whether Father should wear white shirts to the office. Other families are ruled solely by parental edict. Again, nothing about any of this is easy. We have to fall back on judgment—knowing when to do what.

Varying job assignments can do a lot toward minimizing the "chore" aspect of family functioning. Adults also need to accept the child's work at his or her own level, and give up the expectation of perfection. Children who hear the comment, "It's a sloppy job," do not get a boost to their self-esteem.

Another trap is expecting that a plan, once made, will stay in force forever. An example of this is expecting a child to be in bed by 8:30 no matter what—or whether the child is four or fourteen. This is an out-of-date rule as far as the fourteen-year-old is concerned.

I know how tempting it is to look hard for the "one right way" and then use that forever. I believe that well-worked-out plans include a specific termination time—one week, one month, one year, 3:30 today, when Mother gets back, or when you are three inches taller.

When a family is very young and the child is not yet old enough to walk, some adult has to pack the child around. As soon as the child can efficiently walk alone, parents should encourage it. The wise parent takes advantage of each evidence of growth in the child. The child can then do things alone and even help with other tasks. One concern is not to let the evidence of growth get lopsided. When a child first starts to walk, he or she may walk slower than the parent is willing to put up with. The adult might be tempted to pick the child up like a baby and stride off even though the kid could really do it alone.

Here's another example. By the time children reach ten (and very possibly before) they could probably iron their own clothes. They certainly can help with the washing.

With the washing machines of today, a child of four could probably run the machine. The creative family makes use of all of these hands and arms and legs and brains, as soon as they are available, in the interests of both themselves and of the family.

Many children have told me that they think adults are in some kind of conspiracy to shove all the dirty jobs on kids and keep the pleasant jobs for themselves. Maybe there is something to this. If this is happening in your family, change it. It will be well worth it. No matter who is stuck with the drudge jobs, there can be creative, humorous, light ways to make fun out of the work. If not, you can at least feel a sense of accomplishment. Whoever has the dull jobs just shouldn't be asked to look happy while doing them.

Again, I make a plea for flexibility and variation. The engineering in a family goes a long way toward providing each family member with some concrete evidence of value. Every person needs a feeling of mattering, of counting, as well as a feeling of contributing to what is going on. A child who sees herself or himself as someone who matters also gets the feeling that his or her contributions are honestly valued, are being considered, and are really being tried out by someone who needs help.

Now I think we need to talk about *family time.* We all have twenty-four sixty-minute hours available to us every day. But we work, go to school, and have many other activities that take this time from the family. How much family time does your family have? How much of it do you use for the family chores?

Some families use so much of their time for family *business* that they have no time left to enjoy one another. When this happens, family members often feel that the family is a place where they are burdened. The engineering begins to deteriorate.

Here's a way to avoid this. *Go over your job list and ask yourself two questions. Is this job really necessary? If it is, could it be done more efficiently or with more fun?*

You may find that when you ruthlessly look at *why* you are doing this job, you'll find that it was just "always done," yet it really serves no purpose. If that is true, use your good sense and stop doing it.

This brings us to *priorities.* If the problem in your family is that family business squeezes out time for family members to enjoy one another, then I think you need to look carefully at your priorities.

I recommend that you start with the bare bones of what is necessary. Select those jobs that make the difference between life and death—the survival needs. Then, as time permits, other less pressing jobs can get done. Of course, this means you can feel free to change your priorities. To bring this into focus, I'm asking you to divide your family business into two categories: now and later. Obviously, the now category has the highest priority. How many family items of business do you have in this category? More than five items are too many. You may find that each day differs in terms of what is in which category.

The second category, "It would be nice and could be done later," can be woven in as the situation permits.

Now let's look at how you spend the rest of your family time. *How much time is available in your family for contact with individual family members? Of the time spent in this contact, how much of it is pleasant and leads to enjoyment?* When a large amount of contact becomes unpleasant, there is trouble. My experience is that in many families, by the time people get the work done, they actually spend very little time with each member of the family that yields any enjoyment, which makes it easier to see family members as burdensome and uncaring.

Every person needs time to be alone. One of the anguished cries I hear from family members is the need to have some time for oneself. Mothers in particular feel guilty if they wish to have time alone. They feel as if they are taking something away from the family.

Family time needs to be divided into three parts: time for each person to be alone (self time); time for each person to be with each other person (pair time); time when everyone is together (group time). It would be great if every family member could have each of these kinds of time every day. Making this possible requires first being aware that it is desirable and, second, finding ways to do it. With the external pressures we have, we can't always manage all three.

Some extra special factors influence the use of family time in certain families. Some have to arrange their time in terms of the way they make their livings. Firefighters and police officers are examples. Some firefighters are on duty twenty-four hours, then off twenty-four hours. In police work, shifts change and can be irregular. People in other jobs may work on night shifts, as in bus and airline facilities that are open around the clock. People who work special hours have to invent new ways to participate in their share of family planning and family business.

Many families include a parent who travels for long periods of time. This arrangement can put great strain on the family unless members maintain a superb system of communication and make the greatest use of their time when the traveling parent is home. Otherwise this arrangement throws extraordinary weight on the parent left at home, decreasing his or her opportunity for self time and sometimes leading to chemical abuse, extramarital affairs, or overindulgence or overstrictness with the children.

Another special factor is the family's size. The bigger the family, the more complicated the engineering. Time management can be pivotal. To help families take a look at this particular aspect of engineering, I have created a *time /presence inventory.*

Have each person keep track of her or his whereabouts at certain times on two days, one a weekday, and one a weekend day. For each family member, divide a sheet of paper according to the hours in the day, starting when the first person gets out of bed and going on until the hour when the last person goes to bed.

If the first person gets up at 5:30 A.M. and the last one goes to bed at 12 A.M., your sheets would be divided as follows:

5:30 A.M.	12:30 P.M.	7:30 P.M.
6:30 A.M.	1:30 P.M.	8:30 P.M.
7:30 A.M.	2:30 P.M.	9:30 P.M.
8:30 A.M.	3:30 P.M.	10:30 P.M.
9:30 A.M.	4:30 P.M.	11:30 P.M.
10:30 A.M.	5:30 P.M.	12:00 A.M.
11:30 A.M.	6:30 P.M.	

Have each member enter his or her location at these different times of the day. The next day, one person puts these all together, showing very dramatically what opportunities each family member had for self time, pair time, or group time.

I remember one woman saying after we had done her inventory, "My God, no wonder I feel lonely! I never see anyone but the cat!" (She had a very active family.) Indeed, families I've seen rarely have more than twenty minutes a day when all their members are together and can have group time. Twenty minutes to an hour a week is more like it. This means family business has to be transacted in twenty minutes, usually during mealtime. Everybody has to eat; transact past, present, or future business with one another; and take care of anything that comes up during that time, such as phone calls, people dropping in, or Junior falling off the chair. That's a big load to put on twenty minutes, and an even bigger load for people who want to grow in their knowledge, awareness, and enjoyment of one another.

If a family transacts family business without all members present, chances for misunderstanding are greatly multiplied. From time to time, of course, this does happen. When it does, problems can be minimized if someone is responsible for carefully noting what is going on so that she or he can give a clear report to the absent member, for example, "Last night when you were babysitting, Mother told us she is now going to work full time. We wanted you to know so you could start thinking about how this might affect you."

Once we realize how important it is to keep all family members informed about all family business, we can make a practice of seeing who is absent and working out ways to give information to the absent member. Ways to do this include nominating a reporter or writing a note. This kind of thing goes a long way toward cutting down on the alienation of "I didn't know" and "They do things behind my back."

Passing on information is only a substitute for having someone there in person. But it does help. If trust among family members has slipped badly, it will be better to try to transact business only when all members are present, at least until new trust has been built up.

If the family habitually transacts business without all members present and also has little pair time, then some family members get to know each other primarily through a third person. I call this *acquaintanceship by rumor*. The problem is that most people forget that something's a rumor and treat it as fact.

For instance, husbands often learn from their wives how their children are, and vice-versa. One child may tell a parent how another child is. In a family, regardless of whether one actually experiences the other members, everyone thinks he or she knows the others. How many children know their fathers through their own experiences with them? How many children get to know their fathers through their mother's eyes? You can see what a dangerous practice this could be. It becomes something like that old parlor game, "Gossip," in which someone whispers something in the ear of the person next to him, and it gets passed all around a circle of people. When the last person reports what she heard, it is nearly always totally different from what was originally said.

This communication-by-rumor often goes on in families. When families do not agree on group time to transact

family business, it is the best that can happen. In troubled families, this kind of communication is very frequent. There is no substitute for checking out your own perceptions and facts, hearing and seeing for yourself.

Communication affects how well the engineering is working. For instance, a wife announces to her husband that their son Tony, who is not present, did not cut the lawn today. The father may feel called on to discipline Tony. He may discipline without information or without considering why *he* is called on to do the discipline.

Having group time, of course, is no guarantee that family business will be transacted effectively. *When you are together as a group, what happens? What do you talk about? Does most of the conversation concern faults of other persons, lectures by one or more members on how things should be? Does one person monopolize the time with long recitals of aches and pains? Is there silence? No talking? Are people perched on their chairs waiting for a chance to get out?*

One of the best ways to find out about this is to make a tape recording of your family (videotape is even better, if you have the equipment) and then play it back. If you don't have a tape recorder, ask each member to take a turn observing what goes on and reporting back. Another way to do this is to ask a trusted friend to take over this duty. This can be an extremely revealing exercise, and will point out to you how easy it is for us to be unaware of how our family process is taking place.

Do you find that you use this time to get reacquainted with your family members, getting in touch with what life is like for each now and maybe what it was like this day? Is this a time when the individual joys and puzzles as well as the failures, pains, and hurts can come out and be listened to? Can you talk about new plans, present crises, and so on?

Few families realize that every day they, as a group, go through a splitting-up and reconciliation process. They leave each other and come back together. While they are apart, life goes on for them. Getting together at the end of the day provides an opportunity for sharing what happened in the world "out there" and renewing their contact with each other.

A typical kind of day in many families could be something like this. The father gets up at, say, 6:30. He shaves and showers and then comes to the kitchen, where his wife had put out coffee the night before. He may grab some cereal. When he's ready to leave the house, he awakens his wife.

She gets up about 7:15 and makes breakfast for the six-year-old boy, who has to leave on the 8:00 bus. In the meantime, the fourteen-year-old girl got up early and is out doing some running practice. She will leave for school at 8:30 A.M.

Between 7:15, when Mother gets up, and 7:45, the middle child, a twelve-year-old boy, is in the bathroom getting ready. He pops into the kitchen just as little brother starts his breakfast. Having not quite finished his homework from the night before, the older boy sits at the other end of the table. They both take the same bus. They are quiet, thinking about what's going to happen in school that day.

Mother is in the kitchen urging the children to eat. She's watching the clock and is afraid that the children will be late. Finally, the older son gets off, giving mother a little peck on the cheek, and the younger son says, "Good-bye, Ma." The daughter returns from running, prepares for school, and leaves on foot. Maybe a few minutes after this, Mother leaves for her job. Everyone has gone now.

In a few hours, the family members will start returning. The six-year-old will come back at 2:30 in the afternoon and go over to the neighbor's. Mother comes home at 3:00 and calls the neighbor, who tells her her son is there. Then she gets busy with some laundry that she knew had to be done. After all, her husband needs some clean shirts, and the children need underwear.

The twelve-year-old boy is going to be at a Boy Scout meeting that day; the fourteen-year-old is going to have some kind of athletic practice.

At 6:00 when the husband comes home, the six-year-old is back from play, the twelve-year-old is out with the Boy Scouts, and the fourteen-year-old is expected home at 7:30. Wife, husband, and six-year-old all have a hurried dinner. Most of the conversation is about which bill should be paid first.

Then Father goes out to his poker game. The daughter comes home before Father returns and is asleep when he comes in. Father goes for a whole day without sharing anything of substance with his children. Although he is busy, he is interested in his children and might ask his wife how the children were. Of course, she doesn't really know too much either—she's seen them here and there. What she tells him might depend more on *her* feelings than her experiences or observations of the children. Many, many days can go on like this.

Such days form a continual parade of half contacts. It is easy to lose track of people and the relationships. The separation can be continual and prolonged. The result is that people feel isolated from one another. I have worked with families that found no reconciliation until they all came together in my office.

Families in this spot know that although they live together in one house, they do not have much real experience with one another. It is wise to get together once a day for everyone to touch base with each other. In the busy lives that most of us lead, *this kind of meeting needs to be planned.* It cannot be left to chance.

I believe the idea that families live together is more illusion than reality. This helps me understand much of the pain I encounter in families whose communication-by-rumor and half contacts pave the way for all kinds of distortions about how things really are in the family. Filling out a time/presence inventory is a first step to making clear how much of your idea of your family is an illusion and how much is real. With a little planning, once you know what the problem is, you can make opportunities to really contact your family members. Maybe you can go on to make some changes, too.

Another aspect that plays a big part in how well the engineering works has to do with how each person experiences time. For instance, if you're excited about something that's coming up, time often seems to drag. When you are busy and involved with something you particularly like, time flies. The experience of clock time has no direct relationship to the experience of self time. Five minutes can seem like an hour, or it can seem like a minute. How different family members experience time is related to how things get done.

Experiencing time is an important part of predicting time. Predicting time is basic to carrying out commitments and directions. Many people get into difficulties with each other because one is often late. The immediate assumption, that the late one just wanted to bug the other, isn't necessarily the case. It could represent a difference in the way each experiences time.

When little attention is paid to the individual's experience and his management of time as part of the problem people often explain it as follows: "If you loved me, you would be on time." This is a form of blackmail.

Children are often criticized for being late. And a lot of families try to deal with this tardiness by punishment rather than teaching.

When we come into the world, though, we know nothing about how to predict our time. This is something we learn slowly, over a long period. I think that learning about and using time is a very complicated kind of learning. Many adults still have difficulty with it.

Just think of all the factors we have to consider if we announce at 8:00 A.M. that, "at 5:30 tonight I will be at such and such a place." We then face a constant process of selecting, rejecting, and managing all through the day with whatever comes up so that we can be on time. How can we fill the time demands of the day? Can we gauge the transportation circumstances? What allowances can we make for interruptions? We set out to know enough about how this day can or will go, so that at 8:00 A.M. we can assure ourselves and others that we'll arrive at 5:30 P.M. It is really quite a miracle, if you think about it.

Think about yourself and your relation to time. Go back and look at your family's time inventory. If the complexity of using time were more widely understood, people would show more understanding and less blame. Meanwhile, I would be willing to wager that in a great many families, children are asked to handle time in a way that the adults can't do.

Many homemakers, female and male, get in trouble here. They agree to have the dinner ready at 5:30 P.M. As they go through the day, somebody calls up or comes to visit. Or the homemaker sees something that needs cleaning, or gets engrossed in a book. Suddenly it is 5:30, and he or she realizes supper is not ready. This creates situations that cause irritation. Others might call this person lazy or irresponsible.

The way each person experiences time is related to awareness, motivation, knowledge, and interests. It is an aspect of each person's uniqueness. Getting acquainted with how each person uses time is an important factor in every relationship—no two people use it in exactly the same way.

If time schedules can be used as desirable guides rather than evidence of good character, we might come a little closer to eliminating some of the problems of scheduling. After traveling thousands of air miles, I find the airplane that is scheduled to depart at 3:47 sometimes doesn't leave until 8:10. So I have developed a guide for myself, which goes like this: I will use the best judgment I have in making a time commitment. Then I will do the best I can to meet it. If it turns out that things don't work out so I can keep my commitment, and I can't change my circumstances, I don't bug myself.

I was brought up on the sacredness of being on time. If I were late, I would be punished. No matter what, I *had* to be on time. The result was, of course, that I was frequently late. With my current guide, things flow. I am rarely late. I don't fight with myself anymore.

Without our knowing it, the clock runs many of our lives. Instead of being our aid, it becomes our master. Our

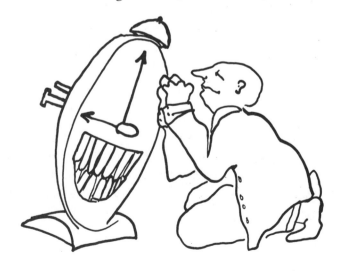

attitudes about time greatly influence our effectiveness in getting the job done.

For instance, many people follow a plan of rigid eating times. That means that at a certain clock time, everybody is expected to be at the table and the cook is expected to serve the food. Unfortunately, not everyone may be hungry. And the person who cooked may feel that people who don't eat heartily at that moment don't love the cook. I know this happens frequently. To avoid offending the cook, family members may grow fat or vomit after meals.

Not eating has nothing to do with loving the cook. It has to do with where that person is in terms of appetite. I am not necessarily making a plea for people to eat or not eat. What is important to me is that people do what fits for them. If they're not very hungry, then they don't have to eat very much. If they're hungry, they can eat more. Clock time and self time do not always coincide. Happy people are flexible about this dilemma.

It's rare that any two people are at exactly the same point at the same time. This goes for sex as well as food, and certainly for desires and wishes. When people are really aware that they can be in different states at different times, they make allowances. Instead of feeling put down, they can usually negotiate and come to some agreement. This may not always represent everyone's druthers, but both people have a chance to have something.

I know a woman who sometimes wants to shop in the evening. She tells her husband of her wish, and he responds that he is a little tired but will go along if she doesn't expect him to be too exciting. If she replies that that's all right with her, the two of them sometimes also go to a movie.

Given that he can tell her about his fatigue, his feeling of having participated in the decision to go shopping may make his energy flow more, and he can end up enjoying a movie as well. He doesn't have to fight the battle of who has the right to tell whom what to do, nor does he concede just to keep peace.

The idea that you have to be where I am is very expensive emotionally. In contrast, if this gal said to her husband, "I want to go shopping, and you'd better come," he might go to avoid an argument but would probably not be a good companion. Then she could feel put upon, and the battle would be on.

If we waited for everyone to be exactly at the same point as everyone else, we might wait forever. If we require that other people be where we are, we run the danger of developing interpersonal difficulty. If we ask where people are and tell them where we are and then enter into some kind of negotiation, accepting each person's current reality, something better can evolve.

The question then becomes: How can we let each other know our whereabouts, and how can we then find a place for each other so that we both benefit?

Every member of the family needs to count on some space and some place for privacy, free of invasion from anybody else. Whether it is little or big doesn't matter, just so it is your own. It is easier for me to respect and value your place if I also have one that you likewise respect and value. Feeling that I have a place that's assured tells me that I count. Not having this assurance often leads to the attitude, "I don't care. So what? What difference does it make? I clean up the kitchen, and you mess it all up."

How many times, for instance, have you heard bitter comment from one child about how another child has taken things or has invaded some personal space? Or have you heard a parent (perhaps yours) yelling because someone removed a tool from its "right" place? The same is true for anyone who is looking for something somebody else took and didn't put back. Just let yourself imagine how you feel when you worry about someone misplacing your belongings.

Being able to count on managing your own things and participating in decisions about how and when others will use your things is very important. This lets you feel that you count.

A clear, reliable experience in ownership paves the way for eventual sharing. It is a message of self-worth and therefore removes fears about sharing. I think a child needs to understand clearly, "This is mine and I can do what I want with it." Some parents buy one child a toy, for instance, with the expectation that the toy will be shared with another child. Then they get upset because the sharing doesn't work. If the toy is to be a house toy, a shared toy, then it should be so designated from the start. Very often conflicts erupt because neither child feels assured in matters of privacy and ownership.

Sharing, to me, is the decision by one person to let another person *in*—to belongings, to time, to thoughts, or to space. It is another one of those complicated learnings that take a long time to grasp fully. People can share only if they feel trust. Parents often ask children to share before they know how to, and then punish them for bad results. In these same families, I rarely see evidence that the adults have learned to share successfully.

At this point, you may have done the necessary work that enables you to have a clear, firm list of the jobs it takes to make your family run. You may also have some new awareness about your priorities. No engineering would be necessary if no people existed. Engineering is necessary only because it can make the lives of people better. If it makes the lives worse, then you need new engineering.

Through what I have asked you to focus on in this chapter, you may now have more ideas about how you can be less burdened and more hopeful. What ties the whole engineering aspect together is an efficient, well-understood information system, which operates in a context of trust and humanness.

To make all of the above easier, I recommend a family temperature reading. I developed this process to keep the emotional climate clear in a family (or any group of people who work or live together) so that the group's necessary business can be transacted and the lines of communication among the members can be kept open. The aim is to put words to areas of life that are present with all of us yet are not often talked about directly. For lack of a better word, I will call these areas *themes.*

The first theme is *appreciation.* We feel good when we share our feelings of appreciation toward others and ourselves. To give a voice to these feelings is to keep a balanced internal state. To share appreciations with others is to give them an unsolicited gift. How often do we take these feelings for granted and not express them? This theme enables us to make conscious, verbalized, appreciation messages.

The second theme deals with the *negatives* of life: complaints, worries, and so on. We all have these too. I invite the person who has a complaint to accompany that complaint with a recommendation for change. The next step will be to ask for the help to make that change. This is quite a different approach than expecting someone else to deal with your complaint or defend themselves against you.

The third theme concerns *puzzles,* which are the gaps that come about naturally when many people are together. Who can think of telling everyone everything that is going on? To do that, we would need a very sophisticated message system. Even businesses goof in this way. To meet this, give yourself permission to say what your puzzles are. Puzzles often occur when people forget, misspeak, or don't hear. It is hardly ever because people are perverse. The important part is to keep things straight. This is a way to do it.

Because of the interactions between family members and the outside world, or between other family members, individual persons often have *new information,* which is a fourth theme. This is often related to puzzles. It is easier to remember what you have in the way of new information if you have a structure to remind you of it.

The last theme is the theme of *hopes and wishes* for ourselves, which are dear to all of us. Many times, we shortchange ourselves because we choose not to put words to our hopes and wishes for fear they might not happen. We will never know what can happen until we do articulate our desires. The other important part is that when you put words out, your loving family members may be able to help you. You may be able to do the same for them when they put out their dreams. We do little alone.

Five themes occur on the thermometer for our family temperature:

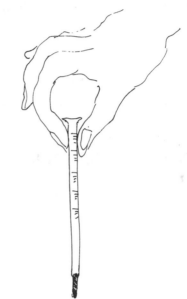

appreciation
complaints
puzzles
new information
hopes and wishes

Make a large "thermometer" with these five readings. Paint it; or make it out of cloth or felt. Make it colorful. Have fun with it. Hang it in a room where your family is likely to sit together and do temperature readings.

Invite all family members to sit comfortably, preferably in a circle. Have a tape recorder handy in case you want to record and listen back later. Agree ahead of time how long you want to take—a half hour, fifteen minutes, or an hour. Have someone be a time-keeper. Ask someone else to write down those things that might not get finished and have to be dealt with later.

While you are learning, it is helpful to take the temperature themes in order. For example, each person who wants to can speak about appreciations. Then ask for the complaints and continue with all the other themes.

It is important to remember that this is all voluntary. Not everyone will have something to say about each theme each time you have a temperature reading. The spirit is to listen and, when responding, to clarify and add rather than correcting or influencing. Apply this to tough things as well.

The most important aim is to give a voice to all the themes by everyone who wants to talk. Be flexible. Do not hurry! A hug by all members at the beginning will show good will. A hug at the end will be a thank-you.

At the beginning, it will be helpful to plan temperature readings at least once weekly. After you have some experience and doing this seems familiar, comfortable, and helpful, try to have ten-minute temperature readings every day.

I said this would keep the emotional climate clear. Regular temperature readings raise everyone's trust and self-esteem. We also continue learning about each other and becoming closer and freer. You will find as a result that your engineering tasks become more creative as well.

18

The Extended Family

Everybody has heard the old saw, "You can pick your friends, but you're stuck with your relatives." Relatives—in-laws, grandparents, aunts, uncles, nieces, nephews—are people who are related legally or by blood, or both. They exist by the nature of things, and no amount of wishing will make them not related. They are part of each person's extended family.

Do you enjoy your in-laws, grandparents, grandchildren, nieces, or nephews? If you do, then you can treat them as real people, sharing criticisms, doubt, pain, and your love. Maybe it is the other way around, too: if you treat your relatives as real people, then maybe you can enjoy them. All people have some parts that can be enjoyed at a given point in time.

Many times, though, we meet our relatives after we have been conditioned by someone else's opinions. It is common, for example, for children to hear their parents saying to each other:

"Your father is a tightwad."

"Your father is just wishy-washy. He does everything your mother tells him to do."

"Your mother is never going to babysit my children."

"My mother just loves *her* grandchildren."

Parents may even give children direct comments, such as:

"Be careful of your language when your grandmother is around."

It is easy to see how children get one-dimensional ideas about their relatives. Before ever coming to know them, the children may hear them presented as saints, devils, burdens, or nothings. Each child begins seeing grandparents through the eyes of parents, and this presents some pretty serious handicaps in ever trying to see them as human beings.

Heaven only knows there are plenty of traps among relatives. In some cases there is virtual war; in other cases, simply avoidance. Some people try to handle an existing problem by estranging themselves. I hear people say, "I wish my children could know their grandparents. I feel bad about that sometimes. But it is so painful to visit them."

Or, "My mother is always spoiling the kids, yet I want them to know her."

Or, "My father shows partiality to my son and ignores my daughter" or vice-versa.

You have probably heard these remarks and many more like them. I hear these kinds of things as extensions of whatever the speaker hasn't worked out in his or her feelings about self. This person not only doesn't consider the adults in the family as people, but confuses these relatives with their roles. This is very common.

Husbands and wives do this kind of thing to their parents, too, by labeling them "the old people." Once you hang a label on someone ("old," "auntie," "grandpa," whatever), it is easy to stop thinking of him or her as a person. Such labels form a large part of the atmosphere in which the extended family finds itself. The generation gap, then, exists as much between parents and grandparents as it does between parents and children. I define the generation gap as an area of strangeness that has not yet been bridged.

On the other hand, if the spouses have become peers to their parents, then all of them can be people together. Each can be treated as a unique, valued person. They can respect one another's privacy, enjoy what is enjoyable about one another, and try to change the parts of life that are less pleasant.

These people take the *people* point of view instead of the *role* point of view. The husbands and wives of today are the grandparents of twenty years from now. The children of today are the husbands and wives of tomorrow, and the grandparents of the future. And throughout all of this, it is *Jane* who is a wife, *Jane* who is a mother, and *Jane* who is a grandmother. No matter what role she assumes, she is Jane, the person.

In other words, husband, wife, parent, child, grandparent, and grandchild are names of roles that people assume as they go through life. The roles describe two things: how one person is related to another, and how this particular role is lived out. Essie Hawkins is my grandmother on my father's side; or Essie Hawkins says that Jane Sutter is her grandchild, the daughter of her son, Harry. When Essie and Jane meet, who are they meeting? People or roles? Roles are sterile and awesome; people are exciting and human.

Once realized, this is pretty obvious, yet so many miss it. Underneath every role name is a personal, given name—

Alice or Marco or Leilani or Wadsworth—and a person who lives that role. Roles are like different clothes or hats one wears, depending on what one is doing at any moment.

Let me illustrate. Alice Sweetworth, forty-six, is married to Guy Sweetworth, forty-seven. They have been married twenty-six years. Alice and Guy have three children: Margaret, twenty-five; Bruce, twenty-three; and Allan, seventeen. Margaret is married to Hans, thirty. Bruce is married to Anita, also twenty-three years old, and they have one child.

When Guy is with Alice, he calls himself husband because he and Alice are married and do marital things together. When he is around Margaret, Bruce, or Allan, he wears his father hat, assuming that he is doing something that fits into his idea of what fathering is all about. When he is with Hans and Anita, he is a father-in-law, doing whatever that role asks of him. When he is with Margaret's kids, he is a grandfather.

Now, suppose he is in the presence of all these people. He then can put on any one of these hats. Yet I know people

who, by the time they get as far as Guy is in life, wear only grandfather hats. Their father-in-law, father, husband, and self parts somehow just went away.

I remember a family who came in to see me once. Ethel, the wife in the family, brought her seventy-three-year-old mother, who was introduced to me as Grandma. I looked at her when I took her hand, and I asked her what her name was. At first she looked at me blankly, and then finally, after a few moments, said very softly, "Anita."

So I said, "Hello, Anita." At this point, the tears streamed down her face. She said it was the first time she had heard her given name in almost twenty years.

Seeing Anita as a person, not just a grandmother, was a very important factor in this family's opening up to some new ideas about how they could work together as people.

Any role name is merely descriptive. Why not let people be who they are, and do what they do, and never mind their titles, whether aunt or uncle, cousin or parent? First and foremost, these are people. I don't know of any universal behavior that means mothering, fathering, husbanding, wifing, aunting, or uncling, and I've never found anybody who did. To live a role is an invitation to squeeze the life out of oneself; to live as a person invites flexibility and fullness.

An important adjunct to all this is that people in families almost always think they really know one another. You know this. What parent doesn't feel he or she knows each child up to the age of fourteen or fifteen? What individual doesn't think she or he knows mother and father? I have found that family members who feel this way are the most likely to be strangers to one another. What they think is a given person is more likely to be his or her role.

The cure for this gap is for each family member to get acquainted with the others as persons. This process needs to be consciously updated from time to time. Let's face it: doing this with people to whom you are legally or blood related is quite hard because of the pesky assumption you already know them. Few people who feel they know each other really share their deeper feelings.

Family members often get stuck with one of their roles, and then that role seems the same as their identity. I am convinced that many of the problems among older people and other members of the family arise because the oldsters' feelings about themselves are tied up in their role of being older people. They forget, and people around them forget, that the heart still beats and that they still wish and need to be loved and valued and to have a purpose.

Like the dreams we pursue, this sense of purpose guides us through the day. A person starts out at birth into a new area of growth that continues until death. If we were to do what is possible for us as human beings, we would be constantly evolving as well as aging. A great deal of evidence now shows that one's body follows one's feeling of worth: the state of one's skin, bones, and muscles is more related to how one feels about oneself than almost any other single factor, with the possible exceptions of nutrition, exercise, and interactions with the people with whom one lives. Furthermore, people who are more prone to illness very often have incomplete, distorted, and undesirable images of themselves.

Just as ironclad roles are inhumane, family ritual and traditions become troublesome when people regard them as demands rather than celebrations. An effective use of ritual is to develop ways of doing things that reflect a certain family's life-style. A family I know has a ritual that when each child becomes fifteen, she or he automatically gets a watch; at sixteen, he or she can drive a car; and so on. Rituals such as these serve as indications of what is significant in a family, but they aren't written in blood; they can be changed from time to time.

Another use of ritual is to indicate a sense of belonging—a kind of clan symbol. Furthermore, a ritual does not require that everybody be present. Some of the worst kinds of things that happen in families are demands that every member of the family be present—at holidays, let us say, at the home of the older generation. I know some young couples who absolutely ruin their holidays because they feel they must spend Christmas with both the husband's parents and then the wife's parents. And so they busy themselves with eating two dinners, enjoying neither.

Such young couples experience a terrible frustration. They feel the pull of having to go to either or both sets of parents and, at the same time, wanting to have something of their own. One couple I know believed they had to go to his mother's home every Friday night or terrible things would happen: his mother or grandmother would have a heart attack and then punish the couple by never speaking to them again or cutting them out of her will. That's a pretty heavy price to pay for peace in the family.

When you make choices to count your own preferences on a par with others', you may encounter some negative reactions. People can survive this, even if they vehemently resist your changes at first.

The most hurtful thing my daughter could do would be to come to my home for dinner on Christmas so my feelings wouldn't be hurt. I would feel I had failed miserably in helping her develop as an autonomous person.

A large portion of things that make for difficulty involve adults who haven't learned to let go of the parent-child relationship with their own parents. This relationship needs to be transformed. The two generations need to develop a peer relationship with each other, in which each respects the other's privacy and autonomy and both can come together when it fits. In this way, the adult children are also well situated to parent their own kids.

To turn this around, I have had many people in their sixties seek my help to get their grown-up offspring off their backs: "They are always bossing me around and telling me what to do." It is a new idea to some adults that their parents might not automatically welcome their advice.

Many binds occur from our awareness of others' loneliness, which we may feel we have to relieve. This can turn into a burdensome chore. That is, you are my mother and I see you as lonely; you don't have any friends, and I don't find much joy with you because you're always complaining. But I go over to see you and sit through the visit with clenched teeth, or else I bug you with telling you what you should do and then get frustrated because you won't do it. Many people attempt this and then pay for it with their anger and guilt. A person who is grown up is free to say yes and no realistically and, at the same time, able to feel balanced about standing up for self.

This leads to another point: helping. Because of disability or illness, many people need the help of their children. How can two people give and receive help from one another and yet feel like equals? Sometimes the effort to help ends up in the familiar old blackmail (the "clutch"): "You must help me because you are my sons. I can't do anything, I'm so little and feeble," or, "You are my parent and you must let me help you."

Again, this kind of thing represents two people who have not yet learned to stand on their own feet and so are handling their transactions by trying to control others instead of attracting them. Anyone looking around at families today can see hundreds of examples of people blackmailing one another under the guise of helplessness and helpfulness. Success for parents means feeling valued, useful, cared about, and liked but not clutched by their children. I think the converse is true for the children. If they feel their parents value them, find them useful, care about them, like them, and don't clutch at them, they too feel that their parents are successful.

At times, of course, people need bona fide help. But the times "help" is used to clutch are far more numerous. I can

just hear some of you as you read this: "How else could I have contact with my daughter-in-law, my son-in-law, my mother-in-law, my father-in-law, my mother, my father, my daughter, my son? The kind of thing you're describing could never happen between us because there has never been any joy between us. My mother-in-law never wanted me to marry her son anyway. My father doesn't like my husband. [My mother didn't want me to marry my wife.] My mother-in-law is always wanting my husband to do things for her." And on and on.

It doesn't happen overnight, and it is not easy. It is possible. All I can say to you is that no people are 100 percent one way. Do some exploring and discovering of these people and yourself with a fresh view.

There are varying degrees of how much one can enjoy others. I don't mean to imply that everybody can enjoy everybody else equally. That would be quite unrealistic. However, most families can come together and work together in new ways once each member knows to the bone that all people are made up of parts and no one *has* to love the unlovable parts. Furthermore, these parts do change from time to time.

People can have honest, real relationships with one another, and they can live in harmony. As I've said before, it is simple, but it is *not* easy. This is an important point to remember. In particular, children often get caught in the middle between parents and grandparents. This is an almost overwhelming spot for a child. How can he or she go against a grandmother who gives a great deal of joy when the mother is saying that the grandmother is no good? The child's experience is quite different: the mother may be talking about her relationship with her *mother-in-law.* Conversely, a grandmother may tell the child that his or her father is no good, when the child's loyalty and maybe even experience do not validate this.

It is all too easy to project onto another person some of your problems, and then ask someone else to go along with you to make you feel right about your conclusion. Lots of problems in the extended family come about this way.

Other difficulties arise for people who are just beginning new roles as auxiliary members in the families of their grown-up children. Many grandparents like to babysit and freely offer to do so. However, I've known other grandparents who felt uncomfortable telling their children they did not want to sit for them. If this bind is present, there's going to be trouble. Sometimes the life-needs or the life-plans of the people who are grandparents don't allow for babysitting. Sometimes grown-up children who don't have a peer relationship with their own parents exploit them; and then the parents, having settled for only a grandparenting role in life, respond by feeling resentful inwardly. And sometimes people in the family—the current parents and grandparents—do not get along, and when Grandma or Grandpa sits with the children, there is really apt to be difficulty.

I see nothing wrong in extending help to family members if it is done as a result of two people coming together and considering the life needs of each. Requests such as "You have to do this because you're my mother" or "You have to let me do that because I am your daughter" change the whole negotiation for help into one of control. Unfortunately, the children are often the ones who get sacrificed. As mentioned, family members frequently blackmail each other in the name of love and relationships. This is one of the reasons so much pain exists in families.

When we look at it, any extended family is composed of three generations, sometimes four. All of these generations are relating somehow and affecting each of the other generations. It's hard for me to think of a family without including the third generation—the people who are the parents or grandparents of the current husband and wife. After all, we become the next family architects by learning from the previous ones.

I can foresee the time when families will conduct themselves so that grown children will be peers to their own parents: self-reliant and autonomous, instead of remaining children to them or becoming parents to them. To me, this is the end point of peoplemaking: that children become autonomous, independent, creative people who are now peers to the people who introduced them into the world.

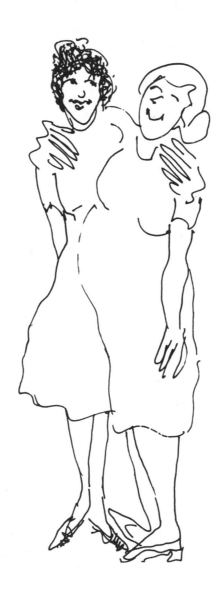

19

The Life Cycle

To help you develop a perspective on your life, I want to
show you images of the life cycle.

In gardening terms, we get planted, we sprout, grow a
main stem, bud, flower and/or fruit, and set a new form in
motion. All of this happens for most people within approxi-
mately seventy to eighty years. To simplify matters, I will
name our five stages, which cluster into three parts of life.
These stages and parts simply remind us that we are different at different times of our lives. What is constant is our
life force.

PART I

Stage 1. Conception to birth. This takes 9 months.

Stage 2. Birth to puberty. This takes 10 to 14 years.

Stage 3. Puberty to adulthood. This lasts 7 to 11 years.

The day we enter into our legal majority, we change
our relationship with regard to dependency and responsibility. We are legally adults and responsible for everything we
do. To be successful, we need to acquire—or to already
have—the learnings that make that possible.

PART II

Stage 4. Adulthood to senior status. This stage lasts from 44
to 47 years and can be divided into young, middle-
aged and older adults.

PART III

Stage 5. Senior status to death.

This too could be divided into stages: new, evolving, and evolved.

Each part has specific growth tasks, responsibilities, and privileges connected with it. It also has a different form. For example, think of a caterpillar and a butterfly being the same energy in a different form.

Each part is a foundation for the next part as well as a link to it. When any part ends before completion—as when someone enters adult life still feeling like a child—the stages unfold out of sync, and the growth cycle becomes distorted. Energy is derailed and causes problems. From physicists, we learn that energy can never be destroyed; it only changes form. Therefore, the energy one uses for a slap can be used instead for hugging. This again raises a very significant question: shall we use our energy for growth, health, and happiness for everyone, or sickness, despair, and destructiveness? Finding out and learning all the ways that we can be constructive means taking a careful look at what we are now doing, then being willing to let go of those ways that defeat and limit us.

Certain learnings are universally necessary to become more fully human. These need to take place at every stage and every part of our life in some form, in every human being, starting with the first stage, infancy. I submit this list of learnings that constitute necessary personal competence.

Differentiation: Distinguishing between you and me.

Relationships: Knowing how to connect to you and others.

Autonomy: Relying on myself, separate and distinct from anyone else.

Self-esteem: Feeling worthy about myself.

Power: Using my energy to initiate and guide my behavior.

Productivity: Manifesting my competence.

Loving: Being compassionate, accepting of others, and giving and receiving affection.

The development of each stage will determine the new form that the universal learnings will take. For example, one would not teach personal competence to a child by demanding that she or he become skillful at driving a car. The child's level of competence could be better developed by learning to use a spoon. Car driving is a competency more appropriate for older teenagers.

The following shows the stages in a life span.

	PART I		PART II	PART III
Stage 1	Stage 2	Stage 3	Stage 4	Stage 5
(9 mos.)	(10–14 years)	(7–11 years)	(44–47 years)	(7–25 years)
conception to birth	birth to puberty	puberty to to adulthood	adulthood to senior status	senior status to death

How we think about and approach these stages determines the outcomes of our lives. The approach shown in this next figure is based on the dominant–submissive pair model. With this we come into the world helpless and go out useless.

Part I	Part II	Part III
Infancy through Adolescence	Adulthood	Senior Status
"Too young to"	"Supposedly in your right place"	"Too old to"

In terms of power and accomplishment, only the adult phase has any positive value in this figure. Pre-adult is too young, and post-adult is too old. This leaves two parts of life essentially devalued, potentially unacceptable, thoroughly disenfranchised, and alienated.

With this picture, it is easy to see how adolescence becomes so frustrating, and old age so abhorrent, to many people. The life line is disempowered at two major points: at the beginning and at the end. The only acceptable place is in the middle. Power is conferred only on adults. It is denied to youth and seniors.

Having spent the first eighteen to twenty-one years learning how to be "too young to," the night before our twenty-first birthday can be a very long night. Among other things, we have to learn how to have high self-esteem, how to use power constructively, and how to make wise choices and decisions in order to handle what faces us in this new stage. This is a big order for a night's sleep.

Of course, we don't accomplish this in one night. We wake up on our birthday pretty much the same as when we went to sleep. Many of the skills and attitudes we need to negotiate the adult stage successfully still have to be learned. And we struggle to do so.

Probably the greatest reason for finding ways to help adolescents feel valued, capable, and effective is to give them the courage, judgment, healthy self-esteem, and other necessary tools with which to meet the responsibilities of their adulthood. Unfortunately, many children are born to parents who have not yet learned what they need to teach. After all, adults can only teach their children what they know. So they continue passing on old attitudes and themes, often mistaking them as innate instead of learned.

By this time the parents have probably arrived at the end of their adult stage. Now they have to look at their impending senior status, wherein they will be "too old to." This change in status often coincides with menopause and retirement, and is responsible for much depression. Fear sometimes takes over and renders many older persons vulnerable to physical, social, and mental disease.

Interestingly, adolescents respond similarly to their new status. They are more likely than older people to engage in aggression and violence, however. Their abundant energy may have no healthy place to express itself, and their self-worth is low.

Almost all of our current educational, medical, social, and psychological practices are based on this dominant–submissive model, categorized by age instead of personhood. This needs to be reevaluated so that each person in each phase of each stage can fully be a human being. The figure below depicts a model that offers very different and hopeful outcomes. The stages and parts of life are the same; however, the approach differs vastly.

Death

Birth

Part I	Part II	Part III
First-rate	First-rate	First-rate
FULLY HUMAN	FULLY HUMAN	FULLY HUMAN

In this fully human model, each person is always in the right place at every stage. We still come into the world helpless, yet we go out gloriously at a high point in our development. This model's relationships are based not on power but on healthy self-worth, equality of value, love, and behavior that reflects personal and social responsibility.

In this model, we approach life with the idea of making every stage first-rate. Each stage reveals a marvel. It expresses the magic of growth. Each stage is treated as a time to be enjoyed, learned from, given to, taken from, and looked at as a whole within itself. Remembering that people are live beings in constant movement, we treat them accordingly.

By the time we reach senior status, we have had so much experience in being whole that our later years are yet another arena in which to develop new possibilities. Won't it be great when, at the sunset of our lives, we can say we lived each part fully, deepening and broadening our understanding and appreciation of ourselves as we went along?

The modern challenge is to empower ourselves so that we can be models and leaders of this process for ourselves and others for each stage of our lives.

20

Adolescence

The teenager's job is a huge one. Moved by the energy released through puberty, the psychological necessity for becoming independent, and social expectations for becoming successful, the adolescent has tremendous pressure while finding a way around a new world. Put this together with the fact that there are no marked paths to follow, and you have the wonder and the scariness that adolescence produces.

We need to recognize this condition. It is tricky for both the adolescent and the parents. Adults need to create a context in which this growth can take place, in much the same careful way we made the house safe for the children when they were toddlers. We need to do it in a way that preserves the adolescents' dignity, develops their sense of self-worth, and gives them useful guidelines, all of which will help them become more socially mature.

An adolescent's psychological context needs to be able to accommodate mood swings, seemingly irrational ideas, occasional bizarre behavior, new vocabulary, and awkward performances. Each or all of these arise as adolescents play with their power, their autonomy, and their dependence and independence.

To successfully negotiate the adventure of adolescence, both parents and teenagers need positive images. Teens have made some great accomplishments requiring great risks. Yours may be among them. Make a scrapbook with pictures and stories about adolescents who used their energy for wonderful purposes: starting backyard businesses, organizing visits to elders, or overcoming obstacles to achieve a goal. This will help to dissolve some of your fear. Enlist the help of your teenager to find these stories. Celebrate the risks teens take that pay off.

I have heard parents complain about their teenagers, "They never sit still. They always have to be doing something." This is par for the course. Wise parents accept this restlessness and find graceful ways to live while temporary storms rage. They carefully choreograph new contexts that nurture the buds which can then become blossoms. The result is the bearing of good fruit.

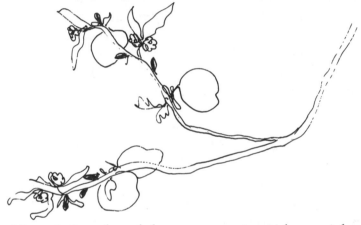

Negotiating the adolescent stage is neither quick nor easy. Both parents and adolescents need to develop patience, and keep talking and loving, to make it work. In this period of tremendous change, everyone becomes new to each other, and people have to get to know one another all over again. Approaching this with more love than fear will often be the difference between success and failure.

I have often said to parents, "If it isn't illegal, immoral, or fattening, give it your blessing." We do much better with helping people if we find and support all the places we can appropriately say yes, and say only the no's that really matter.

Every adult who is reading this book has survived adolescence—some with scars, some with still-open wounds, and all with texture. The differences between texturing and scarring can be explained as follows. Texturing comes from using oneself to accumulate wisdom through learning to deal with one's frustration and conflicts, become responsible, and meeting other of life's realities. Scarring comes as the result of a broken spirit. The open wound shows there has been no healing; not even the thin skin has grown over. This results in seriously handicapped psychological and social conditions. My experience is that parents will do all they can to avoid leaving open wounds with their adolescents. Sometimes the parents' wounds are still open too, and it is hard for them to deal well with their teenagers.

One approach is for parents to form their own groups for support, brainstorming, and practicing congruent communication. This may be especially useful for families in which both parents are away during the day and so need to find other people and resources in the community for support.

Parents often meet this period with negative fantasies stemming from memories of their own adolescence as well as from horror stories about teenage abuses of alcohol, drugs, sex, and violence. The problems of sex and violence seem forbidding, but we need to remember that teenagers are more like adults than they are different. If I pinch an adult hard enough, he or she will hurt just like any adolescent. Much experimenting with sex comes out of a hunger for touch, the need to be held and stroked. And much teen violence comes out of a desperate desire not to appear weak or needy, just as it does with adults.

Addicted teenagers represent a growing percentage of our total adolescent population. These behaviors are so dramatic that it may feel like many more persons are involved than really are. Aside from percentages and statistics, though, many parents have cause for concern about their particular child. Parents who ignore the signs of possible addiction to alcohol and drugs are perpetuating the problem by the same avoidance that is characteristic of people who behave in these ways.

Excellent help exists in programs all over the world as outgrowths of Alcoholics Anonymous, Alateen, Alanon, and Adult Children of Alcoholics are groups that can help and are listed in the telephone directories under Alcoholics Anonymous. In many communities, hotlines also exist to handle calls about parental stress, sexual health, sexual abuse, domestic violence, suicide prevention, and other crises. If you do not find the number in your directory or with the help of a Directory Assistance operator, your community's Mental Health department may be able to refer you to the resources available in your area.

Dealing with serious problems and minor problems both involve finding positive images. Once we can see our way out of a situation, we're half way there. The same holds true for general feelings of anxiety about adolescence. Look around and you will see scores of fine things going on with teenagers. One of these teens could be yours. Have you taken the time to tell your adolescent what you like about what he or she is doing? If not, do it now! Do it every time you notice positive actions. And do it when your teenager shows greater awareness or makes positive choices while trying to resolve a mistake, as well.

When parents and adults take a balanced attitude toward what is a wonderful, exciting, and sometimes a frightening journey, they increase their prospects of being successful guides to their adolescents. We are a different kettle of fish in this period than in any other stage of development, so both parents and teens start out in the dark.

As mentioned, one very big change during puberty is the awakening of a level of energy previously unknown to that individual. This energy is scary and calls for safe, appropriate, and fulfilling ways to have healthy expression. Sports, exercise, and stimulating mental and physical work are effective and nourishing ways to express it. Organized programs and working for causes are two other ways. Adolescents are often idealistic and will work hard to achieve their goals. Help them find a context where this can happen. Programs such as Outward Bound, for example, help people to navigate through the tough parts of their adolescence. This program takes place in the wilderness, creating opportunities for young people to meet their fears, develop their courage, and learn teamwork. While this particular program was developed to help adolescents who were having a rough time, it is good for any teenager. For that matter, similar programs now exist for adults, who can also benefit from these learnings.

Meeting the challenge of harnessing energy and directing it successfully is one aim of adolescence. The picture of excited, energetic race horses pacing nervously at their stalls

as they are forced to wait for the starting gate to open is an apt analogy for the average teenager. They are spirited and want to win the race. I think adults, without meaning to, contribute to teenage difficulties by not providing adequate purposeful activities. Adolescents are not monsters. They are just people trying to learn how to make it among the adults in the world, who are probably not so sure themselves.

I think it is this energy that frightens adults the most. To handle their fears, parents often inundate their teenagers with "don'ts" and other forms of control. Just the opposite is necessary. Adolescents need to be encouraged to create adequate channels to direct their newfound energy. They also need clear boundaries. They need love and acceptance. The important skill to learn is to accept the person's value while at the same time helping to modify his or her behavior.

For example, rather than tossing off admonishments such as "Now, be careful. Remember you're a good girl" to a daughter going out on a date, parents can help by teaching her how to set her own priorities, in advance of the situation. A young person who has carefully thought out his or her attitudes can respond to pressure by saying, "Thanks for asking me, but what you ask at this point doesn't fit for me, so the answer is no."

When I have been privy to parent–adolescent collisions, the most successful way I have found to be helpful is to establish a positive relationship between them based on each person's humanness and caring. It is largely futile to attempt change through control or threat. When each person can be regarded as an individual of worth, real changes can take place and do. I would like parents to see themselves becoming a laboratory of resources for their children.

Adolescents are neither stupid nor perverse; nor are parents. Both only seem like that in the eyes of the other when they can't make contact, when they present each other with implied threats of estrangement, and when they trigger catastrophic expectations.

To develop a foundation for change, I suggest the following steps:

1. You, the parent, need to spell out your fears so your teenager can hear them.

2. You, the adolescent, need to be able to say what is happening with you and be believed. You need to be able to tell your fears and know you will be heard without criticism or ridicule.

3. You, the parent, need to show willingness to listen and to show that you understand. Understanding does not equal excusing. It simply provides a clear basis from which to go forward.

4. You, the adolescent, can make it clear that you need your parent to listen, not to give advice unless you ask for it.

5. You, the parent, need to understand that your teenager may not act on the advice you give.

Now a meaningful dialogue can take place between people who feel equal in value and therefore can develop new, constructive behavior. A stronger relationship can also develop as a result.

Many adults have not mastered the skill and art of being congruent, so even when they want to be congruent, they seem to be controlling (see Chapter 2 on self-esteem). I have never seen parents lose credibility in their teenager's eyes when they admit honestly what they don't know or when they indicate they identify with some pain or negative feeling their teenager may have ("I was scared, too . . ." or "I know what it feels like to lie," etc.).

Through conducting hundreds of repair processes between parents and teenagers, I learned most parents have not completed their own adolescence. They really don't feel like the wise leaders they are supposed to be. Under these circumstances, it is hard for them to help their adolescents learn what they have not themselves yet learned. They have my compassion. Many adults try to handle this by faking. That is, they try to act like they know when they don't. That works sometimes but is ill advised as a blanket technique. Teenagers almost always know what is going on.

I encourage parents to take credit for their inadequacies and limitations, making their acknowledgment into a badge of honesty and therefore high self-worth. The parent and child can then become a team and work together in the interests of both.

One instance that I remember concerned a teenager who was not attending school. Both parents had pleaded and threatened, all to no avail. I learned that neither of these parents had completed their education, and they vowed their son would complete his. They wanted to give to him what they had not received. It was a love act on their part toward their son; but because of the way it was presented, he interpreted it as control. When I facilitated a trust between the parents and their son, all were able to hear each other. It turned out that everyone agreed on the goal. Once he understood his parents' fears, the son was able to trust them and to invest his energy in going back to school because he wanted to, and not because he felt compelled to.

The troublemaker in this scenario was not the goal of education, but the prevailing win–lose attitude. This is inherent in the power messages of "I will tell you what to do and you will do it," "It is good for you, you have to," and so on. Predictably, the teenager answered, "You can't tell me what to do"; "I won't do it"; and "I don't care about education." Many parents and children get into this fix. I call it cutting off your nose to spite your face. The words were about school; the counter- or meta-message was about power and control ("Who has the right to tell who what to do?"). The parents intended to be helpful, yet their effect was to create a war (see chapter on Communication).

I find this particular behavior is the biggest troublemaker between parents and teenagers. In fact, when a conflict over power and control exists between any two people, regardless of age, rank, or sex, trouble will brew. It manifests itself in the familiar communication stances I described earlier: blaming, placating, being super-reasonable or computing, and being irrelevant.

This win–lose attitude makes up the power struggle. The underlying issue in every power struggle is who will win; and people usually assume that only one will. I believe that it is a personal tragedy if either loses: their relationship suffers, and their self-esteem drops. Parents and teenagers need each other, and they can learn to use win-–win attitudes. For example, the young person says, "It's only Wednesday, and I'm out of money. I need some more." The parent who practices win–lose will say, "Too bad. I have no more, so you don't get any." In a win–win approach, the parent says, "That's happened to me, too, and it doesn't feel very good. I won't have any money until payday, but let's see how we can get what you want, and maybe we can learn how to budget your money better."

In the first way (controlling), the parent is trying to teach by punishment. In win–win, the parent teaches negotiation and creativity, and reinforces caring. Money was not a solution in either mode.

Teenagers have a right to expect their parents to be leaders in the growth process, and honesty is extremely important in such dealings. It is actually the only basis for trust. Teenagers will not be honest with adults who are not honest with them. In this case, it is emotional honesty that counts most.

A big part of the adolescent period is to find out what the world is all about. Adolescents become philosophical, questioning everything under the sun. I think this is good. Adults can benefit by the scrutiny that adolescents give our sacred cows and their eagerness to try out lots of things.

Adults need to support this discovery process so that everyone enjoys maximum outcomes with minimum disruptive risk. Families with people in the adolescent stage can thus refresh their lives if they choose to. A lot of adults have become jaded about hope and about their conclusions.

Their adolescents' quests and questions give them a chance to review and renew.

Adults need to be clear about their boundaries and bottom lines and act in accordance with them. Each needs to know where she or he stands with the other. This is what respect is all about. Each of us has limits.

For example, if you, the parent, figure out from your best reality that you can spare your car once a week for your teenager to use, stick to that. If you give the car out on a whimsical basis ("You can have it sometimes") or on a punitive basis ("You didn't do such and such, so you can't have it"), you are likely to run into trouble. Be honest and real about your own boundaries.

One goal for adults that gains respect from the teenager is keeping agreements. Don't give a promise unless you mean it. If you sacrifice your boundaries so your child will love you, the chances are the child will mistrust you and you will resent the child. Everyone loses.

Have you noticed that parents and teenagers rarely enjoy the same activities? Teenagers want to go off in different directions and often with their peers. This is quite normal. It does not mean that the teenager is deserting or rejecting the family. Peers often assume a stronger role than parents during this time. Parents need to find genuine ways to receive their adolescents' friends. Parents also need to recognize that adolescents are dissolving their basic dependence on parents and are preparing for the adult stage. Instead, parents have to give up being control figures in their child's life. Parents need to become helpful guides. In this spirit, parents and adolescents can continue to have in common their humanness and mutual respect.

Remember that when one is an adolescent, one feels forty years old one minute, and five the next. This is, of course, how it needs to be. When adults say critically to adolescents, "Act your age," they forget the confusion teenagers experience in this stage. When adolescents know they are loved, valued, and accepted unconditionally, they can accept responsible adult leadership more easily. They desperately need to have adults who care for them who can and will discreetly plan this journey with them.

Instead of surrounding the adolescent with a lot of restraints and restrictions, concentrate instead on developing a relationship based on honesty, humor, and realistic guidelines. *More than anything else, adolescents need sensitive, flexible relationships with trusted adults.* If they have this, they can weather the storms that are sure to rise from time to time through this exciting, scary, turbulent period. At the end awaits a wonderful jewel: a newly evolved person. Give your blessings to the good relationships your adolescents have with other mature adults. Teens may need explicit permission to do this (so that they do not feel disloyal).

Give all you can when you have your adolescent's listening ear, which you will have when you are trusted. When you don't have that attention, don't demand it. It won't work anyway and will only build walls if you insist. Wait until the ambience is better. You may remember how little enthusiasm you had for the adults who insisted that you follow their advice, instead of helping you to discover what you needed to learn.

Above all, adolescents are striving to accomplish their autonomy and identity. They endure many false starts, unrewarding paths, and, often, hormonal storms. These are natural steps in development. In hormonal storms, teens experience intense feelings. It's important that parents refrain from discounting these strong emotions. ("It's only puppy love," for example, or "Yeah, yeah, *every*body goes through this. C'mon, snap out of it and get on with your life!").

I once heard a famous sculptor say that he waits to see what the stone will bring forth instead of imposing his ideas on it. Parenting adolescents is even more like that.

I want to switch now to the teenager's perspective. "What I need most is to feel loved and valued, no matter how foolish I may seem. I need someone who believes in me because I do not always believe in myself. Frankly, I often feel terrible about myself. I feel I am not strong enough, bright enough, handsome or pretty enough, for anyone to really care about me. Sometimes I feel I know everything and I can stand against the world. I feel intensely about everything.

"I need someone who will listen to me uncritically for what helps me to center myself. When I have a defeat, lose a friend or a game, I feel like the world has collapsed. I need a loving hand to comfort me. I need a place to cry where no one will make fun of me. On the contrary, I need someone who will just be with me. I also need someone to say 'stop' to me clearly. But please don't give me a lecture and remind me of all my past goofs. I already know them and feel guilty about them.

"Above all, I need you to be honest with me about me and about you. Then I can trust you. I want you to know I love you. Please don't have your feelings hurt when I love others. That won't take away from you. Please keep on loving me."

When we love people, we tend to want to make them perfect, in our eyes. This often results in meddling, which no one—adult or adolescent—likes. Using the congruent forms of communication you've learned in this book, you know you can stop meddling. You need to learn to recognize meddling when you are doing it.

You will know that the journey of an adolescent has been successfully completed when he or she shows to handle dependence, independence, and interdependence; has a high sense of self-worth; and knows how to be congruent. These new attributes will probably include a transformed relationship to you, the parents. It will reflect a willingness to work together as a team.

I suggest that at the end of the adolescent stage, the guides (usually the parents) give a party. Its purpose will be to clearly validate the new place between parents and child. The person is no longer adolescent; he or she is adult. This ritual celebration brings parents and child together as peers in the world.

I feel that adolescence has served its purpose when a person arrives at adulthood with a strong sense of self-esteem, the ability to relate intimately, to communicate congruently, to take responsibility, and to take risks. The end of adolescence is the beginning of adulthood. What hasn't been finished then will have to be finished later. I am counting on more enlightened guidance through adolescence by parents and other adults to bring forth young adults who will be capable of being better people and making this world a safer, more exciting, and more human place to live.

21

Positive Pairing

This chapter is written especially for all people who are part of a pair. That means just about everyone: we have sisters, brothers, mothers, fathers, husbands, wives, friends, and coworkers. Each of these constitutes a pair for us.

The skills in *positive pairing* make an important difference in our lives. Conversely, pain or trouble of any sort is usually a symptom of negative pairing. In the following pages, I would like to give you both the flavor and substance of what I mean by positive pairing.

Let us start our learning about positive pairing by thinking of each transaction as a creative act worthy of our total attention and focus. Let us further consider that each person is a human treasure and miracle, rare and irreplaceable. If we remember this, then we can invent each interaction specifically for that one occasion. The next interaction will be in a different time, context, and state of being, and will call for a different kind of exchange.

As we saw in the chapter on couples, any pair consists of three parts: two individuals (you and me) and the relationship between those two individuals (us). Positive pairing allows room for each of these parts. Each part is of equal value. Positive pairers know that if any one of the parts is denied, suppressed, or pushed into the background, the positive nature of the relationship disappears.

For each person to flourish, each needs psychological permission to be him- or herself, to develop these interests and parts that especially fit. Furthermore, each partner willingly and knowledgeably supports the other in this regard and, in turn, is supported. Each is respected by the other, each is autonomous, and each is unique.

The "us" part is where the partners deal with each other. Here they experience the joy, the pleasure—and sometimes the struggle—of being with each other, making decisions and operating as teammates. This relationship has a life of its own. The nature of the relationship will be greatly influenced by the way each partner feels about her- or himself (self-worth) and the way they communicate.

Think of the way the different pairs in your family operate. Are you in some relationships within your family where you would like to practice more positive pairing?

Various forms of submission and domination characterize the pair model that most of us grew up with. I will henceforth refer to this model as the *threat-and-reward* model. The stances in this model are: one person kneels below, looking up; the other stands above, looking down. Symbolically, one is on top and the other is on the bottom. The communication is likely to include some form of blaming and placating. In the extreme form, this is the picture of the victim–victimizer pair.

In a variation of this, one person carries the other on his or her back. This stance epitomizes dependency.

To make pairing positive, each person has to stand on his or her own feet. In relationships modeled on threats and rewards, each person holds the attitude that she or he is unequal to the other in value. For example, they might describe themselves as little in relation to big, poor in relation to rich, powerless in relation to powerful, and so forth. These designations are then rationalized in terms of role, precedent, background, and prejudice. For example, a child and an adult might value themselves differently, as might a woman and a man, student and teacher, or non-white and white.

Relationships based on an equality of value include such distinctions as a description of only a part of the person, not a definition of the person. Whether people are little, big, poor, or rich diminishes neither their value as human beings nor their potentials or possibilities. Positive pairing is based on the gut-and-bone acceptance of this idea. When we change our consciousness to fit this, we can create real safety and peace in the world.

We are still poorly prepared for being living models in relationships of equality. People's hearts have always wanted to feel accepted by other people but somehow their minds could not always comprehend how to do this. Not having this deep-seated sense of human equality is probably the real source of war. We have a lot of new learning to do about positive pairing.

The central factors in equality are giving value to one's self and being really responsible through standing squarely on one's own feet.

"My Declaration of Self-Esteem" says it well (see the end of chapter 3).

How long does it take and what has to happen for someone who was brought up to say "yes" to everything (placate) to become autonomous and say their real "yes's" and "no's"? Similarly, how long does it take someone who has always been in charge to share his or her power? The good news is that it will probably take only as long as you need to create a picture of what you want, take courage, and create the plan to make it happen. I hope this book will help you with your picture and strengthen your courage to act.

Specifically, make a map that shows all your family pairs. If you are a member of a family or other living group, you are paired in some way with each other member. I am doing the following map from the vantage point of Eloise, a 16 year old. You can vary your map any way you need to include all the members of your family.

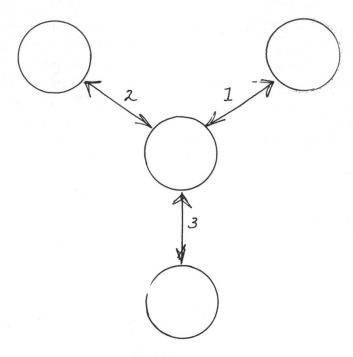

ELOISE'S MAP

Eloise is part of three pairs. Each of her pairings is likely to be different. This is true for each person in the family.

It will be helpful and informative for each person in the family or group to do this and then share findings with each other. After finishing, each person looks at each pair. Notice in which ones you feel equal. In which ones do you feel submissive or dominant? In which ones do you feel dependent? In which ones do you feel you are a caretaker? Can you already see some ways that you can change that will make a difference? (To remind yourself of possibilities, re-read chapters 4, 5 and 6 on communication.)

As we go through further descriptions of positive pairing, you may see some further ways to reshape your relationships. The goal is to feel equal and valued in your various pairs, to hold that feeling toward each pair mate, and to meet issues with honesty, courage, and creativity. You don't have to get anyone's permission to do this, any more than the sun needs permission to shine. You are in charge of your own contribution to positive pairing.

You may feel that your relationships are embedded in concrete and could never change. Chances are you feel that way only because those patterns have gone on so long. However, if it really turns out that there are no further possibilities, let go of the relationship. We need to know when to stop trying. There is no point in continuing to bump your head against a stone wall. Too many people have pinned themselves on the cross of completing what they started without asking themselves whether it fits, is feasible, or is even desirable.

It is also important to exhaust all possibilities before we let go. Overhauling a relationship sometimes takes patience, imagination, and innovativeness. Many times all that has to be done is to give it time and attention.

If you have such a relationship now, start by inviting your partner to join you. Then share your wishes with that partner. Most of the time your partners will be happy to help. Some partners will be shy or fearful at first and need to be reassured. Many people are afraid they will be blamed. Your partners need to be reassured that this is not an exercise in scolding. Rather, it is an experience in loving.

With your pair mate, read through the various points in this chapter's earlier description of positive pairing. Picture yourself and your partner as already having achieved what you want. When you do this, you send hope to yourself and are no longer sending negative energy.

Learning how to pair positively is new to many of us. Let us give ourselves support, love, and patience while we enter a relatively new world of equality of value with all other human beings. Each relationship is as we experience it, pair by pair, and person by person. The stakes are high: replacing the threat-and-reward model with one of positive pairing could improve global as well as personal relations.

Teach yourself to become receptive and aware whenever you interact with another person. Let all your attention be focused for that time on that partner. Remember the position that facilitates good contact: being at arm's length and eye level, with each person feeling physically comfortable. If there is a height difference, find something for one to stand on to put yourselves at eye level. This position will help each of you see, hear, understand, and listen better. This position also gives you maximum freedom to move. You are free to touch, to move closer or farther away. Creating this context for children often produces miracles in their feeling of acceptance and thence changes in any negative behavior.

Once you have established your communication context, focus on being clear and congruent. This means being honest and direct. Give yourself permission to be fully present: to let your mind and attention stay with your partner and not with something outside, such as the call you need to make to Aunt Elsie.

If you can't be present, don't attempt contact. You will be disappointed in your results if you do. It is very unnerving to be with someone whose body is present, but whose attention is somewhere else. If someone asks to engage you when you can't be present, simply say so and arrange another time.

Prepared to be liberal with humor, love, respect, and good will, you will hit the jackpot. The more serious the situation, the more you will need the above. Remember that a relationship lacking any occasional stimulation and excitement gets jaded. A little horsing around can be a big help.

A relationship is like a bud opening a little at a time, or like the universe gradually revealing its secrets. It does it through love, timing, and exploration.

I believe that having fun, playing the clown, being the child, or doing silly things together also give the same adrenalin response as, and are much healthier than, fighting. Appreciate the child within you and each other. Especially in families, let the child in each of you romp. Your kids don't need to have all the fun. Having fun together is a

positive bonding. Preparing for your interactions in this way adds wonderful possibilities; you can also be clear-headed and clear-thinking when you are willing to follow the simple steps I have just presented.

To summarize this chapter, the ingredients of all successful and satisfying pairing are the same, whether the two people are lovers, parents, children, siblings, friends, or co-workers. These roles merely decide the form and context in which interaction takes place. Likewise, factors such as age, race, nationality, gender, and status serve simply to individualize each person. When pairing occurs between people who occupy unequal power positions, it is important to remember that their positions are not the same as their personal value. Personal value remains the same.

In any stage of any relationship, each interaction includes an opportunity for clarifying, strengthening, broadening, and reshaping the pairing. This in turn nourishes the participants.

As you contact your pair member, see that person as a unique being. Do the same for yourself. Recognize further that the uniqueness of each partner can continue to emerge: change is frequent, and new possibilities constantly open up. When we accept this, we significantly enlarge the boundaries of ourselves, as members of the pair, and of the relationship itself. This paves the way for that exquisite experience of feeling in tune with another, and perhaps even dancing to similar drummers.

The factors in a positive pairing relationship are:

1. Each person stands firmly on his or her own feet and is autonomous.
2. Each person can be counted on to say real "yes's" and "no's"—in other words, to be emotionally honest.
3. Each person can ask for what she or he wants.
4. Each acknowledges and takes responsibility for her or his actions.
5. Each can keep promises.
6. Each can be counted on to be kind, fun to be around, courteous, considerate, and real.
7. Each takes full freedom to choose to comment on what is going on.
8. Each supports the other's dreams in whatever way possible. Together, they cooperate instead of competing.

All of this is doable. It is sensible and simple. The difficulties center around the pull of old experiences from the *threat–reward* model, from ignorance and lack of a positive model. Positive pairing can help us shift to a new way of being together.

We live in a world that seems to foster alienation, competition, and suspicion instead of connectedness and trust. Many of us fear that what we yearn for can never happen, so we resign ourselves to doom or something second rate. Yet positive pairing can happen; it is happening, and it can happen more.

This is the scope, flavor, and substance of positive pairing. Join me in making it a more frequent reality.

22

Spirituality

Fifty years ago, no one except those connected with religion would have thought that spirituality was an appropriate subject for discussion in a nonreligious context. Some may still see spirituality as naive or irrelevant to the business of living. I believe it is our connection to the universe and is basic to our existence, and therefore is essential to our therapeutic context.

My personal ideas and understanding of spirituality began with my own experiences as a child, growing up on a dairy farm in Wisconsin. Everywhere I saw growing things. Very early, I understood that growth was life force revealing itself, a manifestation of spirit. I looked at the tiny seeds I planted and watched them grow into big plants. Little chickens emerged from eggs and little piglets came from a sow's belly. Then I saw my brother being born. I marvelled. This was something grand and wonderful. I felt the mystery, the excitement, and the awesomeness. Those wondrous feelings remain with me today, and I think they have guided me in finding ways to help people grow.

We know how growth works, but we do not know how it starts. No one, as yet, has been able to invent an egg or seed capable of reproducing itself in any living thing. I respect the power of life; I know it to be both frail and tough. Any life can be snuffed out in a second, and it can also endure through impossible odds.

My reverence for life was set early in life. No plants

ever grew better because I demanded that they do so or because I threatened them. Plants grew only when they had the right conditions and were given proper care, which, for me, includes loving them and sometimes talking to them. Finding the right place and the proper nourishment for plants—and people as well—is a matter of continual investigation and vigilance.

Each of us emerges as a bud on a universal spiritual tree. That tree links *all* human beings through its roots. Each of us can learn how to become a wise leader who will love, take care of, and nurture the precious life we have been given.

When we ourselves have been nourished, we can then be appropriate in our nourishment of others. This is one reason that I recommend every community have a "cuddle room" where people can come to get spiritual and psychological nourishment. Fortunately, some churches have done something in this direction, providing a room for respite and personal connection.

Creating such caretaking approaches and crystalizing the inner recognition (what I call bone knowledge) is the realization that we are spiritual beings in human form. This is the essence of spirituality. How we apply our spiritual essence shows how we value life.

The creation of life comes from a power much greater than our own. The challenge of becoming more fully human is to be open to and to contact that power we call by many names, God being one frequently used. I believe that successful living depends on our making and accepting a relationship to our life force.

The physical connections to our spirituality are safely housed in our human seeds. Only when sperm and egg unite is the human seed complete and capable of becoming a human being. An egg and sperm alone are only storage tanks awaiting the great meeting. For me, seeds and birth are spirituality in action.

When the union between sperm and egg takes place, a fantastic event occurs. Powerful energy is released and a new human being—unique, no exact duplicate of anyone else, ever before—begins getting ready to burst forth onto this earth. I feel overpowered when I try to comprehend how this very tiny human embryo can produce something as big, complicated, and multifaceted as a person.

Moreover, this tiny seed contains all the ingredients for the intricate systems that make up a living, breathing human being. The life force not only oversees the growth in each seed, but channels the energy so each part gets what it needs.

Is this not a miracle? We need to find ways to cherish, enjoy, nurture, and effectively use this miracle. Your birth, my birth, everyone's birth is a spiritual event and a cause for celebration. Obviously, we need to provide the richest context possible so that each child can grow up to be fully

human. We are not at that point yet. For many, the miracle of birth is eclipsed by the grim conditions into which children are born. Nonetheless, when we accept the fact that each child contains the ingredients of a "walking and waking" miracle, we have a foundation for positive behavior on a world scale. Certainly, the family is the first place this happens. We are slowly moving to that kind of reverence for life.

In the effort to change behavior, it is easy to crush the spirit, thus crippling the body and dulling the mind. This approach is largely due to equating the value of a person with the nature of his or her behavior. Remembering that behavior is something we learn, on the other hand, we can simultaneously honor the spirit and foster more positive behavior.

Recognizing the power of spirit is what healing, living, and spirituality are all about. Many pay lip service to spirituality without living it. Conversely, the very effective Alcoholics Anonymous programs are built on the premise that when individuals accept and face their higher power, their life force is called upon and their healing begins. Literally thousands of people have shifted their lives from agony to joy and have become changed human beings through living this philosophy. No other approach has ever accomplished so much.

We are all unique manifestations of life. We are divine in our origins. We are also the recipients of what has gone before us, which gives us vast resources from which to draw. I believe that we also have a pipeline to universal intelligence and wisdom through our intuition, which can be tapped through meditation, prayer, relaxation, awareness, the development of high self-esteem, and a reverence for life. This is how I reach my spirituality.

We can more easily reach this wise part of ourselves when we are calm inside, when we feel good about ourselves, and when we know how to take positive approaches. I refer to this as being centered.

I work on learning to love the spirit unconditionally while at the same time recognizing, reorienting, and transforming behavior to fit ethical and moral ideals. This is one of the most urgent challenges of our time. My spirituality equals my respect for the life force in myself and all living things.

The following centering exercise is one that I practice; by doing it, you too can deepen your experience of spirituality.

Sit comfortably on a chair with your feet on the floor. Gently close your eyes and simply notice your breathing.

*Now silently go inside and give yourself a message of apprecia-
tion that might sound something like this: "I appreciate me." This
is to give your spirit strength from your actions.*

*Next, visualize yourself affirming your connection with your
creator.*

From time to time as you continue this exercise, be in
touch with your breathing.

*Now go deeper inside and locate the place where you keep the
treasure known by your name. As you approach this sacred place,
notice your resources: your ability to see, hear, touch, taste, and
smell, to feel and to think, to move and to speak and to choose.*

*Linger long enough at each of these resources to remember all
the many times you used them, how you are using them now, and
know that they will be available to you in the future. Then let
yourself remember that these resources are part of you and are capable of many new sights, sounds, and so forth. Realize that you can
never really be helpless as long as you recognize you have these
resources.*

*Let yourself remember that as a creature in this universe, you
are the recipient of the energy from the center of the earth, which
brings you your ability to be grounded, and to make sense; the energy from the heavens, which brings you your intuition, imagination,
and inspiration; and the energy from other human beings who are
ready to be with you and have you with them.*

*Remind yourself to be free to look at and listen to everything,
but to choose only that which fits you. Then you can clearly say yes
to those things that fit you and no to the things that don't. You will
then be able to do positive things for yourself and others instead of
negative things such as fighting.*

Now again, give yourself permission to breathe.

This can take one minute or five minutes. You decide.
Commit this exercise to memory and practice it often. Every time I do this, I am again reminded who I am and given
an opportunity to feel a new sense of strength which becomes my link to life.

I want to end this chapter with another autobiograph-
ical note.

I started a private practice over thirty-five years ago. Because I was a woman and had nonmedical training, the people who were available to me were the "rejects" of other therapists and the very "high-risk" persons, those who had been abused, were alcoholic, "psychopathic," and generally seen as untreatable. But many of these people began to blossom as the treatment proceeded. I think now that this happened because I was working to contact their spirits, loving them as I went along. The question for me was never whether they had spirits, but how I could contact them. That is what I set out to do. My means of making contact was in my own congruent communication and the modeling that went with it.

It was as though I saw through to the inner core of each being, seeing the shining light of the spirit trapped in a

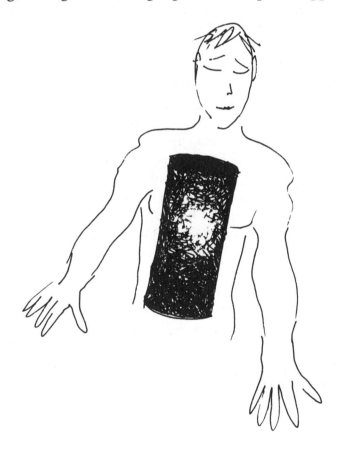

thick black cylinder of limitation and self-rejection. My effort was to enable the person to see what I saw; then, together, we could turn the dark cylinder into a large, lighted screen and build new possibilities.

I consider the first step in any change is to contact the spirit. Then together we can clear the way to release the energy for going toward health. This too is spirituality in action.

23

The Later Years

Successful living in the later years begins with a process of transition, saying good-bye to what was, in order to say hello to what will be. Among the big events that herald the beginning of the later years are menopause and retirement. These are concrete manifestations that cannot be denied.

The energy released by these endings can be put to new uses when we are ready to do so. For example, when a woman has achieved menopause, she no longer has to worry about pregnancy and can enter into sex with new abandon. Likewise, not having to go to work every day frees that time to be used for something else. This is all quite logical. However, to make this happen freely, one must go through the steps of transition. Going through the transition process is always unsettling in the sense that we are making changes; a plan helps provide the structure.

The following five steps will help you to complete transition and create a new foundation for living in your later years.

1. Acknowledge that an end has occurred. This means you are facing a reality: "It is true. I am retired."
2. Grieve the loss. This means putting words to the feelings about the loss, the resentments, fear, and rejection.
3. Acknowledge the positive parts of that which has just ended. This means to honor your experience by openly

appreciating what you got from it. Very few things are entirely bad.

4. Notice and acknowledge that your life now has spaces open to be filled with new possibilities. By the time you have finished this step, you will probably be feeling more balanced and centered.

5. Now you are ready to welcome new possibilities. Take action. Center yourself, focus your energy, create what you want, and move on. Go forward with your life.

Put on your explorer's hat and ready yourself to make another of life's journeys. As on previous journeys, you will look for the meaning that fits your life now. Thinking about it, you realize you have done this many times before. Going to school for the first time, menstruating or shaving for the first time were such journeys. They were landmarks after which life had different possibilities. You came through with new learnings and, consequently, you came to a different place in your life. The same will be true now. However, this time you may be more conscious of the steps involved.

Going through transition is often intimidating and produces anxiety. Give yourself time and patience. Increase your level of awareness, and strengthen your resolve. Don't hurry. Each transition develops its own rhythms. Sometimes it may take a year or more to complete all the steps. Arriving there, you will feel ready to take on new challenges.

To give energy to your transition process, give some transition parties from time to time. Pick something you are ready to say good-bye to and then something you want to say hello to. Develop a loss–gain ritual. Invite your friends who may be involved in the same process. You can support each other and have fun at the same time. Each transition must be wrestled with if your subsequent years are to be successful.

I have noticed that when people do not go through an appropriate transition, they can't seem to focus on a new

start. Their energy and attention still seem directed toward the past, which leaves little for the present. This may result in a feeling of enduring life rather than enjoying it. It also creates a feeling of depression, which is exacerbated by negative images and fantasies of what living in the later years will be like.

A composite of commonly held negative pictures of the later years goes something like this: "When I am old, I will no longer be interested in or capable of sexual satisfaction. I will become physically feeble, unsteady, and perhaps hard of hearing or have difficulties in seeing. I will be sick because old age and sickness go together. My brain will deteriorate; I will be intellectually dull. I will be unattractive, wrinkled, and fat. I will annoy people with my neediness, my complaining, or withdrawal. I will have to relegate myself to TV soap operas and busy myself with make-do work. I expect to be lonely and rejected. After all, who wants an old person like me around anyway?

"I will sit in a rocking chair, gazing vacantly out the window, muttering to myself, ignoring my surroundings, and looking stupid. I will feel defeated, dependent, and useless. Everything that is important for me will have already happened. I will resign myself to waiting for the ultimate end, death."

If I thought this was the fate that awaited me in my later years, I would do *anything* and *everything* to avoid it, even if it killed me. I am over seventy as I write this book. In many ways, I feel my life is just starting. For people who really believe the gruesome picture sketched above, getting older must hold terrible dread. Many handle these paralyzing fears by valiantly trying to ignore and deny the signs of aging.

This just adds to the self-increasing tension and develops strong self-hatred which, in turn, makes one vulnerable to disease, depression, and unhappiness. Our selves do not like to be put down; they fight back. The self wants to grow older gracefully and be loved unconditionally during the process. We are made to be healthy at any age.

Another kind of fantasy comes from people who are caught up in the drudgery of their day-to-day work. They live for the day when they will retire. Then, as in fairy tales, their dreams will come true. They will not have to work. There will be no ticking clocks and no unreasonable bosses to deal with. They will be able to do what they please. Life will be wonderful.

People with these fantasies who did not develop the skills they needed to enjoy retirement may soon find that retirement becomes a nightmare. Harry worked hard all his life, pushing and shoving to get ahead. He prepared for retirement by buying and outfitting a trailer in deluxe style so he could be his own boss and travel wherever he wished. He was determined to be a free man. Selling the house over his wife Ellen's objections, he reassured her that all would be wonderful. In the end, she unhappily resigned herself to those assurances.

With their house sold and their trailer ready, Harry and Ellen set off for *his* nirvana the day after his retirement party. Within two months of living in such a confined space, they were not speaking to each other. Within six months, Harry became terminally ill; by year's end, he was dead.

Actually, Harry was a dictatorial man who wanted everything his way. He had few skills for congruent communication, little patience, and very low self-esteem. He made no allowance for the important and necessary transition between the life he had lived and what was ahead. The outcome was ghoulish. During his illness, Ellen refused to take care of him. When he died, her anger was still so great that she did not go to his funeral.

His plan might have worked had he and Ellen planned this new stage in their lives together. They then would have consciously and realistically prepared for this very different way of being together. After years of spending only one waking hour together in the morning and two in the evening, they now were together twenty-four hours a day. From a spacious three-bedroom house which included a workroom for each, they now were in a space about the size of one medium-sized room. It takes a lot of self-worth, a very special relationship, and lots of humor to be happy under these circumstances. They asked the impossible of each other.

Given their available resources, what else might have been possible? What if Harry or Ellen had experimented with life in a trailer for a month to find out what that kind of living was like? They could have kept their home meanwhile and continued to have options.

They might have become aware that the two of them were not ready for this drastic step; they might have made other plans. Or, they might have found out what they needed to live in this new way and taken time to learn it.

The experience of Ellen and Harry points to the need for keeping options open and carefully considering any radical change in lifestyle. To have happy and productive experiences in later years, it is important to let yourself know clearly what your pictures and fantasies really are. These pictures have a strong influence on your adjustment. Knowing them consciously enables you to deal with them and compare them with reality as you know it. These pictures are sources of thought, and thought is powerful.

Let yourself really know these fantasies. Paint them, write them down, tell them to a friend, share them with your partner, or record them on tape and then listen back. You can be sure that if

these fantasies are negative, they will become the inner voices that will inhibit and prohibit you from having what you want.

If your images are positive, they will support you and cheer you on when you get discouraged. Negative pictures rattle around inside of you, affecting you without your knowing it. We need to give these fantasies an airing.

Until we let them out, some fantasies are not even apparent to us. We may not know we have them. *If you have never let yourself be conscious of your fantasies, let them emerge now. Ask yourself, "What will it be like when I . . . ?" and simply see what comes to mind.*

Interesting, positive effects may follow. As you listen to your fantasies, consult your inner wisdom and ask yourself if you believe what you are saying. You may find that even other parts of you think you may be talking nonsense. That is one of the concrete benefits of giving a voice to your fantasies.

The following questions may help you find the source of these fantasies. As you consider these questions, you may even loosen your attachment to certain images or ideas and free yourself to evaluate them in the light of reason, common sense, and your present desires.

Who have you known who was old?

What was the nature of your relationship to that person?

What did you hear from and observe about that person?

What were you told about what it is like to be old?

How did you imagine yourself being when you reached your later years?

Now check out your information against current facts and feelings.

Through researching the process of aging in healthy people, we now know that we are not doomed to decrepitude, disease, and degeneration simply because of our age. Those are outcomes of illness, not of age.

As people move into later life, they will, of course, experience physiological changes. That is life manifesting itself.

John W. Rowe, M.D., a professor of medicine at Harvard Medical School, states that "the person who ages successfully has a life style, an economic status, and personality that enhance, rather than impair, his or her ability to cope with the few changes that do accompany age" (in Robert Henig, "Aging Successfully," *AARP News Bulletin,* Jan. 1988).

A separate article, coauthored by Dr. Robert Kahn, states that "Within the category of normal aging, a distinction can be made between usual aging . . . and successful aging."

This fits in with my clinical experience. The foundation of anyone's ability to cope successfully is high self-esteem. If you don't already have it, you can always develop it. The aging experience is an individual affair. As in former changes, successful outcomes rest almost totally on the creative coping that comes from someone with high self-esteem. The negative picture I drew earlier is more likely to be rooted in low self-worth than in age. Age has little to do with our unsatisfying interactions with others, our dissatisfaction with ourselves and our work, or the way we dishonor life, which includes our own and that of the universe. We can learn anew at any age how to love ourselves (have high self-esteem), develop satisfying relationships, find work and other activities that are enriching, and honor life and the universe. *Learning* will go a long way not only to relieve pain and troubles, but also to open doors to a more wonderful life.

I keep coming back to my old allies, high self-worth and congruent communication. For most of us, learning these skills is a life-long process. I repeat, our *skills and attitudes are all learned.* Our limitations lie in our resistance to learning something new. For many, change is a scary process. Some people immobilize themselves with the adage that you can't teach an old dog new tricks. It is hard for them to grasp that our brains continue to function throughout our lives.

We now have reliable information that challenges the negative assumptions of the past. Research findings on the aging process of healthy people show the following:

1. Our capacity to learn increases as we age. The mind continues to grow when it is stimulated.

2. The capacity for sexual excitement and satisfaction continues and, under some conditions, increases. We don't lose our sexual interest just because we are older.

3. The body demonstrates great regenerative power when it teams up with high self-esteem, purposeful activity, physical movement, and satisfying love relationships. It is living tissue, and it responds well to good care.

The big challenge for the later years is to act on what we know about health. Acquaint yourself with research findings on aging and trade in any negative pictures for some positive, exciting ones. A new picture based on health would be something like this: "When I am older, I expect to be healthy. I will be wiser. Having time and interest, I will create stimulation to enjoy my life. I will experiment with new things.

"I will be able to enjoy myself alone. I will also continue being able to connect with other people when I choose.

"I will be physically active. I will wear beautiful colors. My body will be supple and good looking.

"I will have energy. I will shine from the reflection of myself."

The challenge now is: What do I have to *learn* to accomplish this? *Please remember your thoughts, attitudes, and perceptions have great power.* Seeing a glass filled halfway, you can describe it as being half full, which will direct your energy upward and will give you positive feelings. Or you can see it as half empty, which will send your energy downward and give you negative feelings. Both descriptions are accurate,

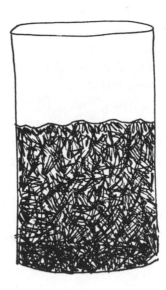

but they bring up quite different feelings. I recommend that we picture the glass as half full.

It makes sense to look at things positively. I believe that reframing our attitudes from negative to positive creates an invitation to attract other positive energy. Smiling at someone who smiles back is an example of this.

I would like to promote the idea that one possible outcome of growing older is becoming wiser. Healthy people can be fountains of wisdom and experience and can be helpful partners to younger people and to each other. What if every community had an "Elders Council"?

I know of some exciting programs that bring older people together with young children and adolescents to form a kind of grandparent–grandchild relationship. In these days when families are so scattered, this can be a valuable opportunity for all.

One's attitude and spirit are powerful factors in physical, emotional, and spiritual wellness at any age. Of course, the body will show signs of use and wear as we grow older: we get gray hair and our metabolism changes. Our reaction times change, and recovery from illness takes longer. But the human spirit, attitude, self-worth, and emotional responses only get better with age. These are like good wine.

Very few communities have done much to organize innovative programs based on the resources of the older person. Almost every community has Senior Citizen programs and health-care facilities, but too few have programs through which older people can contribute in a meaningful way to the community. Perhaps you, a reader of this book, might organize such a service through your church or other community facility—a program in which everyone benefits.

I have often been impressed by how quickly older people become more vital, creative, and healthy once they begin to be excited by their possibilities and decide to live their lives, rather than "dying" them. At funerals, I feel the saddest for those who really never lived.

I believe research will prove what we already know clinically: that age is a concept in our heads. Low self-worth, poor nutrition, lack of stimulation, inadequate living conditions, isolation, friendlessness, and negative relationships all contribute to making us vulnerable to physical and mental ill health. The antidote is high self-worth, good nutrition, mental and physical stimulation, attractive and healthy living conditions, satisfying connections with other people, intimate human contact, nourishing relationships, and clear purposes.

Structure is another important dimension of the later years. Retirement is new and unknown. Just as in adolescence, you have not been there before. There is no one who tells you what to do. The clock and the calendar become superfluous. The 8-to-5 workday dividers are removed, and you are responsible for structuring your entire day. After outside authority has done it for so long, designing your own life is a monumental challenge. Now you have to develop a structure that is tailor-made to support you.

Retirement is a testing ground for your personal coping skills, your maturity, and the nature of your relationships.

You can look at this as a wonderful opportunity to find out what you need. For instance, you can learn about your flexibility to adjust, your level of self-esteem, your triggers to low self-esteem, your entrenched habits, and the rhythm of your moods, in ways that were not apparent before.

Many people in relationships flounder seriously at this time. Not only does the new situation create a new context, but it may challenge the effectiveness of what currently exists. All your relationships come up for scrutiny. If your relationships need help, find a way to give it to them. Be your own Sherlock Holmes. Do what you need to do when you see the problem; don't let your shyness or fear get in the way (see the chapters on self-esteem and couples). When you find you are floundering, join (or create) a self-help support group, where you can get new perspectives. Talking things out with a group of caring people is healing as well as bonding. Professional counseling also helps.

Perhaps it is becoming more clear that our context does not automatically limit our opportunities. How we operate and how we cope in that context ultimately determine what happens to us. Living in the later years is simply another context for creative living.

If you already have developed high self-esteem and congruent communication, going into your later years is another opportunity for further growth. You know that your high self-worth depends on you and not your job, your money, or your connections. You can take a positive attitude or a negative one. The image that comes to mind again is of the sculptor who approaches the rough stone. What comes out will be what he finds there, rather than any preconception.

Many people reach their later years after being outwardly successful; inwardly, though, they may carry a chronic feeling of emptiness and loneliness. Deprived of the outer trappings of success—money, authority, status, etc.— these persons often experience depression or start acting out inappropriately when they enter their later years. What they counted on to be their strength is gone. If this is happening to you now, treat it as a discovery and look for ways to develop your self-worth. This need not be a lonely pursuit: relatively few people are brought up with high self-esteem and congruent coping skills.

Recently I gave a talk to a group of retired male executives. A man over seventy, formerly a bank president, told me, "I have no title. I have no office. I am nobody." (Within minutes, three other men told me versions of the same thing.) From an observer's point of view, this man really had achieved all the outward signs of success. What had yet to be developed was a sense of his *inner* worth. Since these four people regarded their titles and big offices as definers of their self-worth, retirement signified being ruthlessly torn apart and lying there bleeding and helpless.

When youth and young looks fade, when money, power, and position have gone, people can suffer great agonies if they equated these factors with personal value. Until they learn other ways to live, many take the paths of alcoholism, illness, divorce, depression, or suicide. Outside help is often needed at this time to discover how life can be transformed.

People don't have to wait until their later years to discover their inner worth. Beyond any outer evidence of success, the meaning and value of life are central to human existence. Once we can value life, we can experience our own spiritual awakening.

The first step is high self-esteem. This is an attitude we can learn at any age, and it's especially useful in our later years. For example, learning or having high self-worth enables us to continue uncovering our untapped resources. We can finish old dreams if they still seem appealing, or invent new ones. We are limited only by our ability to dream, and the energy to make the dreams manifest.

The later years are a time when you can take on new purposes in your life, perhaps something you have always wanted to try. If the yearning is still there, try it out. If you are looking for some entirely new direction, you may want to turn back to the fantasy exercises earlier in this chapter.

Our common human needs, present at any age, are listed below to remind you of what you already know but may have forgotten momentarily.

We need to love and be loved, to be noticed, recognized, and respected, to be literally and figuratively touched.

We need to matter and have a purpose.

We need to be stimulated and to learn new things.

We need to have satisfying and intimate relationships.

We need to have fun and humor.

We need to be economically secure.

We need to be mentally and physically healthy.

We need to belong.

We need to be part of a vital community of friends and colleagues.

We need to be in touch with our life force, our religion, our divinity.

These needs are present in all stages of our life, from infancy onward. We don't always learn them as we go along. In some stages, they are more in the foreground than in others. In our later years, it is important to ask ourselves where we are on all these points and then take steps to improve and acquire what we do not yet have.

Pause for a moment now and make a mental inventory of your present lifestyle.

Are you eating nourishing foods?

Are you exercising?

Are you paying attention to your emotional needs?

Are you continuing to develop your skill of congruent communications?

Are you having nurturing relationships?

Do you have a support group?

Are you developing your ability to listen, to be honest with yourself, to ask for what you want?

Have you developed effective ways to handle conflict?

Are you excited about your life and enjoying it?

Are you further developing your sense of humor and having fun with life?

Are you developing satisfying ways of loving and valuing yourself?

Are you cultivating an interest in learning new things?

Do you have good ways to relax?

Are you allowing yourself to learn from your mistakes?

Are you giving yourself full permission to love openly and deeply?

If you have reached the later years and cannot say "yes" to these questions, it is time to begin. Forgive yourself if you haven't learned before; your world has not been geared toward focusing on these ideas. Accomplishing these learnings will pay handsome dividends: profound positive effects on you, your health, and the way you approach the world. It is important to know that we have choices about what we want to do with our lives. We can choose to take a positive attitude or a negative one.

Make a list of the people you know personally, or have read or heard about, who have made significant contributions to their lives and the world in their later years. Learn about them. These can give you positive models for later life. Form a study group to pool your resources. We need to find positive, healthy models to counterbalance the effect of the terrible negative images from the past.

Find healthy people in their sixties or beyond. Look for them in health spas, church groups, YWCA and YMCA classes, Elder Hostels, travel clubs, square-dance groups, Senior Citizens groups, outdoor events, neighborhood organizations, and retirement associations. Notice their beauty, aliveness, and zest for living. Learn about their philosophy and their approach to life. Experience the richness and excitement of their company.

You might even get excited about interviewing some of these people, recording them on tape, and giving them a copy of your interview. We need a lot of positive exposure

to healthy people in their later years. Ugly, negative images of the older person are still quite powerful and need to be supplanted by powerfully positive, attractive images.

If you are a younger reader who has relationships with parents or other relatives in their later years, give them support. Treat them as responsible, responding human beings. Do not limit them by treating them as over the hill, pampering them, or being condescending to them. See them instead as human beings who are entering a vast arena in life that contains many unknowns and opportunities for taking new risks. Make room for the fact that they may feel anxiety, as people often do when going into new things.

I remember a family of grown-up children who brought their 84-year-old mother to me because she was showing signs of sexual interest in a "strange man" very near her age. She was "caught" sitting in the park with him. When I was able to convince the grown-up children that their mother, Anita, was acting responsibly toward her loneliness and her wish to grow, they could see her as a person: as Anita, not merely "Mother" or "Granny." She was more like them than different, but their images had affected their thoughts, perceptions, and behavior. These children had denied their mother her personhood.

Vitality is the outcome of high self-esteem. It goes a long way toward a positive outlook which nourishes the whole self. People of high self-esteem have eyes that shine; their spirits are round and inviting. They are open, have a wonderful sense of humor, and meet life with dignity and enthusiasm. They are efficient and knowledgeable as well. All of this is created by their positive attitude, which can be cultivated at any point in life with any person who is willing.

I have already mentioned the power of your thoughts to affect your health and outlook on life. Isn't it miraculous that a change in thinking can produce so many fine results?

Through their modeling, the older people of today are torchbearers for new images of what our older years can be.

Older persons are beginning to be recognized as one of society's great pools of resources, energy, wisdom, and creativity. This is good. It is also timely: by the year 2000, 30 percent of our population will be over the age of sixty. We will need their energy. The challenge for older persons of today is to show, by their example, the magnitude of their potential contribution to their own lives, their community, and the planet.

24

The Family in the Larger Society

Put together all the existing families and you have society. It is as simple as that. Whatever kind of training took place in the individual family will be reflected in the kind of society that these families create. And institutions such as schools, churches, businesses, and government are, by and large, extensions of family forms to nonfamily forms.

Families and societies are small and large versions of one another. Both are made up of people who have to work together, whose destinies are tied up with one another. Each features the components of a relationship: leaders perform roles relative to the led, the young to the old, and male to female; and each is involved with the process of decision-making, use of authority, and the seeking of common goals.

Some families teach individual conformity, some teach individual rebellion, some teach group responsibility, some teach *laissez-faire,* by default. Every family teaches something about how to deal with the outside world: how to get along, what to do about injustice and the ugly things in the world, and how to relate to all of it.

Parents can easily teach the *laissez-faire* attitude by building a cocoon around the children, guiding their steps so they won't see ugliness and injustice. In short, they protect their children from seeing any part of the seamy side of life. The world then becomes only what the children know, what they have been allowed to see.

Television is making this kind of protection a little

more difficult. It's pretty hard to stay in a cocoon when you can look at what is going on in the world through the window of TV. However, it is still possible to discount much of this because, after all, if you don't know too much about the world and haven't experienced what is going on, you can say it's foreign to you and forget it. Believe it or not, I still find people in the twelve-to-eighteen age bracket who have never seen a person of another race, have never seen a poor person or a rich person, or have not taken a bath in an honest-to-goodness bathtub. In the ghettos and high-rent districts of some cities, children can be isolated in their own neighborhoods and economic levels.

To understand fully what is going on today in terms of families and society, a little historical perspective might help. Once upon a time, in ancient society, the family was the only source for teaching its members what they needed to know to make it to adulthood. This meant learning how to care for and maintain themselves, how to care for and treat others, and how to treat the world of things. Available knowledge was limited, and one person—perhaps two—could know it all.

Initially the content of this learning was probably very simple. Life then was much more a matter of simple survival: how to stay alive, how to get enough to eat, how not to freeze to death or be killed by wild animals, and so on. One had to watch others and then learn for oneself.

Obviously, many of what we consider basic needs today would have been inappropriate and even irrelevant then. Why would early humans need to read and write, study proper nutrition, or prepare for retirement? Many aspects of life and the human race were still locked in the unknown. People didn't know what they didn't know.

For example, at one time people did not know that babies were the result of sexual intercourse. Sexual intercourse took place, perhaps as a response to an instinct, and led to an awareness of pleasure, but was in no way thought to be associated with the development of the child. The large belly of the pregnant woman was connected with producing babies—that was a little easier to see. The explanation of how the baby got there was not related to intercourse, but instead may have been related to what a woman ate, some thoughts she had had, or a divine or evil intervention of some kind. Once people understood the connection between sexual intercourse and pregnancy, the way was open for new discoveries.

I cite this as an example of the simplicity of information then and how far we have come since. We would have to agree that informing girls and boys today about the intricacies of pregnancy involves much more than proper diet!

In the complexity of our society today, no family can be expected to teach its children everything. We have developed institutional specialists to take on part of the teaching process for us, and the wealth of our technological advancement has propelled us into an age of specialization. Because we have had to parcel out learning experiences to institutions outside the family, we often lose sight of the fact that our real wealth lies in our people. As things have turned out, the family gets what's left over after business, school, church, and government get through training us. These institutions (which we created ourselves to help us in peoplemaking) are actually moving against the health of the family. Schools separate children from parents, business blithely expects men and women to be away from home much of the time, and our government extracts our young men and women to serve on foreign soil.

Of course, I would like to see all institutions relate themselves to the welfare of the family. It's entirely possible for institutions to do this without having to forfeit their own goals.

Meanwhile, I'm afraid that we are a power- and thing-oriented society. And our families have become accustomed to going along with this. We teach our children how to be grabbing and powerful in order to cope in the outside world. But what happens? After you win over someone else, where are you really? You are left with the fear that if you don't watch out, someone will win over you, and you live out your life in insecurity, guardedness, caution, and fear. Suppose you retain your power and get all you want of material things. Can these things talk to you, or have arms to comfort and support you? I've never seen possessions or money that were affectionate. Nor do I think it is a matter of either–or (either we have human values and we don't have power and material things, or we are powerful and have no human values).

Again, we need to examine and recognize the relationship between family training and the development of our institutions. The whole question centers around the use of power; *use* is the key word. Too often we confuse powerfulness with the person ("I am powerful, I am something; I am powerless, I am nothing"). Compare that kind of thinking with, say, my using my power for my growth and your growth. This kind of use of power doesn't exclude human values; it enhances them.

Teaching skills to children is a good example of how we can use—or misuse—our power. Most adults in families feel that they are the best authorities to teach their youngsters about discipline, sex, ways of dealing with money, and so on. Then the kids go off to school, where a different set of adults feels that they know best how to teach in certain areas. If the parents and the schoolteachers are presenting very different information, the question arises as to how these two sources of information and learning can be put together for the child. And what happens to the people involved because of these differences?

I am thinking of a boy whose father is an automobile mechanic. The son goes to a trade school and then frequently runs into clashes with his dad about the right way to fix cars. This kind of conflict is more than a disagreement between an old-fashioned way of car repair and newfangled trade-school ideas; it reflects the widespread belief that there is one right way to do whatever is required. Some of us may realize this is faulty reasoning, yet many of us go right on using it.

Let's take another example. Joannie, a precocious five-year-old in a local kindergarten, could read, do simple arithmetic, and was a highly creative child. Kindergarten bored her and she said so at home. Mother sent a note to the school saying the curriculum was too boring for her child, and that the teacher should make kindergarten more interesting.

Joannie happened to be one of forty kindergarteners—one the teacher noticed was "always disruptive." So the teacher sent a note telling the parents that if they didn't do something about Joannie, she would ask her to leave.

These notes happened to cross each other in the mail. Incidentally, the teacher did not know that Joannie knew how to read; the parents didn't know that Joannie was disrupting the class. Both parties had incomplete information, and a fight and hurt feelings were in the making. Principals in the drama were "those permissive parents" from the teacher's view and "that incompetent teacher" from the view of the parents. Joannie was sure to lose as long as this kind of thing was going on.

What was needed was a system that made it possible for information to be shared by all involved. This kind of feedback paves the way for appropriate changes because it recognizes that no one can know everything. I certainly cannot know the full effect of what I do to you unless you tell me. And what hope does a teacher have for changing parents already labeled permissive? How can a parent hope to reach, let alone change, a teacher already labeled incompetent? In this regard, the attitude of "I know that I don't know everything" is very useful. Also, whenever anything happens, there are many parts to the happening, not all of them readily apparent. Without feedback, attack, capitulation, and indifference inevitably follow. Feedback systems are thus vital in families, institutions, and areas where the two combine in some mutual goal.

Insidious and hurtful misunderstandings arise when people cannot find a way to share information. The ensuing hostility lowers self-esteem and creates true deterrents to any kind of problem-solving. The misunderstandings, the walls around people, and the gaps grow even greater. Thus human beings who feel misunderstood and violated suffer loss of self-worth, which in turn cuts down on their productivity and joy of living. And this happens whether the one who misunderstands and violates is a parent, teacher, pastor, business executive, congregation member, or whatever.

All right. At this point I think it would be useful to recap the components that society and individual families hold in common, as discussed earlier in this chapter. Each contends with relationships between leaders and followers, young and established, male and female, together with the processes of making decisions, using authority, and achieving common goals.

Today these components are being challenged in families and institutions all over the world. People are beginning to recognize the common thread basic to all relationships, and they are beginning to demand that our institutions recognize it, too. This basic thread is that every leader is a person, every youngster is a person, males and females are persons. Decisions, authority, and goals are basically personal means of getting along together.

Finally, we must all recognize that life is run with people, and what goes on among people is the chief determinant of what happens to them and the environment around them. What people know, what they believe, and how they handle their differences begin in the family. At this time, our institutions reflect these family learnings. Further, we realize that some of these learnings have deterred growth, and so the time has come to change the basis on which we operate. It will not surprise you that all this has to do with self-worth—how it is manifested, how you communicate about it, and what kind of group relationships emerge among people with high pot, who communicate in a leveling way, who know how to be intimate, and who can trust openly.

I see a need for families to ask to become partners in any institution in which any of their members are involved and to be considered as part of that establishment. The family is *the* integral unit in society. Actually the family is one of the few units whose geographical area and membership are small enough so that everyone can sit in one room and can be known. Rare is the family numbering over fifteen. Fifteen is a recognized, good-sized, full group. So when a group is no larger than fifteen and gathers on the same premises, everyone can expect (within a reasonable time) to be known, heard, and seen, and to know, see, and hear.

Remember the family meetings we talked about many chapters ago? *Sit down with your family for the express purpose of finding out where everyone is in relation to outside institutions: school, business, church, Camp Fire, Boy Scouts, the track team, whatever. Use this family meeting as the one place where you can each look at lacks, oversights, injustices, rewards, and experiences, in the frame of everyone's needs. Talk over any adjustments that might have to be made. This will provide you with the feedback system we mentioned before.*

So what am I actually saying to you? Start with your family. You all know about self-worth, communication, and process; now put these powerful forces to work in your family. And when they start to function in your family, making it a more nurturing one, these same forces will be applied in society. It could even be the beginning for a new kind of society. After all, the family unit is the synthesizing

link to its parent: society as a whole. As such, the family and what it teaches are central to the achievement of peace.

25

Peace Within, Peace Between, and Peace Among

I want to build on the idea that the world is a family of nations, made up of people like you and me. These nations are led by people, just as any other family is. They happen to be people in governments, but they face the same issues, challenges, and possibilities that individuals in families face.

Creating peace in the world strongly resembles making peace in the family. We are learning how to heal families, and we can use those learnings to heal the world. Our global family is dysfunctional and, in effect, operates with the same themes as any other dysfunctional family. In many governments, power is concentrated in one person or role. Identity is seen in terms of conformity and obedience, and autonomy is subject to someone else's approval.

In and between countries, conflict is often dealt with by blame and punishment. Solutions are reached by decree, threat, force, and avoidance. Trust is frequently betrayed and therefore suspect. Relationships are based on dominance and submission.

We know that the child who discovers he or she gets results by threat, force, or manipulation will likely use those methods as an adult, unless there has been an intervention. The threat used by a child might be a fist or a stick. As an adult, it might be a gun or a bomb; it will still be the same process.

Since a majority of people are brought up with these learnings, it is no surprise to find that most leaders of the world practice them. Through war crises, hunger, and economic depressions, the world family cries out to us for help in much the same way the dysfunctional family shows its pain through symptoms.

At this point, all people on Earth are living under the shadow of the threat of nuclear war. Paradoxically, we also have more information and technology regarding human beings than at any other previous time. We are living in a time of great opportunity as well as potential peril. Our choices will make the difference. You and I will make those choices.

In today's world, we can reach almost any person almost anywhere on the planet in seconds, through satellites and other communication vehicles. Through television, we can see what is going on everywhere, as it happens. Computers can calculate vast amounts of information in fractions of a second. We can fly to almost any place on the globe in seventeen hours. We can make space bridges between continents. We have put astronauts on the moon. We are even talking about putting dwellings in space.

We have the intelligence and skill to create splendid and sometimes awesome technology. We have yet to work out a reliable way for the people of the world to live and work together. Now we need to use our intelligence to achieve this. Once we decide down to our very bones that the time is now, that it is necessary, we will succeed.

I wonder what would happen if suddenly during one night, all five billion persons in the world learned the essentials of congruent living:

To communicate clearly

To cooperate rather than compete

To empower rather than subjugate

To enhance individual uniqueness rather than categorize

To use authority to guide and accomplish "what fits" rather than force compliance through the tyranny of power

To love, value, and respect themselves fully

To be personally and socially responsible

To use problems as challenges and opportunities for creative solutions

I think we would wake up in a very different world, a world in which peace is possible. It is only a matter of change in consciousness. What will cause each of us to change our minds? I believe it will be when we love and value ourselves enough and recognize that we are spiritual beings.

When we think of changing our world, the task seems so enormous that it is intimidating. Where could one person start? Among five billion people, one person seems like only a straw in a haystack, feeling powerless to change anything. I am not so brash as to think that one person could do

this job alone. However, many persons of like mind coming together could begin the change.

I recently saw a button that said, "Peace begins with me." When one lives peace, the change starts. This is how a solitary person can start—with himself or herself. When I model peacefulness and harmony, all who are around me are affected. The same is true for you and others. Margaret Mead said, "Change has always come about by a few committed people."

If we had all been brought up differently, the world would be a peaceful place. Our job is to embrace the new learnings that can create new individual awareness.

My thesis is both simple and logical. If we bring up children in a peaceful context in which adult leaders model congruence, the children will become peaceful adults who, in turn, will create a peaceful world.

Most parents unwittingly defeat themselves by creating an unpeaceful family context and consequently do not model what they preach. Therefore, the old learnings live on. Our challenge now is to interrupt these old patterns and develop new ones that will enable us to help one another rather than making war on each other.

War as a means of acceptable conflict resolution now belongs in museums with the other relics of antiquity.

There are people who already are discovering the secret of congruence. They are learning to treasure their own miraculousness and that of others. They connect with each other on the basis of sameness and grow and enjoy each other on the basis of differentness. They believe in their capacity to grow and change. They know how to be emotionally honest. They are vital, engaging human beings with a sense of purpose and the ability to laugh at themselves.

These are the people who are qualified to be leaders for peace. They are scattered about the planet and are often unknown to one another. Networks are beginning to form, and bridges are being built between them. As these people come together, they create a positive critical mass which, because of its nurturing force, will attract similar energy.

Until a strong force emerges for positive change, society will remain as it is. We are all members of society and have the power to change it if we choose. Each of us can make a difference.

You can help by developing a network, enlisting your friends. You will soon see who is ready. For those who are not yet ready, simply love them, be open to them, and be prepared to welcome them when the time comes.

In your effort to connect with other people, you may be surprised to find that there are many "closet believers" who have been too shy to speak out for what they believe. Your contact with them may be just enough to give them the support they need to come out into the open so you can join each other.

Today, rather than having a positive critical mass, we have a negative one which has been building over many years. Its origins and support come from attitudes manifested in violence, distrust, greed, coercion, and apathy. These conditions engendered fear, which reinforces the helplessness of people who already feel that way.

People who are strong and have a sense of high self-worth will not support such a negative mass nor act as its victims. This does not mean that the negative critical mass is made up of bad people. They are just ordinary individuals who feel unworthy within or dislike themselves. They meet the world through blaming problems on others, ignoring trouble, or denying what is going on.

For example, it is easy to think of human beings as numbers, categories, or statistics instead of as people. We read that 40,000 people are killed each year by automobiles whose drivers were drunk, or that 500 people die in a warring country. We may feel a momentary shock and sadness, yet we soon go about our lives as though nothing momentous had occurred. We remain basically untouched. In many instances, we do not take action because we feel totally helpless.

What a difference experience it becomes when one of those 40,000 or 500 is a wife, husband, child, parent, or close friend. When the experience is a personal tragedy, we are touched. Only then are we moved to do something.

What do we have to do to personalize these tragedies when they do not affect one of our loved ones? If we saw each statistic concerning human beings in terms of a person who had a name, had dreams and yearnings, and was someone's father, mother, sister, brother, spouse, or friend—who felt, breathed, thought, tended machines, toiled the ground, cried when hurt, bled when cut, and laughed when amused—would we not feel a sense of identification?

Would we do more to change the political, social, economic, and personal tyranny that is responsible for these deaths? I believe we would.

Today, "I" may not have been the target, but what about tomorrow? We are slowly realizing that the place to start a new consciousness is with each individual, in the family. There we can learn how to love and value ourselves, which will be reflected in how we love others. As I have stated elsewhere in this book, when one cares deeply about the life force within oneself, one would do nothing to injure that self or another self.

In other words, people who really care about and value themselves move toward engaging and contacting others in loving, respectful, and realistic ways. They use their energies to develop possibilities for all human beings.

There has never yet been a society whose priority and prevailing value was the worth of all human beings. We who are living now are the first to even attempt it. Our future in the world needs to be one in which all countries feel first-rate about themselves. This requires the same learnings that are needed to stop war and create peace. Each of us can make a difference in this matter.

Whether or not we acknowledge it, all people are connected as manifestations of life, symbolized by the universal presence of a sperm and egg and supported by a cosmic spirituality. Similarly, all nations are connected. The relationships between nations form a giant network through which the energy of five billion souls surges constantly and daily. The quality of that energy affects the health of the planet in much the same way that the quality of blood and oxygen affect the health of a person.

I believe that the quality of human energy rests on the value society places on individuals and the value individuals place on themselves. Strong, congruent, vital people cope creatively, realistically, and fairly with what life hands them. Throughout this book, I have shown how one becomes strong, congruent, and vital. These qualities are available for everyone. That makes peace available to all, once we change our consciousness and our minds. With that change, we will be able to create a social and political world that serves the needs of all people, respecting differentness and forming bonds based on sameness.

26

Family of the Future

To prepare a context for looking at the family of the future, let us turn the calendar back and peek at the American family of 1900, at the turn of the present century. Two separate worlds existed then: one was of men; the other, women. There were very few bridges between them. The men's world was considered superior and out of the reach of women. It was a world of competition, physical stamina, sexual prowess, intellectual pursuit, dominance, toughness, power, strength, and protection of the weak.

To fulfill this picture, men had to suppress their feelings and exaggerate their intellectual and physical prowess. This made them vulnerable to the ills that befall people who tie themselves up emotionally. Statistically, men have died earlier than women ever since the Industrial Revolution. To keep their worlds separate, the roles of both men and women were clearly defined.

The women's world in 1900 was largely one of propriety, softness, sweetness, childbearing, caring for children, serving husbands, and being good cooks and homemakers. The woman was expected to make her world full through her home, husband, and children. The worst thing that could happen to a woman then was to become a spinster, or old maid, which was the same as being a social outcast. Many women chose unhappy marriages as a lesser evil. Today many women choose to remain unmarried if the choice is between marrying for marriage's sake or remaining single. Women of today are waking up to the fact that they are no longer willing to settle for second-best.

The woman of 1900 repressed her intellectual side to remain marriageable. Society contended that men did not want to marry intellectual women. (Women are still crawling out from under this one.) Only the bravest and most venturesome women dared pursue higher education. Men, on the other hand, were encouraged to become as well educated as possible. Today, women are free to choose careers; it is part of the social ethic for women as well as men to be educated.

Turn-of-the-century women were expected to be virgins when they married. Men, on the other hand, were considered unmanly if they had not had sexual experience before marriage. The double standard was in full force. Today sexual expression prior to marriage is fast becoming the norm in many parts of society. We are still very naive as far as managing our sexual selves. We have not yet found a healthy balance.

The acceptable woman of 1900 was expected to go from her parents' home to her husband's bed. She was to accept the fact that her husband would be totally in charge of the family, the supreme authority. Laws barred women from owning property in some states. They depended totally on their husbands, fathers, brothers, and sons for their financial transactions and support. Today many women are heads of families or partners in their financial support.

At the turn of this century, men literally owned both women and children. Even the marriage vows reflected ownership. The woman was to love, honor, and obey her husband. He promised only to love and cherish her. Today people have many choices for making the marriage vows, and women and children are no longer anyone's legal property.

Since early-century brides were expected to be virgins, husbands were supposed to educate them sexually. Not all men had enough information to be good teachers, though, and sex was therefore often unappealing. Appeal notwithstanding, women had no legal right to refuse their spouses sexually; in fact, not until the 1970s did state legislatures begin outlawing marital rape.

Family planning and birth control were other topics about which we knew little. Abstinence was the only birth control; abortions were illegal, very dangerous, and considered immoral. Today family planning is widely available, and many consider birth control acceptable and desirable. Abortions are legal, though controversy still abounds.

In the 1900s, families were large, infant mortality was high, and many women died in childbirth. Because of the ravages of disease and accidents, many men also died early. These events created a large number of totally or half-orphaned children. Since women and children could not manage by themselves, second families were often necessary. When a spouse died, the remaining parent was expected to remarry as soon as possible, creating what I have called a blended family.

Today we perhaps have even more blended families than before. However, they are now more often the result of divorce rather than death. This means men are often in the position of bringing up other men's children. Psychological problems often result for fathers as well as their children. As more men get custody, women are coming into the same boat.

In general, blended families—both then and now—have been considered not quite first rate. Since so many exist today, though, much work is under way to create a first-rate attitude toward these families.

Social stigma also used to plague anyone born to an unmarried woman. Adoption was one answer to this situation; the circumstances of the birth were kept secret by law, supposedly to give the child a better start in life.

Many jurisdictions still require birth information of adopted children to be kept secret, although many states have provisions to help people get their birth information. The stigma of being born to unmarried parents still exists in some places; in others, it is so reduced that single women sometimes seek to become mothers without being married. This practice carries with it serious challenges for bringing up healthy children.

Looking back on the family of the 1900s, one gets the following impression. Men were in the dominant position; women were subservient, dependent, and treated as—and expected to be—inferior. The relationship was one of domination and submission. It was either benign or malevolent. Even though women were the heart and soul of the family, that role was inferior to the role of men. Feeling, heart, and soul were not given much value in the affairs of the world.

This is beginning to change. New medical and psychological information clearly shows it is a matter of health and longevity for men to handle their feelings openly and honestly (this goes for women as well, of course). The roles of men and women have also changed considerably in the direction of equality of power and value. Stereotypes of dominant males and submissive females are now being replaced by relationships of equality. Some men still feel threatened. They are not sure how to deal with women who want equal power, nor do they know the benefits possible for them. The many other men who have been able to go beyond their past training have experienced more freedom for themselves. To their delight, they can share the responsibilities and burdens that formerly they had to carry alone.

Recently I overheard the following conversation between two men sitting behind me in an airplane. The subject was a tender one; perhaps that accounted for the long pauses between their comments.

First man: Is your wife involved in that women's lib stuff?

Second man: Yeah.

First: How is that for you?

Second: You really want to know?

First: Yeah!

Second: I love it. I have only two feet. Until my wife got on her own, I had to behave as though I had four feet. Now we really are partners.

I regard the emerging balance between women and men as being as earthshaking as the discovery that the world is round instead of flat. Many changes will have to occur before the majority of people will know how to assert and attain equality of value in their relationships. When we achieve that equality, the family will become stronger. We will be raising more competent people. Children who grow up experiencing models of male and female equality can more easily become whole adults. In turn, these adults will be able to parent and guide their children to a healthy adulthood. Achieving this will represent a monumental social milestone and confirm that human development is on a more positive course.

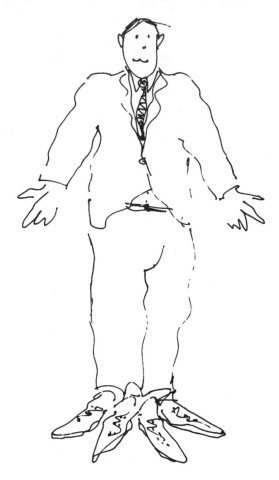

To hasten this development, we need to reshape our spiritual, psychological, emotional, social, physical, legal, and intellectual perceptions. To date, we have had few guidelines and few models for equality between people: male and female, young and old, black and white, rich and poor. The ideal has been in our hearts but not our actions. We have been steeped in conformity and obedience, subordination and superiority, submission and dominance for so long that we sometimes think this is how human relations really are.

Now we need to learn about equality and how, within this context, we conceptualize and live autonomy, freedom, responsibility, empowerment, leadership, decision-making, and satisfying conflict resolution. We will need patience and creativity to make the needed changes.

We are in a shifting and sorting time. The current chaos, especially with regard to the family, is essential to reach the next step in our evolution of becoming more fully human. We have made a dent in the status quo.

Whenever change occurs, the old order is disturbed and a period of upheaval follows. During this chaos, it may be hard to see what has been gained. One other stumbling block to rapid progress arises when people try to accomplish new goals using an old process. It takes time to learn a new process.

Families have always wanted to be happy and healthy. They have wanted to live fuller and more meaningful lives. However, few people ever really expected that to happen. Now we are closer than ever before to developing the kinds of persons who can make that happen.

One hundred years ago, people probably would not have asked themselves if they were happy. They would more likely have been conscious of whether they were living their roles properly. Today the question of happiness is an important one. We are beginning to realize that personal happiness is a major component in health and strength. We are not yet a society that knows how to practice happiness and at the same time be increasingly competent. Many people still seem to act as if being happy will reduce the incentive to work hard.

At the turn of the century, the only family form given first-rate status was the one in which a man and a woman chose each other and stayed together until death. The challenge of today is to make every family and every person in the family feel first-rate. There are thousands of happy, well-adjusted persons in *all* family forms. There are also thousands of persons living in families that do not work. The difference is not in the form, but in the relationships within the family. Specifically, we need to replace the dominant-submissive mode of relating.

The relationships that succeed can be described simply. Within the family, the adults work as a team, are open with each other, demonstrate their presence as individuals, and show their respect and esteem for each other. They treat each other as unique, are aware of and build on their sameness, and grow and learn from their differences. They model the behaviors and values they wish to teach their children. Conflict resolution (dealing with differentness) becomes one vehicle by which new growth occurs. The new generation learns how to do this as children, by watch-

ing the adults around them. To practice what they preach, to model in this way, the adults need to have developed a high degree of self-esteem.

Learning to feel equal to all other human beings will also help us live in accordance with our higher natures. Our long history of dominance and submission may be the biggest impediment to being in touch with our higher natures. Living in this way has required us to divide ourselves and live through negative forms of power more than through love and respecting our spiritual selves and others. As the adults of today learn how to be more whole people, they will provide the models for new, more fully human adults of tomorrow and thus create stronger families. Then the old chain will be broken and a new way of being can emerge.

I believe that the path to our higher selves is through the development of high self-worth; this is a family affair. As a therapist, I found that the foundation for releasing symptoms and the emergence of health was the development of high individual self-worth. I, as well as others, have demonstrated this concept over and over again. Many people already live their lives according to their higher natures. *All people can learn to behave in accordance with their higher natures.* Changing our perceptions from negative to positive is the first step.

Some may feel that it is too much to hope that everyone in the world can learn to have high self-worth. Others may object on the basis that current human behavior represents human nature. I take issue with this. Human behavior largely represents what has been taught, learned, and modeled, and does *not* represent the human potential. We need a change in perceptions as well as and confidence in human possibilities.

Each of us can live out this change. We have to start with where we are and go from there. The family becomes a wonderful place to both teach and practice.

We are at the birth of another evolution in the history of humankind. Never before have so many people been so discouraged and dissatisfied with the state of the human condition. At the same time, many pockets of strong creative energy all over the world are already emerging. The main cry seems to be for greater feelings of individual self-esteem, more honest and loving relationships with others, and creating appropriate contexts.

I think we are beginning to see the end of people relating to each other through force, dictatorship, obedience, and stereotypical categories. We are beginning to relate through cooperation, choice, empowering leadership, and a real understanding of being more fully human.

Let us remember that old, traditional, entrenched, familiar attitudes die hard. We need to have patience and, at the same time, be bold enough to take our courage and move forward. We can be prompted by our compassion and intelligence. I am working on the side of nurturing the new ways, and I invite you to join me. If any of this book makes sense to you, you are already on your way. As we move closer to achieving individual self-worth, the family will be strengthened. In turn, this will produce a more mature society, in which people can have many creative ways to enjoy their lives, making them meaningful as well as socially and personally responsible.

If, as I hope, more people can see what it means to be truly and fully human, and can develop ways to make this happen, the future of the family looks bright. Growing numbers of people know what it feels like to feel whole and real, to love and be loved, to be productive and responsible, and to feel that the world is a better place because they are in it. When I think of what people in the future will be like when they are brought up in nurturing families living in a nurturing world, I am filled with awe and wonder.

Dear Reader:

I am interested in knowing how my book has affected you. If you were aroused or influenced in any way by the communication games, I would like to hear your comments, insights, ideas, and to share in your personal reactions as well. This will help me to continue to grow and learn as I go along.

I will appreciate each of your letters even though I cannot promise to answer personally.

My further hope is that I can somehow help to set up networks that connect people who will help each other grow.

Thank you,
Virginia Satir

Send comments to:

Virginia Satir
c/o Science & Behavior Books
2017 Landings Drive
Mountain View, CA 94043

Bibliography

I regard books as inspirations to new possibilities, spring-boards to trying out new things, and resources that add to information. By the nature of things, books represent the part of the world that the writer sees as well as how that world is interpreted. I enjoy seeing the various ways people view the same things.

This bibliography includes books that have particularly excited, inspired, and informed me. I have grouped them so that you, the reader, might more quickly locate your special interests.

Children & Parenting

Bartz, Wayne R.; and Richard A Basor. *Surviving with Kids.* San Luis Obispo, CA: Impact Publishers, 1978.

Black, Claudia. *My Dad Loves Me, My Dad Has a Disease.* [Alcoholism] Newport Beach, CA: Alcoholism, Children & Therapy, 1979.

Fishel, Elizabeth. *Sisters.* New York: Bantam, 1979.

Griffith, Linda Lewis. *Battle Fatigue: And You Thought You Were Busy Before You Had Children!* San Luis Obispo, CA: Impact Publishers, 1986.

Huxley, Laura A.; and Piero Ferrucci. *The Child of Your Dreams.* Minneapolis: CompCare Publications, 1987.

Kimball, Gayle. *50-50 Parenting: Sharing Family Rewards and Responsibility.* Lexington, MA: D. C. Heath, 1988.

Nicholson, Luree; and Laura Torbet. *How to Fight Fair with Your Kids . . . and Win!* New York: Harcourt Brace Jovanovich, 1980.

Shallcross, Doris J.; and Dorothy A. Sisk. *The Growing Person: How to Encourage Healthy Emotional Development in Children.* Englewood Cliffs, NJ: Prentice-Hall, 1982.

Shapiro, Jerrold Lee. *When Men Are Pregnant: Needs and Concerns of Expectant Fathers.* San Luis Obispo, CA: Impact Publishers, 1987.

Shiff, Eileen. *Experts Advise Parents: A Guide to Raising Loving, Responsible Children.* New York: Delacorte, 1987.

Stewart, Betty. *Growing Up Before Your Children Do.* Evanston, IL: The Haven Corp., 1981.

Couples

Barbach, Lonnie. *For Each Other: Sharing Sexual Intimacy.* New York: Anchor Press/Doubleday, 1982.

Brandon, Nathaniel. *The Psychology of Romantic Love.* Los Angeles: J. P. Tarcher, 1980.

Cameron-Bandler, Leslie. *They Lived Happily Ever After: Methods for Achieving Happy Endings in Coupling.* Cupertino, CA: Meta Publications, 1978.

Garland, Diana R. *Couples Communication and Negotiation Skills.* Workshop Models for Family Life Education Series. New York: Family Service Association of America, 1978.

Kilgore, James E. *Try Marriage Before Divorce.* Waco, TX: Word Books, 1978.

Lederer, William J.; and Don D. Jackson. *Mirages of Marriage.* New York: Norton, 1968.

Miller, Sherod; Elam W. Nunnally; and Daniel B. Wackman. *Alive and Aware: Improving Communication in Relationships.* Minneapolis: Interpersonal Communication Programs, 1975.

———. *Talking Together: Couple Communication I.* Minneapolis: Interpersonal Communication Programs, 1979.

Norwood, Robin. *Women Who Love Too Much.* Los Angeles: J. P. Tarcher, 1985.

Paul, Jordon; and Margaret Paul. *Do I Have to Give Up Me to Be Loved by You?* Minneapolis: CompCare Publications, 1983.

Pelton, Charles L. *The Sex Book for Those Who Think They Know It All.* Aberdeen, SD: C. L. Pelton, 1980.

Shostrom, Everett; and James Kavanaugh. *Between Man and Woman: The Dynamics of Interpersonal Relationships.* Los Angeles: Nash Publishing, 1971.

Families & Communication

Beebe, Steven A.; and John T. Masterson. *Family Talk: Communication in the Family.* New York: Random House, 1986.

Benson, Jeannette; and Jack Hilyard. *Becoming Family* [communication and self-esteem exercises]. Winona, MN: St. Mary's Press, 1979.

Bernhard, Yetta; and George Bach. *Aggression Lab: The Fair Fight Training Manual.* Dubuque, IO: Kendal-Hunt, 1971.

Branden, Nathaniel. *"If You Could Hear What I Cannot Say": Learning to Communicate with the Ones You Love.* New York: Bantam, 1983.

Edinberg, Mark. *Talking with Your Aging Parents.* Boston, MA: Shambala, 1987.

Einstein, Elizabeth. *Strengthening Your Stepfamily.* New York: Random House, 1987.

Kilgore, James E.; with Don Highlander. *Getting More Family Out of Your Dollar.* Irvine, CA: Harvest House, 1976.

Lieberman, Mendel; and Marion Hardie. *Resolving Family and Other Conflicts: Everybody Wins.* Santa Cruz, CA: Unity Press, 1981.

Paul, Jordan; and Margaret Paul. *If You Really Loved Me. . .* [Family communications] Minneapolis: CompCare Publications, 1987.

Schaefer, Nathan. *Families Are Forever.* Saratoga, CA: R&E Publishers, 1985.

Stinnett, Nick; and John DeFrain. *Secrets of Strong Families.* New York: Berkley, 1985.

Wahlroos, Sven. *Family Communication: A Guide to Emotional Health.* New York: Macmillan, 1974.

Wegscheider, Don. *If Only My Family Understood Me. . .* [Family systems] Minneapolis: CompCare Publications, 1979.

Wegscheider, Sharon. *Another Chance: Hope and Health for Alcoholic Families.* Palo Alto, CA: Science and Behavior Books, 1981.

White, Ann; and Deborah Grayson. *Parents and Other Strangers.* Port Washington, NY: Ashley Books, 1987.

Zahnd, Walter F. *Crested Butte Temperature Reading Chart.* Available from author: 217 Valley View Drive, Paradise, CA 95969.

Families: Blended, Single-Parent, etc.

Adler, Robert E. *Sharing Our Children: How to Resolve Custody Problems and Get On with Your Life.* Bethesda, MD: Adler & Adler, 1988.

Anderson-Khleif, Susan. *Divorced But Not Disastrous: How to Improve the Ties between Single-Parent Mothers, Divorced Fathers, and the Children.* Englewood Cliffs, NJ: Prentice-Hall, 1982.

Burt, Mala Schuster; and Roger B. Burt. *What's Special About Our Stepfamily?* [Participation book for children] New York: Dolphin-/Doubleday, 1983.

Einstein, Elizabeth. *Strengthening Your Stepfamily.* New York: Random Hosue, 1987.

Gately, Richard; and David Koulack. *The Single Father's Handbook.* New York: Anchor/Doubleday, 1979.

Lewis, Helen C. *All About Families: The Second Time Around.* Atlanta: Peachtree Publishers, 1980.

Ricci, Isolina. *Mom's House, Dad's House: Making Joint Custody Work.* New York: Macmillan, 1980.

Smoke, Jim. *Growing Through Divorce.* Irvine, CA: Harvest House, 1976.

Visher, Emily B.; and John S. Visher. *Stepfamilies: A Guide to Working with Stepparents and Stepchildren.* New York: Brunner/Mazel, 1979.

Adolescence

Adams, Caren; Jennifer Fay; and Jan Loreen-Martin. *NO Is Not Enough: Helping Teenagers Avoid Sexual Assault.* San Luis Obispo, CA: Impact Publishers, 1974.

Donlan, Joan. *I Never Saw the Sun Rise.* [Diary of a recovering chemically dependent teenager] Minneapolis: CompCare Publications, 1977.

Elchoness, Monte. *Why Can't Anyone Hear Me? A Guide for Surviving Adolescence.* Sepulveda, CA: Monroe Press, 1986.

Personal Growth

Adams, Ramona S.; Herbert A. Otto; and Deane S. Cowly. *Letting Go: Uncomplicating Your Life.* New York: Macmillan, 1980.

Alberti, Robert E.; and Michael L. Emmons. *Your Perfect Right: A Guide to Assertive Living.* San Luis Obispo, CA: Impact Publishers, 1982.

Bernhard, Yetta. *How to Be Somebody: Open the Door to Personal Growth.* Millbrae, CA: Celestial Arts, 1975.

———. *Self-Care.* Brookline, MA: BFI Publishers (251 Harvard St.), 1983.

Branden, Nathaniel. *Honoring the Self: Personal Integrity and the Heroic Po-tentials of Human Nature.* Los Angeles: J. P. Tarcher, 1983.

Buzan, Tony. *Use Both Sides of Your Brain.* New York: E. P. Dutton, 1974.

Carson, Richard David. *Taming Your Gremlin: A Guide to Enjoying Your-self.* Dallas: The Family Resource, 1983.

Gale, Raymond F. *Who Are You? The Psychology of Being Yourself.* Engle-wood Cliffs, NJ: Prentice-Hall, 1976.

Kalellis, Peter M. *A New Self-Image: Restoring a Positive Sense of Self.* Al-len, TX: Argus Communications, 1982.

Lakien, Alan. *How to Get Control of Your Time and Your Life.* New York: NAL/Signet, 1974.

McKay, Matthew; and Patrick Fanning. *Self-Esteem.* Oakland, CA: New Harbinger, 1987.

―――. *Meditations and Inspirations.* Millbrae, CA: Celestial Arts, 1985.

Satir, Virginia. *Making Contact.* Millbrae, CA: Celestial Arts, 1976.

―――. *Self-Esteem.* Millbrae, CA: Celestial Arts, 1975.

―――. *Your Many Faces.* Millbrae, CA: Celestial Arts, 1978.

Shostrom, Everett L. *From Manipulator to Master: Uncovering the Source of Your Power.* New York: Bantam, 1983.

Weinberg, Gerald M. *Becoming a Technical Leader: An Organic Problem-Solving Approach* [professional growth]. New York: Dorset House, 1986.

―――. *The Secrets of Consulting: A Guide to Giving and Getting Advice Successfully.* New York: Dorset House, 1985.

Health

Brown, Barbara. *Supermind: The Ultimate Energy.* New York: Harper & Row, 1980.

Cousins, Norman. *The Anatomy of an Illness.* New York: Norton, 1979.

Green, Elmer; and Alyce Green. *Beyond Biofeedback.* New York: Dela-corte, 1977.

Gross, Stanley J. *Rolework: Dealing with Role Stress and Role Strain.* Avail-able from the author: Roslindale, MA.

Haney, C. Michele; and Edmond W. Boenisch, Jr. *Stressmap: Finding Your Pressure Points.* San Luis Obispo, CA: Impact Publishers, 1982.

Hatfield, Bruce; and Bob Hatfield. *Matters of Life and Death.* Winfield, B.C., Canada: Wood Lake Books.

Lynch, James. *The Languages of the Heart: The Body's Response to Human Dialogue.* New York: Basic Books, 1986.

Pelletier, Kenneth R. *Holistic Medicine.* New York: Delacorte, 1980.

Schwartz, Jackie. *Letting Go of Stress.* New York: Pinnacle, 1982.

Selye, Hans. *Stress Without Distress.* Philadelphia: J. P. Lippincott, 1974.

———. *The Stress of Life.* Philadelphia: J. P. Lippincott, 1956.

Siegel, Bernard S. *Love, Medicine & Miracles.* New York: Harper & Row, 1986.

Simonton, Carl; and Stephanie Simonton. *Getting Well Again.* New York: Bantam, 1980.

Later Years

Kubler-Ross, Elizabeth. *On Death and Dying.* New York: Macmillan, 1969.

Polster, Erving. *Every Person's Life Is Worth a Novel.* New York: Norton, 1987.

Reuerstein, Phyllis; and Carol Roberts. *The Not-So-Empty Nest: How to Live with Your Kids After They've Lived Someplace Else.* Chicago: Follett, 1981.

Staying Young. Audiotapes available through SyberVision, Inc. (P.O. Box 13875, Denver, CO 80201–9908).

Spirituality

Fox, Matthew. *Original Blessing: A Primer in Creation Spirituality.* Santa Fe: Bear & Co., 1983.

Friends of Peace Pilgrim. *Peace Pilgrim: Her Life and Work in Her Own Words.* Santa Fe: Ocean Tree/Peace Press, 1983.

Gibran, Khalil. *Prophet.* New York: Alfred A. Knopf, 1923.

Johnson, Charles M. *The Creative Imperative: A Four-Dimensional Theory of Human Growth and Planetary Evolution.* Millbrae, CA: Celestial Arts, 1986.

Keyes, Ken, Jr. *The Hundredth Monkey.* Coos Bay, OR: Vision Books, 1982.

Other books by Virginia Satir

SATIR STEP BY STEP:
A Guide to Creating Change in Families

Virginia Satir & Michele Baldwin

Virginia Satir and her colleague Michele Baldwin detail the methods and strategy of Satir's world-renowned family therapy, including some of her newest material.

Part I is an annotated transcript of a family therapy demonstration, in which Satir explains her techniques and interventions step by step. Part II recaps the theoretical foundations of Satir's work. Several fundamental approaches are published here for the first time.

Virginia Satir, the only woman leader in the field of family therapy, is often described as "larger than life." How wrong! Virginia meets life with the largesse of a woman excited by, plagued by, entranced by, and devoted to those aspects of humanity common to all, and loving what is unique to each. Her therapeutic approach is concerned with the joy and pain of experiencing reality—unafraid.

Frederick J. Duhl, M.D.
Director
Boston Family Institute

6×9 inches
269 pages

Cloth: $14.95
illustrated

CONJOINT FAMILY THERAPY, Third Edition
Revised and Expanded

Virginia Satir

Universally recognized as a classic in the field of family dynamics, this book has enjoyed ever-increasing success. In immensely readable outline form, it presents Virginia Satir's unique and nonblaming approach to working with families. Heartily endorsed by therapists, parents, and students, it has been translated into eighteen languages and is widely adopted for classroom use.

This third edition incorporates fifteen additional years of the author's experience, techniques, and models. An exciting new chapter (Part IV) provides an in-depth discussion of Virginia's initial interview with a client family. As she details her impressions, her use of humor, and her various and flexible interventions, readers catch an intimate glimpse of a pioneering therapist at work.

In Part V, "Involving the Larger System," the author takes readers beyond conjoint family therapy. Just as she once helped revolutionize her field by treating individuals within the context of their families, Virginia now explores the benefits of helping families within the context of their communities. As part of this process, she describes how she works with large groups (200–300 people) in a logical extension of systems theory.

This primer's excellence can be ascribed to many factors . . . heartfelt dedication to the families with which [she] has worked . . . absence of psychiatric and psychoanalytic terms . . . [and the fact that it] focuses sharply on the importance of becoming more conversant with what actually does go on in the family.

Norma Paul
in Family Process

You can count on Virginia Satir. Her work is seminal. *Conjoint* is a basic book for anyone working with families—beginners and pros alike. I know of no one who has contributed more to the personal and professional development of family therapists and educators, here and abroad, than Virginia.

Sherod Miller, Ph.D.
Minnesota Couples Communication Program

6×9 inches
269 pages

Paper: $14.95

FROM VIRGINIA SATIR...

I am very pleased to announce something special in my life—the AVANTA NETWORK—which I think will be of interest to you. This is a group of colleagues who have studied, worked, and shared with me over the years. We have joined together to use our skills and gifts to help individuals, families, social agencies, businesses, churches, and political and educational organizations move toward a more human and joyful way of being, living, and functioning. Activities of the Avanta Network include:

- A four-week International Summer Training Institute PROCESS COMMUNITY under my direction with a faculty of Avanta members
- Advanced training programs for persons who have completed Process Community training
- Workshops given by Avanta members across North America and throughout the world.

If you want to know more about the Avanta Network, write to me at 139 Forest Avenue, Palo Alto, CA 94301.

Index

ORDER FORM

Tear out and mail this form with your check to:

SCIENCE AND BEHAVIOR BOOKS
2017 Landings Drive
Mountain View, CA 94043
(415) 965–0954

Please send me:

_____ copies of *Satir Step By Step*   Cloth $14.95 _____

_____ copies of *Conjoint Family Therapy, Third Edition*

                                    Paperback $14.95 _____

_____ copies of *The New Peoplemaking* Paperback $15.95 _____

Subtotal   _____

Tax (add 6.5% for California residents)   _____

Freight & Handling   _____2.00

Total Amount Enclosed   _____

Name _____

Address _____

City _____ State_____ Zip_____

Phone ____(   )_____

Charge to my credit card:

☐ Visa #_____

☐ Master Card #_____

  Expiration Date _____

Signature _____
                    (Credit Card Only)